# Docker and Kubernetes for Java Developers

Scale, deploy, and monitor multi-container applications

**Jaroslaw Krochmalski**

BIRMINGHAM - MUMBAI

# Docker and Kubernetes for Java Developers

First published: August 2017

Production reference: 1240817

Published by Packt Publishing Ltd.
Livery Place
35 Livery Street
Birmingham
B3 2PB, UK.

ISBN 978-1-78646-839-0

www.packtpub.com

# Credits

**Author**
Jaroslaw Krochmalski

**Reviewer**
Pierre Mavro

**Commissioning Editor**
Vijin Boricha

**Acquisition Editor**
Prachi Bisht

**Content Development Editor**
Trusha Shriyan

**Technical Editor**
Varsha Shivhare

**Copy Editor**
Safis Editing

**Project Coordinator**
Kinjal Bari

**Proofreader**
Safis Editing

**Indexer**
Mariammal Chettiyar

**Graphics**
Kirk D'Penha

**Production Coordinator**
Shantanu Zagade

# About the Author

**Jaroslaw Krochmalski** is a passionate software designer and developer who specializes in the financial domain. He has over 12 years of experience in software development. He is a clean-code and software craftsmanship enthusiast. He is a certified scrum master and a fan of Agile. His professional interests include new technologies in web application development, design patterns, enterprise architectures, and integration patterns.

He has been designing and developing software professionally since 2000 and has been using Java as his primary programming language since 2002. In the past, he has worked for companies such as **Kredyt Bank** (**KBC**) and Bank BPS on many large-scale projects, such as international money orders, express payments, and collection systems. He currently works as a consultant at Danish company 7N as an infrastructure architect for the Nykredit bank. You can reach him via Twitter at @jkroch or by email at jarek@finsys.pl.

# About the Reviewer

**Pierre Mavro** lives in a suburb of Paris. He's an open source software lover and has been working with Linux for more than 10 years now. Currently, he is working as a lead SRE at Criteo, where he manages distributed systems and NoSQL technologies. During the last few years, he has been designing high-availability infrastructures, public and private cloud infrastructures, and worked for a high-frequency trading company. He also wrote a book on MariaDB named *MariaDB High Performance*. He's also one of the co-founders of Nousmotards, an application for riders.

# www.PacktPub.com

For support files and downloads related to your book, please visit www.PacktPub.com. Did you know that Packt offers eBook versions of every book published, with PDF and ePub files available? You can upgrade to the eBook version at www.PacktPub.com and as a print book customer, you are entitled to a discount on the eBook copy. Get in touch with us at service@packtpub.com for more details. At www.PacktPub.com, you can also read a collection of free technical articles, sign up for a range of free newsletters and receive exclusive discounts and offers on Packt books and eBooks.

https://www.packtpub.com/mapt

Get the most in-demand software skills with Mapt. Mapt gives you full access to all Packt books and video courses, as well as industry-leading tools to help you plan your personal development and advance your career.

# Why subscribe?

- Fully searchable across every book published by Packt
- Copy and paste, print, and bookmark content
- On demand and accessible via a web browser

# Customer Feedback

Thanks for purchasing this Packt book. At Packt, quality is at the heart of our editorial process. To help us improve, please leave us an honest review on this book's Amazon page at `https:/ / www. amazon. com/ dp/ 1786468395`.

If you'd like to join our team of regular reviewers, you can e-mail us at `customerreviews@packtpub.com`. We award our regular reviewers with free eBooks and videos in exchange for their valuable feedback. Help us be relentless in improving our products!

# Table of Contents

# Preface

Imagine creating and testing Java EE applications on Apache Tomcat or Wildfly in minutes, along with deploying and managing Java applications swiftly. Sounds too good to be true? You have a reason to cheer, because such scenarios are possible by leveraging Docker and Kubernetes.

This book will start by introducing Docker and delve deep into its networking and persistent storage concepts. You will be then introduced to the concept of microservices and learn how to deploy and run Java microservices as Docker containers. Moving on, the book will focus on Kubernetes and its features. You will start by running the local cluster using Minikube. The next step will be to deploy your Java service in the real cloud, on Kubernetes running on top of Amazon AWS. At the end of the book, you will get hands-on experience of some more advanced topics to further extend your knowledge of Docker and Kubernetes.

## What this book covers

Chapter 1, *Introduction to Docker*, introduces the reasoning behind Docker and presents the differences between Docker and traditional virtualization. The chapter also explains basic Docker concepts, such as images, containers, and Dockerfiles.

Chapter 2, *Networking and Persistent Storage*, explains how networking and persistent storage work in Docker containers.

Chapter 3, *Working with Microservices*, presents an overview of what microservices are and explains their advantages in comparison to monolithic architectures.

Chapter 4, *Creating Java Microservices*, explores a recipe for quickly constructing Java microservice, by utilizing either Java EE7 or the Spring Boot.

Chapter 5, *Creating Images with Java Applications*, teaches how to package the Java microservices into Docker images, either manually or from the Maven build file.

Chapter 6, *Running Containers with Java Applications*, shows how to run a containerized Java application using Docker.

Chapter 7, *Introduction to Kubernetes*, introduces the core concepts of Kubernetes, such as Pods, nodes, services, and deployments.

`Chapter 8`, *Using Kubernetes with Java*, shows how to deploy Java microservices, packaged as a Docker image, on the local Kubernetes cluster.

`Chapter 9`, *Working with Kubernetes API*, shows how the Kubernetes API can be used to automate the creation of Kubernetes objects such as services or deployments. This chapter gives examples of how to use the API to get information about the cluster's state.

`Chapter 10`, *Deploying Java on Kubernetes in the Cloud*, shows the reader how to configure Amazon AWS EC2 instances to make them suitable to run a Kubernetes cluster. This chapter also gives precise instructions on how to create a Kubernetes cluster on the Amazon AWS cloud.

`Chapter 11`, *More Resources*, explores how Java and Kubernetes point the reader to additional resources available on the internet that are of high quality, to further extend knowledge about Docker and Kubernetes.

# What you need for this book

For this book, you will need any decent PC or Mac, capable of running a modern version of Linux, Windows 10 64-bit, or macOS.

# Who this book is for

This book is for Java developers, who would like to get into the world of containerization. The reader will learn how Docker and Kubernetes can help with deployment and management of Java applications on clusters, either on their own infrastructure or in the cloud.

# Conventions

In this book, you will find a number of text styles that distinguish between different kinds of information. Here are some examples of these styles and an explanation of their meaning. Code words in text, database table names, folder names, filenames, file extensions, pathnames, dummy URLs, user input, and Twitter handles are shown as follows: "The Dockerfile is used to create the image when you run the `docker build` command." A block of code is set as follows:

```
{
"apiVersion": "v1",
"kind": "Pod",
"metadata":{
```

```
"name": "rest_service",
"labels": {
"name": "rest_service"
}
},
"spec": {
"containers": [{
"name": "rest_service",
"image": "rest_service",
"ports": [{"containerPort": 8080}],
}]
}
}
```

Any command-line input or output is written as follows:

```
docker rm $(docker ps -a -q -f status=exited)
```

**New terms** and **important words** are shown in bold. Words that you see on the screen, for example, in menus or dialog boxes, appear in the text like this: "Clicking the **Skip For Now** will take you to the the images list without logging into the Docker Hub."

Warnings or important notes appear in a box like this.

Tips and tricks appear like this.

# Reader feedback

Feedback from our readers is always welcome. Let us know what you think about this book-what you liked or disliked. Reader feedback is important for us as it helps us develop titles that you will really get the most out of. To send us general feedback, simply email feedback@packtpub.com, and mention the book's title in the subject of your message. If there is a topic that you have expertise in and you are interested in either writing or contributing to a book, see our author guide at www.packtpub.com/authors.

# Customer support

Now that you are the proud owner of a Packt book, we have a number of things to help you to get the most from your purchase.

## Downloading the example code

You can download the example code files for this book from your account at `http://www.packtpub.com`. If you purchased this book elsewhere, you can visit `http://www.packtpub.com/support` and register to have the files emailed directly to you. You can download the code files by following these steps:

1. Log in or register to our website using your email address and password.
2. Hover the mouse pointer on the **SUPPORT** tab at the top.
3. Click on **Code Downloads & Errata**.
4. Enter the name of the book in the **Search** box.
5. Select the book for which you're looking to download the code files.
6. Choose from the drop-down menu where you purchased this book from.
7. Click on **Code Download**.

Once the file is downloaded, please make sure that you unzip or extract the folder using the latest version of:

- WinRAR / 7-Zip for Windows
- Zipeg / iZip / UnRarX for Mac
- 7-Zip / PeaZip for Linux

The code bundle for the book is also hosted on GitHub at `https://github.com/PacktPublishing/Docker-and-Kubernetes-for-Java-Developers`. We also have other code bundles from our rich catalog of books and videos available at `https://github.com/PacktPublishing/`. Check them out!

## Downloading the color images of this book

We also provide you with a PDF file that has color images of the screenshots/diagrams used in this book. The color images will help you better understand the changes in the output. You can download this file from `http://www.packtpub.com/sites/default/files/downloads/DockerandKubernetesforJavaDevelopers_ColorImages.pdf`.

# Errata

Although we have taken every care to ensure the accuracy of our content, mistakes do happen. If you find a mistake in one of our books-maybe a mistake in the text or the code-we would be grateful if you could report this to us. By doing so, you can save other readers from frustration and help us improve subsequent versions of this book. If you find any errata, please report them by visiting http://www.packtpub.com/submit-errata, selecting your book, clicking on the **Errata Submission Form** link, and entering the details of your errata. Once your errata are verified, your submission will be accepted and the errata will be uploaded to our website or added to any list of existing errata under the Errata section of that title. To view the previously submitted errata, go to https://www.packtpub.com/books/content/support and enter the name of the book in the search field. The required information will appear under the **Errata** section.

# Piracy

Piracy of copyrighted material on the internet is an ongoing problem across all media. At Packt, we take the protection of our copyright and licenses very seriously. If you come across any illegal copies of our works in any form on the internet, please provide us with the location address or website name immediately so that we can pursue a remedy. Please contact us at copyright@packtpub.com with a link to the suspected pirated material. We appreciate your help in protecting our authors and our ability to bring you valuable content.

# Questions

If you have a problem with any aspect of this book, you can contact us at questions@packtpub.com, and we will do our best to address the problem.

# 1
# Introduction to Docker

The first thing we will do in this chapter will be to explain the reasoning behind Docker and its architecture. We will cover Docker concepts such as images, layers, and containers. Next, we will install Docker and learn how to pull a sample, basic Java application image from the `remote` registry and run it on the local machine.

Docker was created as the internal tool in the platform as a service company, dotCloud. In March 2013, it was released to the public as open source. Its source code is freely available to everyone on GitHub at: `https://github.com/docker/docker`. Not only do the core Docker Inc. team work on the development of Docker, there are also a lot of big names sponsoring their time and effort to enhance and contribute to Docker such as Google, Microsoft, IBM, Red Hat, Cisco systems, and many others. Kubernetes is a tool developed by Google for deploying containers across clusters of computers based on best practices learned by them on Borg (Google's homemade container system). It compliments Docker when it comes to orchestration, automating deployment, managing, and scaling containers; it manages workloads for Docker nodes by keeping container deployments balanced across a cluster. Kubernetes also provides ways for containers to communicate with each other, without the need for opening network ports. Kubernetes is also an open source project, living on the GitHub at `https://github.com/kubernetes/kubernetes`. Everyone can contribute. Let's begin our journey with Docker first. The following will be covered in:

- We will start with the basic idea behind this wonderful tool and show the benefits gained from using it, in comparison to traditional virtualization
- We will install Docker on three major platforms: macOS, Linux, and Windows

# The idea behind Docker

The idea behind Docker is to pack an application with all the dependencies it needs into a single, standardized unit for the deployment. Those dependencies can be binaries, libraries, JAR files, configuration files, scripts, and so on. Docker wraps up all of it into a complete filesystem that contains everything your Java application needs to run the virtual machine itself, the application server such as Wildfly or Tomcat, the application code, and `runtime` libraries, and basically everything you would install and deploy on the server to make your application run. Packaging all of this into a complete image guarantees that it is portable; it will always run in the same way, no matter what environment it is deployed in. With Docker, you can run Java applications without having to install a Java runtime on the host machine. All the problems related to incompatible JDK or JRE, wrong version of the application server, and so on are gone. Upgrades are also easy and effortless; you just run the new version of your container on the host.

If you need to do some cleanup, you can just destroy the Docker image and it's as though nothing ever happened. Think about Docker, not as a programming language or a framework, but rather as a tool that helps in solving the common problems such as installing, distributing, and managing the software. It allows developers and DevOps to build, ship, and run their code anywhere. Anywhere means also on more than one machine, and this is where Kubernetes comes in handy; we will shortly get back to it.

Having all of your application code and runtime dependencies packaged as a single and complete unit of software may seem the same as a virtualization engine, but it's far from that, as we will explain now. To fully get to know what Docker really is, first we need to understand the difference between traditional virtualization and containerization. Let's compare those two technologies now.

# Virtualization and containerization compared

A traditional virtual machine represents the hardware-level virtualization. In essence, it's a complete, virtualized physical machine with BIOS and an operating system installed. It runs on top of the host operating system. Your Java application runs in the virtualized environment as it would normally do on your own machine. There are a lot of advantages from using virtual machines for your applications. Each virtual machine can have a totally different operating system; those can be different Linux flavors, Solaris, or Windows, for example. Virtual machines are also very secure by definition; they are totally isolated, complete operating systems in a box.

However, nothing comes without a price. Virtual machines contain all the features that an operating system needs to have to be operational: core system libraries, device drivers, and so on. Sometimes they can be resource hungry and heavyweight. Virtual machines require full installation, which sometimes can be cumbersome and not so easy to set up. Last, but not least, you will need more compute power and resources to execute your application in the virtual machine the hypervisor needs to first import the virtual machine and then power it up and this takes time. However, I believe, when it comes to running Java applications, having the complete virtualized environment is not something that we would want very often. Docker comes to the rescue with the concept of containerization. Java applications (but of course, it's not limited to Java) run on Docker in an isolated environment called a container. A container is not a virtual machine in the popular sense. It behaves as a kind of operating system virtualization, but there's no emulation at all. The main difference is that while each traditional virtual machine image runs on an independent guest operating system, the Docker containers run within the same kernel running on the host machine. A container is self-sufficient and isolated not only from the underlying OS, but from other containers as well. It has its own separated filesystem and environment variables. Naturally, containers can communicate with each other (as an application and a database container for example) and also can share the files on disk. Here comes the main difference when comparing to traditional virtualization because the containers run within the same kernel they utilize fewer system resources. All the operating system core software is removed from the Docker image. The base container can be, and usually is, very lightweight. There is no overhead related to a classic virtualization hypervisor and a guest operating system. This way you can achieve almost bare metal, core performance for your Java applications. Also, the startup time of a containerized Java application is usually very low due to the minimal overhead of the container. You can also roll-out hundreds of application containers in seconds to reduce the time needed for provisioning your software. We will do this using Kubernetes in one of the coming chapters. Although Docker is quite different from the traditional virtualization engines. Be aware that containers cannot substitute virtual machines for all use cases; a thoughtful evaluation is still required to determine what is best for your application. Both solutions have their advantages. On the one hand, we have the fully isolated secure virtual machine with average performance. On the other hand, we have the containers that are missing some of the key features, but are equipped with high performance that can be provisioned very fast. Let's see what other benefits you will get when using Docker containerization.

# Benefits from using Docker

As we have said before, the major visible benefit of using Docker will be very fast performance and short provisioning time. You can create or destroy containers quickly and easily. Containers share resources such as the operating system's kernel and the needed libraries efficiently with other Docker containers. Because of that, multiple versions of an application running in containers will be very lightweight. The result is faster deployment, easier migration, and startup times.

Docker can be especially useful when deploying Java microservices. We will get back to microservices in detail in one of the coming chapters. A microservices application is composed of a series of discrete services, communicating with others via an API. Microservices break an app into a large number of small processes. They are the opposite of the monolithic applications, which run all operations as a single process or a set of large processes.

Using Docker containers enables you to deploy ready-to-run software, which is portable and extremely easy to distribute. Your containerized application simply runs within its container; there's no need for installation. The lack of an installation process has a huge advantage; it eliminates problems such as software and library conflicts or even driver compatibility issues. Docker containers are portable; they can be run from anywhere: your local machine, a remote server, and private or public cloud. All major cloud computing providers, such as **Amazon Web Services** (**AWS**) and Google's compute platform support Docker now. A container running on, let's say, an Amazon EC2 instance, can easily be transferred to some other environment, achieving exactly the same consistency and functionality. The additional level of abstraction Docker provides on the top of your infrastructure layer is an indispensable feature. Developers can create the software without worrying about the platform it will later be run on. Docker has the same promise as Java; write once, run anywhere; except instead of code, you configure your server exactly the way you want it (by picking the operating system, tuning the configuration files, installing dependencies) and you can be certain that your server template will run exactly the same on any host that runs Docker.

Because of Docker's reproducible build environment, it's particularly well suited for testing, especially in your continuous integration or continuous delivery flow. You can quickly boot up identical environments to run the tests. And because the container images are all identical each time, you can distribute the workload and run tests in parallel without a problem. Developers can run the same image on their machine that will be run in production later, which again has a huge advantage in testing.

The use of Docker containers speeds up continuous integration. There are no more endless build-test-deploy cycles; Docker containers ensure that applications run identically in development, test, and production environments. The code grows over time and becomes more and more troublesome. That's why the idea of an immutable infrastructure becomes more and more popular nowadays and the concept of containerization has become so popular. By putting your Java applications into containers, you can simplify the process of deployment and scaling. By having a lightweight Docker host that needs almost no configuration management, you manage your applications simply by deploying and redeploying containers to the host. And again, because the containers are very lightweight, it takes only seconds.

We have been talking a lot about images and containers, without getting much into the details. Let's do it now and see what Docker images and containers are.

# Docker concepts - images and containers

When dealing with Kubernetes, we will be working with Docker containers; it is an open source container cluster manager. To run our own Java application, we will need to create an image first. Let's begin with the concept of Docker images.

## Images

Think of an image as a read-only template which is a base foundation to create a container from. It's same as a recipe containing the definition of everything your application needs to operate. It can be Linux with an application server (such as Tomcat or Wildfly, for example) and your Java application itself. Every image starts from a base image; for example, Ubuntu; a Linux image. Although you can begin with a simple image and build your application stack on top of it, you can also pick an already prepared image from the hundreds available on the Internet. There are a lot of images especially useful for Java developers: `openjdk`, `tomcat`, `wildfly`, and many others. We will use them later as a foundation for our own images. It's a lot easier to have, let's say, Wildfly installed and configured properly as a starting point for your own image. You can then just focus on your Java application. If you're a novice in building images, downloading a specialized base image is a great way to get a serious speed boost in comparison to developing one by yourself.

Images are created using a series of commands, called instructions. Instructions are placed in the Dockerfile. The Dockerfile is just a plain text file, containing an ordered collection of `root` filesystem changes (the same as running a command that starts an application server, adding a file or directory, creating environmental variables, and so on.) and the corresponding execution parameters for use within a container runtime later on. Docker will read the Dockerfile when you start the process of building an image and execute the instructions one by one. The result will be the final image. Each instruction creates a new layer in the image. That image layer then becomes the parent for the layer created by the next instruction. Docker images are highly portable across hosts and operating systems; an image can be run in a Docker container on any host that runs Docker. Docker is natively supported in Linux, but has to be run in a VM on Windows and macOS. It's important to know that Docker uses images to run your code, not the Dockerfile. The Dockerfile is used to create the image when you run the `docker build` command. Also, if you publish your image to the Docker Hub, you publish a resulting image with its layers, not a source Dockerfile itself.

We have said before that every instruction in a Dockerfile creates a new layer. Layers are the internal nature of an image; Docker images are composed from them. Let's explain now what they are and what their characteristics are.

# Layers

Each image consists of a series of layers which are stacked, one on top of the another. In fact, every layer is an intermediate image. By using the **union filesystem**, Docker combines all these layers into a single image entity. The union filesystem allows transparent overlaying files and directories of separate filesystems, giving a single, consistent filesystem as a result, as you can see the following diagram:

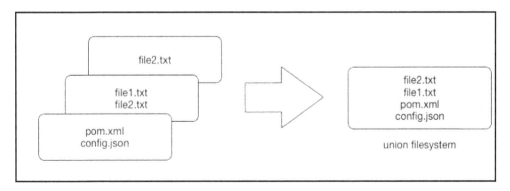

Contents and structure of directories which have the same path within these separate filesystems will be seen together in a single merged directory, within the new, virtual-like filesystem. In other words, the filesystem structure of the top layer will merge with the structure of the layer beneath. Files and directories which have the same path as in the previous layer will cover those beneath. Removing the upper layer will again reveal and expose the previous directory content. As we have mentioned earlier, layers are placed in a stack, one on the top of another. To maintain the order of layers, Docker utilizes the concept of layer IDs and pointers. Each layer contains the ID and a pointer to its parent layer. A layer without a pointer referencing the parent is the first layer in the stack, a base. You can see the relation in the following diagram:

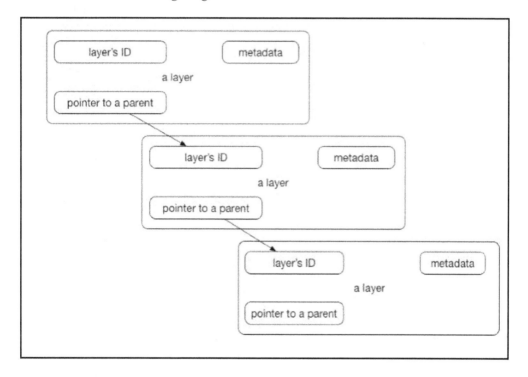

Layers have some interesting features. First, they are reusable and cacheable. The pointer to a parent layer you can see in the previous diagram is important. As Docker is processing your Dockerfile it's looking at two things: the Dockerfile instruction being executed and the parent image. Docker will scan all of the children of the parent layer and look for one whose command matches the current instruction. If a match is found, Docker skips to the next Dockerfile instruction and repeats the process. If a matching layer is not found in the cache, a new one is created. For the instructions that add files to your image (we will get to know them later in detail), Docker creates a checksum for each file contents. During the building process, this checksum is compared against the checksum of the existing images to check if the layer can be reused from the cache. If two different images have a common part, let's say a Linux shell or Java runtime for example, Docker, which tracks all of the pulled layers, will reuse the shell layer in both of the images. It's a safe operation; as you already know, layers are read-only. When downloading another image, the layer will be reused and only the difference will be pulled from the Docker Hub. This saves time, bandwidth, and disk space of course, but it has another great advantage. If you modify your Docker image, for example by modifying your containerized Java application, only the application layer gets modified. After you've successfully built an image from your Dockerfile, you will notice that subsequent builds of the same Dockerfile finish a lot faster. Once Docker caches an image layer for an instruction, it doesn't need to be rebuilt. Later on, instead of distributing the whole image, you push just the updated part. It makes the process simpler and faster. This is especially useful if you use Docker in your continuous deployment flow: pushing a Git branch will trigger building an image and then publishing the application for users. Due to the layer-reuse feature, the whole process is a lot faster.

The concept of reusable layers is also a reason why Docker is so lightweight in comparison to full virtual machines, which don't share anything. It is thanks to layers that when you pull an image, you eventually don't have to download all of its filesystem. If you already have another image that has some of the layers of the image you pull, only the missing layers are actually downloaded. There is a word of warning though, related to another feature of layers: apart from being reusable, layers are also additive. If you create a large file in the container, then make a commit (we will get to that in a while), then delete the file, and do another commit; this file will still be present in the layer history. Imagine this scenario: you pull the base Ubuntu image, and install the Wildfly application server. Then you change your mind, uninstall the Wildfly and install Tomcat instead. All those files removed from the Wildfly installation will still be present in the image, although they have been deleted. Image size will grow in no time. Understanding of Docker's layered filesystem can make a big difference in the size of your images. Size can become a problem when you publish your images to a registry; it takes more requests and is longer to transfer.

Large images become an issue when thousands of containers need to be deployed across a cluster, for example. You should always be aware of the additivity of layers and try to optimize the image at every step of your Dockerfile, the same as using the command chaining, for example. We will be using the command chaining technique later on, when creating our Java application images.

Because layers are additive, they provide a full history of how a specific image was built. This gives you another great feature: the possibility to make a rollback to a certain point in the image's history. Since every image contains all of its building steps, we can easily go back to a previous step if we want to. This can be done by tagging a certain layer. We will cover image tagging later in our book.

Layers and images are closely related to each other. As we have said before, Docker images are stored as a series of read-only layers. This means that once the container image has been created, it does not change. But having all the filesystem read-only would not make a lot of sense. What about modifying an image? Or adding your software to a base web server image? Well, when we start a container, Docker actually takes the read-only image (with all its read-only layers) and adds a writable layer on top of the layers stack. Let's focus on the containers now.

# Containers

A running instance of an image is called a container. Docker launches them using the Docker images as read-only templates. If you start an image, you have a running container of this image. Naturally, you can have many running containers of the same image. In fact, we will do it very often a little bit later, using Kubernetes.

To run a container, we use the `docker run` command:

```
docker run [OPTIONS] IMAGE [COMMAND] [ARG...]
```

There are a lot of `run` command options and switches that can be used; we will get to know them later on. Some of the options include the network configuration, for example (we will explain Docker's networking concepts in Chapter 2, *Networking and Persistent Storage*). Others, the same as the `-it` (from interactive), tell the Docker engine to behave differently; in this case, to make the container interactive and to attach a terminal to its output and input. Let's just focus on the idea of the container to better understand the whole picture. We are going to use the `docker run` command in a short while to test our setup.

So, what happens under the hood when we run the `docker run` command? Docker will check if the image that you would like to run is available on your local machine. If not, it will be pulled down from the `remote` repository. The Docker engine takes the image and adds a writable layer on top of the image's layers stack. Next, it initializes the image's name, ID, and resource limits, such as CPU and memory. In this phase, Docker will also set up a container's IP address by finding and attaching an available IP address from a pool. The last step of the execution will be the actual command, passed as the last parameter of the `docker run` command. If the `it` option has been used, Docker will capture and provide the container output, it will be displayed in the console. You can now do things you would normally do when preparing an operating system to run your applications. This can be installing packages (via `apt-get`, for example), pulling source code with Git, building your Java application using Maven, and so on. All of these actions will modify the filesystem in the top, writable layer. If you then execute the `commit` command, a new image containing all of your changes will be created, kind of frozen, and ready to be run later. To stop a container, use the `docker stop` command:

```
docker stop
```

A container when stopped will retain all settings and filesystem changes (in the top layer that is writeable). All processes running in the container will be stopped and you will lose everything in memory. This is what differentiates a stopped container from a Docker image.

To list all containers you have on your system, either running or stopped, execute the `docker ps` command:

```
docker ps -a
```

As a result, the Docker client will list a table containing container IDs (a unique identifier you can use to refer to the container in other commands), creation date, the command used to start a container, status, exposed ports, and a name, either assigned by you or the funny name Docker has picked for you. To remove a container, you can just use the `docker rm` command. If you want to remove a couple of them at once, you can use the list of containers (given by the `docker ps` command) and a filter:

```
docker rm $(docker ps -a -q -f status=exited)
```

We have said that a Docker image is always read-only and immutable. If it did not have the possibility to change the image, it would not be very useful. So how's the image modification possible except by, of course, altering a Dockerfile and doing a rebuild? When the container is started, the writable layer on top of the layers stack is for our disposal. We can actually make changes to a running container; this can be adding or modifying files, the same as installing a software package, configuring the operating system, and so on. If you modify a file in the running container, the file will be taken out of the underlying (parent) read-only layer and placed in the top, writable layer. Our changes are only possible in the top layer. The union filesystem will then cover the underlying file. The original, underlying file will not be modified; it still exists safely in the underlying, read-only layer. By issuing the docker commit command, you create a new read-only image from a running container (and all it changes in the writable layer):

```
docker commit <container-id> <image-name>
```

The docker commit command saves changes you have made to the container in the writable layer. To avoid data corruption or inconsistency, Docker will pause a container you are committing changes into. The result of the docker commit command is a brand new, read-only image, which you can create new containers from:

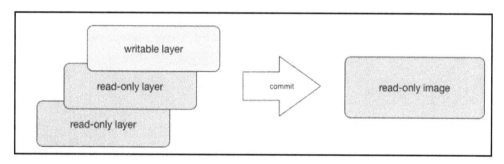

In response to a successful commit, Docker will output the full ID of a newly generated image. If you remove the container without issuing a commit first and then relaunch the same image again, Docker will start a fresh container without any of the changes made in the previously running container. In either case, with or without a commit, your changes to the filesystem will never affect the base image. Creating images by altering the top writable layer in the container is useful when debugging and experimenting, but it's usually better to use a Dockerfile to manage your images in a documented and maintainable way.

We have now learned about the build (Dockerfile and the image) and runtime (container) pieces of our containerization world. We are still missing the last element, the distribution component. The distribution component of Docker consists of the Docker registry, index, and repository. Let's focus on them now to have a complete picture.

# Docker registry, repository, and index

The first component in Docker's distribution system is the registry. Docker utilizes a hierarchical system for storing images, shown in the following screenshot:

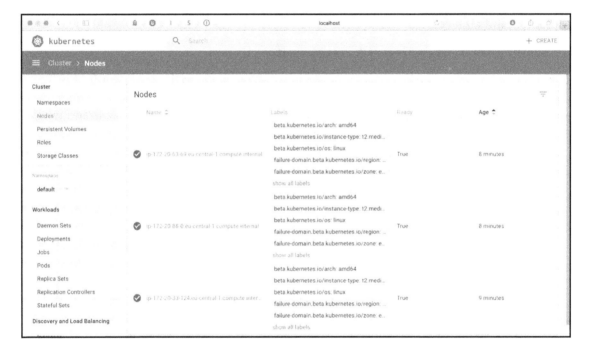

Images which you build can be stored in a `remote` registry for others to use. The `Docker` registry is a service (an application, in fact) that is storing your Docker images. The Docker Hub is an example of the publicly available registry; it's free and serves a huge, constantly growing collection of existing images. The repository, on the other hand, is a collection (namespace) of related images, usually providing different versions of the same application or service. It's a collection of different Docker images with the same name and different tags.

If your app is named `hello-world-java` and your username (or namespace) for the **Registry** is `dockerJavaDeveloper` then your image will be placed in the `dockerJavaDeveloper/hello-world-java` repository. You can tag an image and store multiple versions of that image with different IDs in a single named repository and access different tagged versions of an image with a special syntax such as `username/image_name:tag`. The `Docker` repository is quite similar to a Git repository. For example, `Git`, a `Docker` repository is identified by a URI and can either be public or private. The URI looks the same as the following:

```
{registryAddress}/{namespace}/{repositoryName}:{tag}
```

The Docker Hub is the default registry and Docker will pull images from the Docker Hub if you do not specify a registry address. To search an image in the registry, execute the `docker search` command; for example:

```
$ docker search hello-java-world
```

Without specifying the `remote` registry, Docker will conduct a search on the Docker Hub and output the list of images matching your search criteria:

The difference between the registry and repository can be confusing at the beginning, so let's describe what will happen if you execute the following command:

```
$ docker pull ubuntu:16.04
```

The command downloads the image tagged `16.04` within the `ubuntu` repository from the Docker Hub registry. The official `ubuntu` repository doesn't use a username, so the namespace part is omitted in this example.

Although the Docker Hub is public, you get one private repository for free with your Docker Hub user account. Last, but not least, the component you should be aware of is an index. An index manages searching and tagging and also user accounts and permissions. In fact, the registry delegates authentication to the index. When executing remote commands, such as `push` or `pull`, the index first will look at the name of the image and then check to see if it has a corresponding repository. If so, the index verifies if you are allowed to access or modify the image. If you are, the operation is approved and the registry takes or sends the image.

Let's summarize what we have learned so far:

- The Dockerfile is the recipe to build an image. It's a text file containing ordered instructions. Each Dockerfile has a base image you build upon
- An image is a specific state of a filesystem: a read-only, frozen immutable snapshot of a live container
- An image is composed of layers representing changes in the filesystem at various points in time; layers are a bit same as the commit history of a Git repository. Docker uses the layers cache
- Containers are runtime instances of an image. They can be running or stopped. You can have multiple containers of the same image running
- You can make changes to the filesystem on a container and commit them to make them persisted. Commit always creates a new image
- Only the filesystem changes can be committed, memory changes will be lost
- A registry holds a collection of named repositories, which themselves are a collection of images tracked by their IDs. The registry is same as a Git repository: you can `push` and `pull` images

You should now have an understanding of the nature of images with their layers and containers. But Docker is not just a Dockerfile processor and the runtime engine. Let's look at what else is available.

# Additional tools

It's a complete package with a wide selection of tools and APIs that are helpful during the developer's and DevOp's daily work. There's a Kinematic, for example, a desktop developer environment for using Docker on Windows and macOS X.

From a Java developer's perspective, there are tools available, which are especially useful in a programmer's daily job, such as the IntelliJ IDEA Docker integration plugin (we will be using this add-on heavily in the coming chapters). Eclipse fans can use the Docker tooling for Eclipse, which is available starting with Eclipse Mars. NetBeans also supports Docker commands. No matter which development environment you pick, these add-ons let you download and build Docker images, create and start containers, and carry out other related tasks straight from your favorite IDE.

Docker is so popular these days, no wonder hundreds of third-party tools have been developed to make Docker even more useful. The most prominent of them is Kubernetes, which we are going to focus on in this book. But apart from Kubernetes, there are many others. They will support you with Docker-related operations, such as continuous integration/continuous delivery, deployment and infrastructure, or optimizing images. Tens of hosting services now support running and managing Docker containers.

As Docker captures more attention, more and more Docker-related tools pop-up almost every month. You can find a very well-crafted list of Docker-related tools and services on the GitHub awesome Docker list, available at `https://github.com/veggiemonk/awesome-docker`.

But there are not only tools available. Additionally, Docker provides a set of APIs that can be very handy. One of them is the Remote API for the management of the images and containers. Using this API, you will be able to distribute your images to the runtime Docker engine. There's also the Stats API that will expose live resource usage information (such as CPU, memory, network I/O, and block I/O) for your containers. This API endpoint can be used create tools that show how your containers behave; for example, on a production system.

As we now know the idea behind Docker, the differences between virtualization and containerization, and the benefits of using Docker, let's get to the action. We are going to install Docker first.

# Installing Docker

In this section, we will find out how to install Docker on Windows, macOS, and Linux operating systems. Next, we will run a sample `hello-world` image to verify the setup and check if everything works fine after the installation process.

Docker installation is quite straightforward, but there are some things you will need to focus on to make it run smoothly. We will point them out to make the installation process painless. You should know that Linux is the natural environment for Docker. If you run the container, it will run on a Linux kernel. If you run your container on Docker running on Linux, it will use the kernel of your own machine. This is not the case in macOS and Windows; that's the reason why the Linux kernel needs to be virtualized if you want to run a Docker container on these operating systems. The Docker engine, when running on macOS or MS Windows, will use the lightweight Linux distribution, made specifically to run Docker containers. It runs completely from RAM, using only several megabytes, and boots in a couple of seconds. After the installation of the main Docker package on macOS and Windows, the OS built-in virtualization engine will be used by default. Therefore, there are some special requirements for your machine. For the newest, native Docker setup, which is deeply integrated into native virtualization engines present in your operating system, you will need to have 64-bit Windows 10 professional or enterprise. For macOS, the newest Docker for Mac is a native Mac application developed from scratch, with a native user interface, integrated with OS X native virtualization, hypervisor framework, networking, and filesystem. The mandatory requirement will be Yosemite 10.10.3 or newer. Let's begin with installing on macOS.

## Installing on macOS

To get the native Docker version for your Mac, head to the `http://www.docker.com` and then the **Get Docker** macOS section. Docker for Mac is a standard, native `dmg` package you can mount. You will find just a single application inside the package:

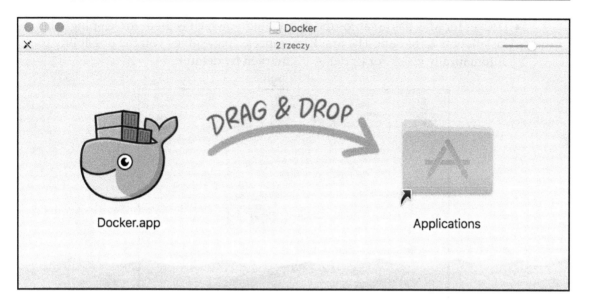

Now just move the `Docker.app` into your `Applications` folder, and you are all set. Couldn't be easier. If you run Docker, it will sit as a small whale icon in your macOS menu. The icon will animate during the Docker startup process and stabilize after it finishes:

- If you now click the **icon**, it will give you a handy menu with the Docker status and some additional options:

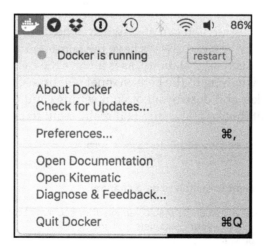

- Docker for Mac has an auto-update capability, which is great for keeping your installation up to date. The first **Preferences...** pane gives you the possibility to automatically check for updates; it's marked by default:

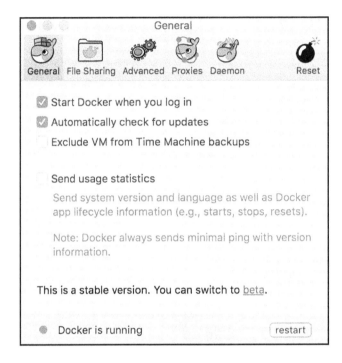

- If you are a brave soul, you can also switch to the beta channel for getting updates. This way you can always have the latest and greatest Docker features, with the risk of decreased stability, as is always the case with beta software. Also take note that switching to the beta channel will uninstall your current stable version of Docker and destroy all of your settings and containers. Docker will warn you about this, to make sure you really want to do it:

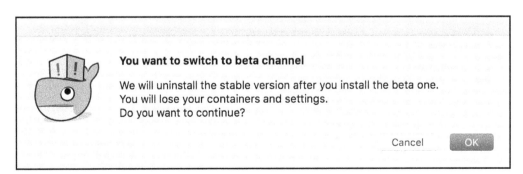

- The **File Sharing** pane of the **Preferences**... will give you an option to mark macOS directories on your machine to be bind mounted into Docker containers you are going to run later. We will explain mounting directories in detail later on in the book. For the time being, let's just have the default set of selected directories:

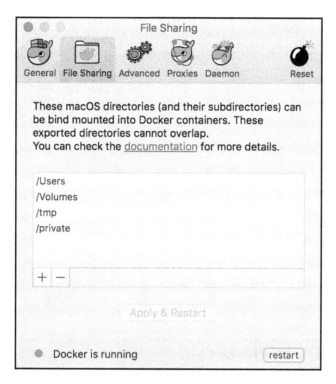

- The **Advanced** pane has some options to adjust the resources of your computer that will be available for Docker, it will be the number of processors and memory amount. The default settings are usually a good start if you begin with Docker on macOS:

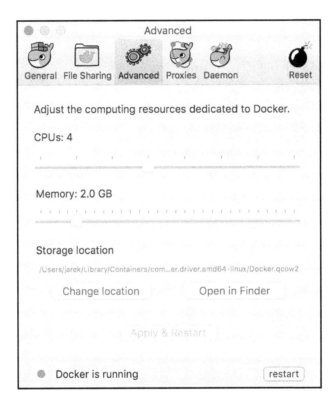

- The **Proxies** pane gives you the possibility to setup a proxy, if you need it on your machine. You can opt for using system or manual settings, as you can see in the following screenshot:

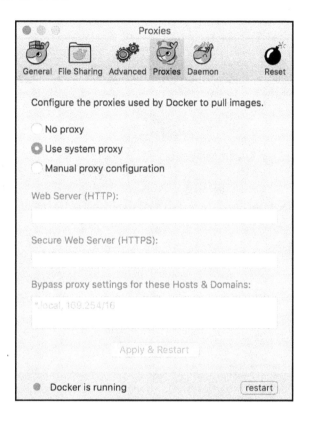

- On the next page, you can edit some Docker daemon settings. This will include adding registries and registry mirrors. Docker will use them when pulling the image. The **Advanced** tab contains a text field, in which you can enter the JSON text containing the daemon config:

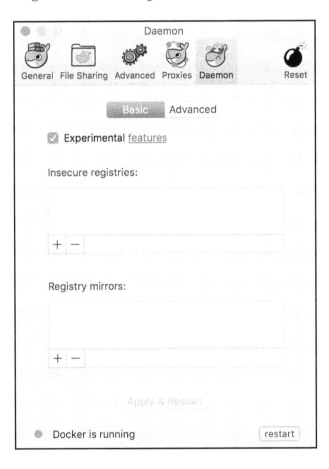

- In the **Daemon** pane, you can also turn off Docker **Experimental features**. For some time now, **Experimental features** have been enabled by default. From time to time, a new version of Docker comes with new **Experimental features**. At the time of writing this book, they will include, for example, **Checkpoint & Restore** (a feature that allows you to freeze a running container by checkpointing it), Docker graph driver plugins (to use an external/out-of-process graph driver for use with the Docker engine as an alternative to using the built-in storage drivers), and some others. It's always interesting to see what new features are included in the new version of Docker. Clicking the link in the **Daemon** page will take you to the GitHub page which lists and explains all the new experimental features.
- The last **Preferences...** pane is the Reset. If you find that your Docker won't start or behaves badly, you can try to reset the Docker installation to the factory defaults:

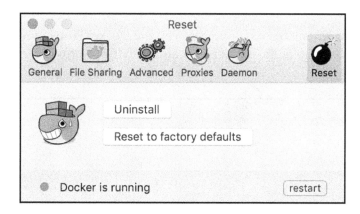

You should be warned though, that resetting Docker to the factory state will also remove all downloaded images and containers you may have on your machine. If you have images that have not been pushed anywhere yet, having a backup first is always a good idea.

The **Open Kitematic** in the Docker menu is a handy shortcut to open the **Kitematic** application we have mentioned earlier. It's a desktop utility for using Docker on Windows and Mac OS X. If you do not have **Kitematic** installed already, Docker will give you a link with the installation package:

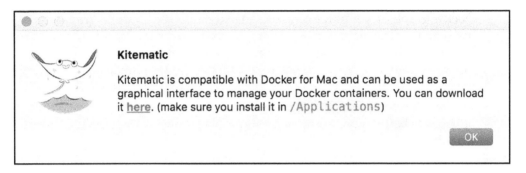

- If you run **Kitematic**, it will present you the Docker Hub login screen first. You can now Sign up to the Docker Hub and then log in providing your **username** and **password**:

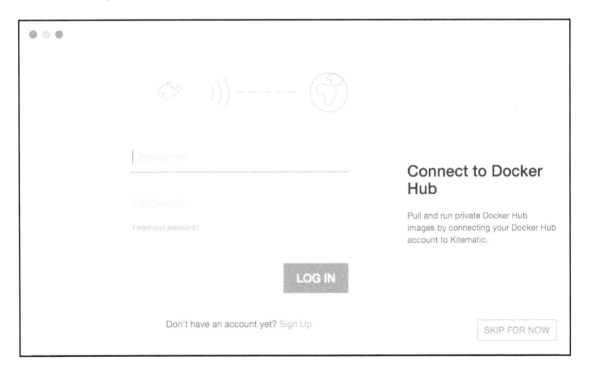

Clicking on **Skip For Now** will take you to the images list without logging into the Docker Hub. Let's test our installation by pulling and running an image. Let's search for `hello-java-world`, as seen on the following screenshot:

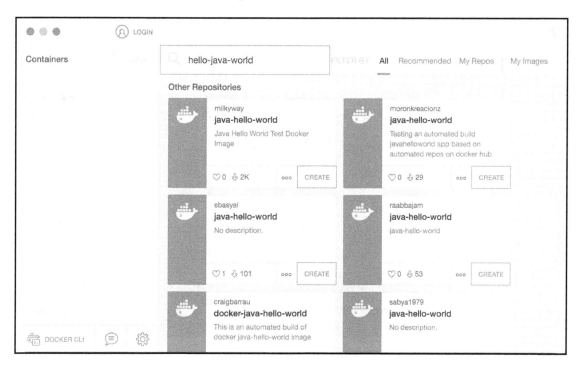

After pulling the image from the registry, start it. **Kitematic** will present the running **Container** logs, which will be the famous `hello world` message, coming from a containerized Java application:

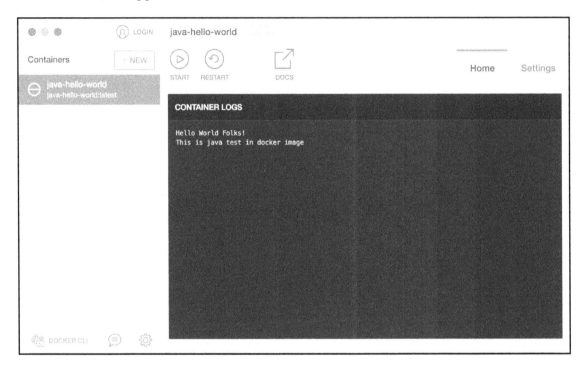

That's it for running the container in **Kitematic**. Let's try to do the same from the shell. Execute the following in the terminal:

```
$ docker run milkyway/java-hello-world
```

As a result, you will see the same greeting, coming from a containerized Java application, this time in the macOS terminal:

```
● ● ●  jarek@ubuntu: ~
Preparing to unpack .../docker-engine_1.13.1-0~ubuntu-xenial_amd64.deb ...
Unpacking docker-engine (1.13.1-0~ubuntu-xenial) ...
Selecting previously unselected package liberror-perl.
Preparing to unpack .../liberror-perl_0.17-1.2_all.deb ...
Unpacking liberror-perl (0.17-1.2) ...
Selecting previously unselected package git-man.
Preparing to unpack .../git-man_1%3a2.7.4-0ubuntu1_all.deb ...
Unpacking git-man (1:2.7.4-0ubuntu1) ...
Selecting previously unselected package git.
Preparing to unpack .../git_1%3a2.7.4-0ubuntu1_amd64.deb ...
Unpacking git (1:2.7.4-0ubuntu1) ...
Processing triggers for libc-bin (2.23-0ubuntu5) ...
Processing triggers for man-db (2.7.5-1) ...
Processing triggers for ureadahead (0.100.0-19) ...
Processing triggers for systemd (229-4ubuntu16) ...
Setting up aufs-tools (1:3.2+20130722-1.1ubuntu1) ...
Setting up cgroupfs-mount (1.2) ...
Setting up docker-engine (1.13.1-0~ubuntu-xenial) ...
Setting up liberror-perl (0.17-1.2) ...
Setting up git-man (1:2.7.4-0ubuntu1) ...
Setting up git (1:2.7.4-0ubuntu1) ...
Processing triggers for libc-bin (2.23-0ubuntu5) ...
Processing triggers for systemd (229-4ubuntu16) ...
Processing triggers for ureadahead (0.100.0-19) ...
jarek@ubuntu:~$ []
```

That's it, we have a native Docker up and running on our macOS. Let's install it on Linux, as well.

# Installing on Linux

There are a lot of various Linux distributions out there and the installation process can be a little bit different for each Linux distribution. I'm going to install Docker on the latest, 16.04 Ubuntu desktop:

1. First, we need to allow the `apt` package manager to use a repository over the HTTPS protocol. Execute from the shell:

   ```
   $ sudo apt-get install -y --no-install-recommends apt-
   transport-https ca-certificates curl software-properties-common
   ```

2. The next thing we are going to do is add Docker's `apt` repository `gpg` key to our `apt` sources list:

   ```
   $ curl -fsSL https://download.docker.com/linux/ubuntu/gpg |
   sudo apt-key add -
   ```

3. A simple OK will be the response if succeeded. Use the following command to set up the stable repository:

```
$ sudo add-apt-repository "deb [arch=amd64]
https://download.docker.com/linux/ubuntu $(lsb_release -cs)
stable"
```

4. Next, we need to update the apt packages index:

```
$ sudo apt-get update
```

5. Now we need to make sure the apt installer will use the official Docker repository instead of the default Ubuntu repository (which may contain the older version of Docker):

```
$ apt-cache policy docker-ce
```

6. Use this command to install the latest version of Docker:

```
$ sudo apt-get install -y docker-ce
```

7. The apt package manager will download a lot of packages; those will be the needed dependencies and the docker-engine itself:

```
jarek@jarek-ubuntu: ~
Unpacking aufs-tools (1:3.2+20130722-1.1ubuntu1) ...
Selecting previously unselected package cgroupfs-mount.
Preparing to unpack .../cgroupfs-mount_1.2_all.deb ...
Unpacking cgroupfs-mount (1.2) ...
Selecting previously unselected package docker-ce.
Preparing to unpack .../docker-ce_17.06.1~ce-0~ubuntu_amd64.deb ...
Unpacking docker-ce (17.06.1~ce-0~ubuntu) ...
Selecting previously unselected package liberror-perl.
Preparing to unpack .../liberror-perl_0.17-1.2_all.deb ...
Unpacking liberror-perl (0.17-1.2) ...
Selecting previously unselected package git-man.
Preparing to unpack .../git-man_1%3a2.7.4-0ubuntu1.2_all.deb ...
Unpacking git-man (1:2.7.4-0ubuntu1.2) ...
Selecting previously unselected package git.
Preparing to unpack .../git_1%3a2.7.4-0ubuntu1.2_amd64.deb ...
Unpacking git (1:2.7.4-0ubuntu1.2) ...
Processing triggers for libc-bin (2.23-0ubuntu9) ...
Processing triggers for man-db (2.7.5-1) ...
Processing triggers for ureadahead (0.100.0-19) ...
Processing triggers for systemd (229-4ubuntu19) ...
Setting up aufs-tools (1:3.2+20130722-1.1ubuntu1) ...
Setting up cgroupfs-mount (1.2) ...
Setting up docker-ce (17.06.1-ce-0~ubuntu) ...
Setting up liberror-perl (0.17-1.2) ...
Setting up git-man (1:2.7.4-0ubuntu1.2) ...
Setting up git (1:2.7.4-0ubuntu1.2) ...
Processing triggers for libc-bin (2.23-0ubuntu9) ...
Processing triggers for systemd (229-4ubuntu19) ...
Processing triggers for ureadahead (0.100.0-19) ...
jarek@jarek-ubuntu:~$
```

8. That's it, you should be all set. Let's verify if Docker works on our Linux box:

    ```
    $sudo docker run milkyway/java-hello-world
    ```

9. As you can see, the Docker engine will pull the `milkyway/java-hello-world` image with all its layers from the Docker Hub and respond with a greeting:

```
jarek@ubuntu: ~

jarek@ubuntu:~$ sudo docker run milkyway/java-hello-world
Unable to find image 'milkyway/java-hello-world:latest' locally
latest: Pulling from milkyway/java-hello-world
df22f9f3e4ec: Pull complete
a3ed95caeb02: Pull complete
1baedbcb8739: Pull complete
8fc9ba848e58: Pull complete
6714492f3def: Pull complete
4533be7d59e7: Pull complete
6edb4dde5ad2: Pull complete
069a03f4fbaf: Pull complete
Digest: sha256:4ea6174262db78a4691c86759bb18a595f7782373ce482c0f7a7eca297ddfd60
Status: Downloaded newer image for milkyway/java-hello-world:latest
Hello World Folks!
This is java test in docker image
jarek@ubuntu:~$
```

But do we need to run Docker commands with `sudo`? The reason for that is the Docker daemon always runs as the `root` user, and since Docker version 0.5.2, the Docker daemon binds to a Unix socket instead of a TCP port. By default, that Unix socket is owned by the user `root`, and so, by default, you can access it with sudo. Let's fix it to be able to run the `Docker` command as a normal user:

1. First, add the `Docker` group if it doesn't already exist:

    ```
    $ sudo groupadd docker
    ```

2. Then, add your own user to the Docker group. Change the username to match your preferred user:

```
$ sudo gpasswd -a jarek docker
```

3. Restart the Docker daemon:

```
$ sudo service docker restart
```

4. Now let's log out and log in again, and execute the docker run command one more time, without sudo this time. As you can see, you are now able to work with Docker as a normal, non-root user:

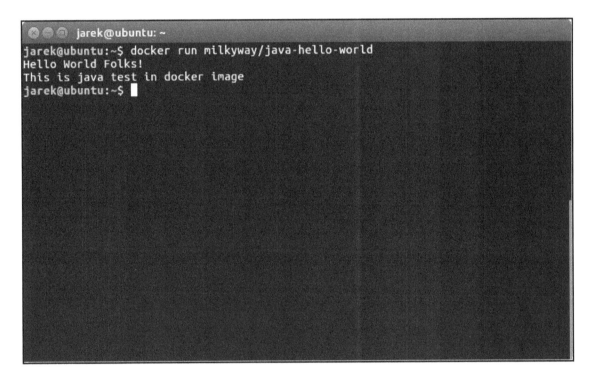

```
jarek@ubuntu: ~
jarek@ubuntu:~$ docker run milkyway/java-hello-world
Hello World Folks!
This is java test in docker image
jarek@ubuntu:~$ 
```

5. That's it. Our Linux Docker installation is ready to play with. Let's do an installation on the Windows box now.

# Installing on Windows

The native Docker package can be run on 64-bit Windows 10 Professional or Enterprise. It uses the Windows 10 virtualization engine to virtualize the Linux kernel. This is the reason that the installation package does no longer contain the VirtualBox setup, as with the previous versions of Docker for Windows. The native application comes in a typical .msi installation package. If you run it, it will greet you with a friendly message, saying that it is going to live in your task bar tray, under the small whale icon, from now on:

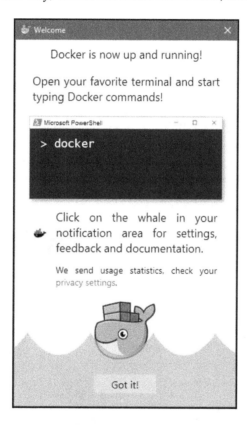

The **Docker's** icon in the tray informs you about the Docker engine state. It also contains a small but useful context menu:

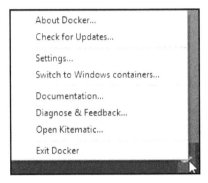

Let's explore the preferences settings and see what's available. The first tab, **General**, allows you to set Docker to run automatically when you log in. If you use Docker daily that may be the recommended setting. You can also mark to check for updates automatically and send usage statistics. Sending usage statistics will help the Docker team improve the tool in future versions; unless you have some mission critical, secure work to be done, I recommend turning this option on. This is a great way to contribute to future versions of this magnificent tool:

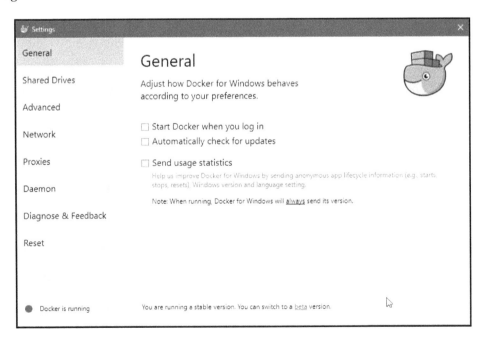

The second tab, **Shared Drives**, allows you to select the local Windows drives which will be available to the Docker containers you will be running:

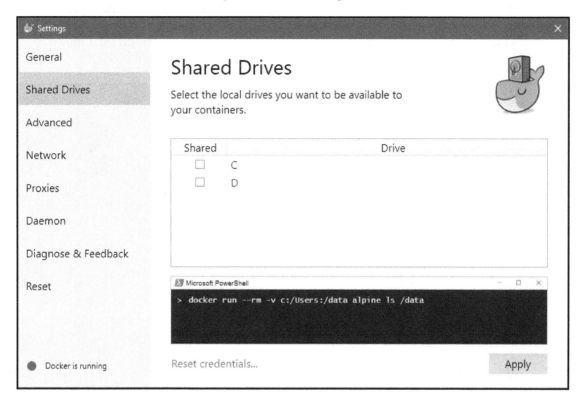

We are going to cover Docker volumes in `Chapter 2`, *Networking and Persistent Storage*. Selecting a drive here means that you can map a directory from your local system and read that as a Windows host machine to your Docker container. The next preferences page, **Advanced**, allows us to make some restrictions on the Docker engine running on our Windows PC and also select the location of the virtual machine image with the Linux kernel:

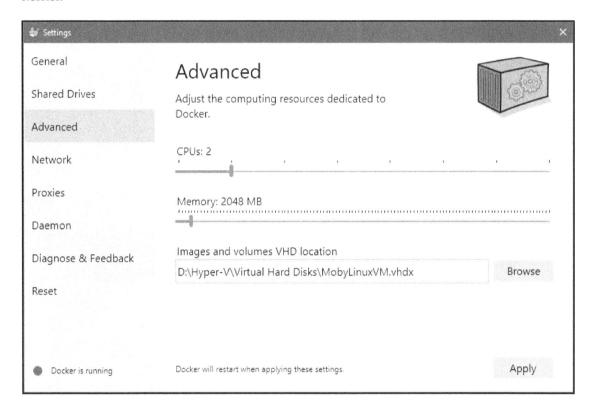

The default values are usually good out of the box and unless you experience problems during the development process, I would recommend leaving them as they are. The **Network** lets you configure the way Docker works with the network, the same as subnet address and mask or DNS server. We are going to cover Docker networking in Chapter 2, *Networking and Persistent Storage*:

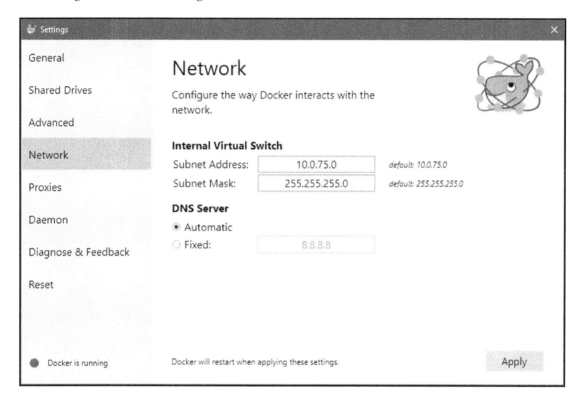

If you're behind a proxy in your network and would like Docker to access the Internet, you can set up the proxy settings in the **Proxies** tab:

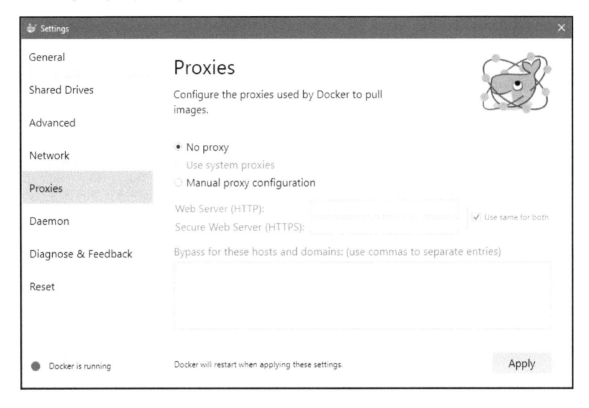

The dialog is similar to what you find in other applications where you can define proxy settings. It can accept no proxy, system proxy settings, or manual settings (with a different proxy for HTPP and HTTPS communication). The next pane can be useful to configure the Docker daemon:

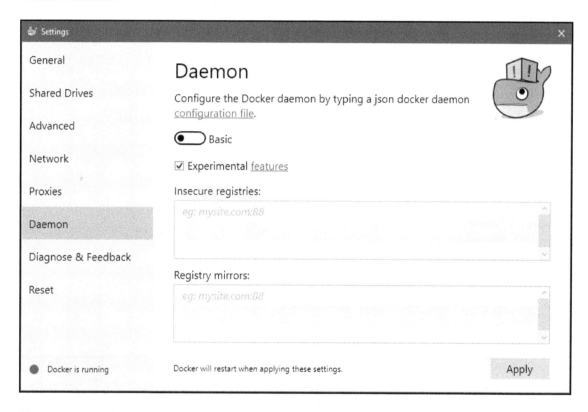

The Basic switch means that Docker uses the basic configuration. You can switch it to Advanced and provide a customized setting in a form of JSON structure. The **Experimental features** are the same as we have already mentioned during the Docker setup on macOS, this will be **Checkpoint & Restore** or enabling Docker graph driver plugins, for example. You can also specify a list of remote registries. Docker will be pulling images from insecure registries using just plain HTTP instead of HTTPS.

Using the **Reset** options on the last pane lets you restart or reset Docker to its factory settings:

Be aware though, that resetting Docker to its initial settings will also remove all images and containers currently present on your machine.

The **Open Kitematic...** option, which is also present in the Docker tray icon context menu, is a quick shortcut to launch **Kitematic**. If you do it for the first time and don't have **Kitematic** installed, Docker will ask if you would like to download it first:

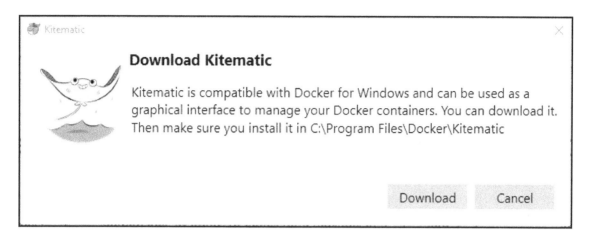

That's it for installing Docker for Windows. It's a pretty painless process. As a last step of the installation process, let's check if Docker can be run from the command prompt, because it's probably the way you will be launching it in the future. Execute the following command in the command prompt or in the PowerShell:

```
docker run milkyway/java-hello-world
```

```
PS C:\Users\jarek> docker run milkyway/java-hello-world
Unable to find image 'milkyway/java-hello-world:latest' locally
latest: Pulling from milkyway/java-hello-world
df22f9f3e4ec: Pull complete
a3ed95caeb02: Pull complete
1baedbcb8739: Pull complete
8fc9ba848e58: Pull complete
6714492f3def: Pull complete
4533be7d59e7: Pull complete
6edb4dde5ad2: Pull complete
069a03f4fbaf: Pull complete
Digest: sha256:4ea6174262db78a4691c86759bb18a595f7782373ce482c0f7a7eca297ddfd60
Status: Downloaded newer image for milkyway/java-hello-world:latest
Hello World Folks!
This is java test in docker image
PS C:\Users\jarek>
```

As you can see on the previous screenshot, we have a Hello World message coming from the Java application started as a Docker container.

# Summary

That's it. Our Docker for Windows installation is fully functional. In this chapter, we have learned about the idea behind Docker and the main differences between traditional virtualization and containerization. We know a lot about Docker core concepts such as images, layers, containers, and registries. We should have Docker installed already on our local machine; it's now time to move on and learn about more advanced Docker features, such as networking and persistent storage.

# 2
# Networking and Persistent Storage

We learned a lot about Docker concepts in the previous chapter. We know that the container is a runtime of an image. It will contain your Java application altogether with all needed dependencies, such as JRE or an application server. But, there are rare cases when the Java application is self-sufficient. It always needs to communicate with other servers (as a database), or expose itself to others (as a web application running on the application server which needs to accept requests coming from the user or from the other applications). It's time to describe ways to open the Docker container to the outside world, networking, and persistent storage. In this chapter, you are going to learn how to configure networking, and expose and map network ports. By doing that, you will enable your Java application to communicate with other containers. Imagine the following scenario: you can have one container running a Tomcat application server with your Java application, communicating with another container running a database, `PostgreSQL` for example. While the Kubernetes approach to networking is somewhat different in comparison to what Docker provides by default, let's focus on Docker itself briefly now. We are going to cover Kubernetes' specific networking later on. The container communication with the outside world is not only about networking; in this chapter, we will also focus on data volumes as a way to persist the data between container run and stop cycles.

This chapter covers the following topics:

- Docker network types
- Networking commands
- Creating a network
- Mapping and exposing ports
- Volume-related commands
- Creating and removing volumes

Let's begin with Docker networking.

# Networking

To make your container able to communicate with the outside world, whether another server or another Docker container, Docker provides different ways of configuring networking. Let's begin with the network types which are available for our containers.

# Docker network types

There are three different network types Docker delivers out of the box. To list them, execute the `docker network ls` command:

```
$ docker network ls
```

Docker will output the list of available networks containing the unique network identifier, its name, and a driver which powers it behind the scenes:

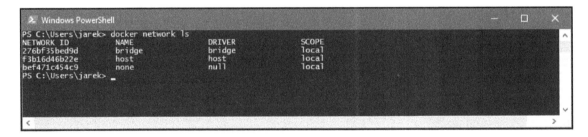

To have an overview of the differences between various network types, let's describe them now one by one.

# Bridge

This is the default network type in Docker. When the Docker service daemon starts, it configures a virtual bridge, named `docker0`. If you do not specify a network with the `docker run -net=<NETWORK>` option, the Docker daemon will connect the container to the bridge network by default. Also, if you create a new container, it will be connected to the bridge network. For each container that Docker creates, it allocates a virtual Ethernet device which will be attached to the bridge. The virtual Ethernet device is mapped to appear as `eth0` in the container, using Linux namespaces, as you can see in the following diagram:

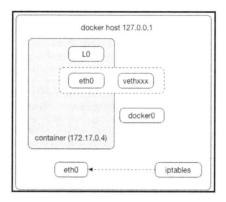

The `in-container eth0` interface is given an IP address from the bridge's address range. In other words, Docker will find a free IP address from the range available on the bridge and will configure the container's `eth0` interface with that IP address. From now on, if the new container wants to, for example, connect to the Internet, it will use the bridge; the host's own IP address. The bridge will automatically forward packets between any other network interfaces that are attached to it and also allow containers to communicate with the host machine, as well as with the containers on the same host. The bridge network will probably be the most frequently used one.

# Host

This type of network just puts the container in the host's network stack. That is, all of the network interfaces defined on the host will be accessible to the container, as you can see in the following diagram:

If you start your container using the -net=host option, then the container will use the host network. It will be as fast as normal networking: there is no bridge, no translation, nothing. That's why it can be useful when you need to get the best network performance. Containers running in the host's network stack will achieve faster network performance compared to those running on bridge networking, there is no need to traverse the docker0 bridge and iptables port mappings. In host mode, the container shares the networking namespace of the host (your local machine, for example), directly exposing it to the outside world. By using the -net=host command switch, your container will be accessible through the host's IP address. However, you need to be aware that this can be dangerous. If you have an application running as root and it has some vulnerabilities, there will be a risk of a security breach, as someone can get remote control of the host network via the Docker container. Using the host network type also means that you will need to use port mapping to reach services inside the container. We are going to cover port mapping later, in this chapter.

## None

To cut a long story short, the none network does not configure networking at all. There is no driver being used by this network type. It's useful when you don't need your container to have network access; the -net=none switch to docker run command completely disables networking.

Docker provides a short list of commands to deal with networking. You can run them from the shell (Linux or macOS) or the command prompt and PowerShell in Windows. Let's get to know them now.

# Networking commands

The parent command for managing networks in Docker is docker network. You can list the whole command set using the docker network help command, as you can see in the following screenshot:

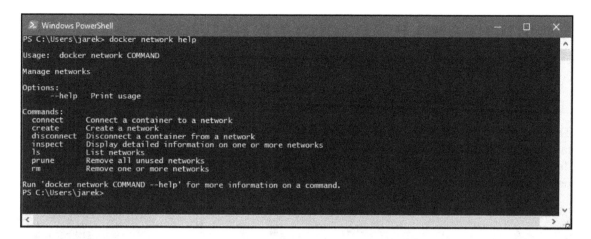

To have a detailed syntax and description of each option available for a specific command, use the `-help` switch for each of the commands. For example, to get the description of parameters available for `docker network create`, execute the `docker network create -help`.

Let's briefly describe each command available:

- **$ docker network ls**: This is the command we have been using previously, it simply lists networks available for your containers. It will output the network identifier, its name, the driver being used, and a scope of the network

- **$ docker network create**: Creates new network. The full syntax of the command is, `docker network create [OPTIONS] NETWORK`. We will use the command in a short while

- **$ docker network rm**: The `dockercnetworkcrm` command simply removes the network

- **$ docker network connect**: Connects the container to the specific network

- **$ docker network disconnect**: As the name suggests, it will disconnect the container from the network

- **$ docker network inspect**: The docker network inspect command displays detailed information about the network. It's very useful, if you have network issues. We are going to create and inspect our network now

The `docker network` inspect command displays detailed information about the network. It's very useful if you have network issues. We are going to create and inspect our network now.

# Creating and inspecting a network

Let's create a network. We are going to call our network `myNetwork`. Execute the following command from the shell or command line:

```
$ docker network create myNetwork
```

This is the simplest form of the command, and yet it will probably be used the most often. It takes a default driver (we haven't used any option to specify a driver, we will just use the default one, which is bridge). As the output, Docker will print out the identifier of the newly created network:

You will later use this identifier to refer to this network when connecting containers to it or inspecting the network's properties. The last parameter of the command is the network's name, which is a lot more convenient and easier to remember than the ID. The network name in our case is `myNetwork`. The `docker network` create command takes more parameters, as shown in the following table:

| Option | Description |
|---|---|
| `-d, --driver="bridge"` | Driver to manage the network |
| `--aux-address=map[]` | Auxiliary IPv4 or IPv6 addresses used by network driver |
| `--gateway=[]` | IPv4 or IPv6 gateway for the master subnet |
| `--ip-range=[]` | Allocate container IP from a sub-range |
| `--ipam-driver=default` | IP address management driver |
| `-o, --opt=map[]` | Set driver's specific options |
| `--subnet=[]` | Subnet in CIDR format that represents a network segment |

One of the most important parameters is the `-d` (`--driver`) option, with the default value bridge. Drivers let you specify the network type. As you remember, Docker has a couple of drivers available by default: `host`, `bridge`, and `none`.

After creating a network, we can inspect its properties using the `docker network inspect` command. Execute the following from the shell or command line:

```
$ docker network inspect myNetwork
```

In response, you will get a lot of detailed information about your network. As you can see in the screenshot, our newly created network uses the bridge driver, even if we haven't explicitly asked for it:

As you can see, the container list is empty, and the reason why is that we haven't connected any container to this network yet. Let's do it now.

# Connecting a container to the network

Now we have our `myNetwork` ready, we can run the Docker container and attach it to the network. To launch containers, we are going to user the `docker run --net=<NETWORK>` option, where the `<NETWORK>` is the name of one of the default networks or the one you have created yourself. Let's run Apache Tomcat for example, which is an open source implementation of the Java Servlet and JavaServer pages technologies:

```
docker run -it --net=myNetwork tomcat
```

It will take a while. The Docker engine will pull all of the Tomcat's image layers from the Docker Hub and then run the Tomcat container. There's another option to attach the network to the container, you can inform Docker that you would like the container to connect to the same network as other containers use. This way, instead of specifying a network explicitly, you just instruct Docker that you want two containers run on the same network. To do this, use the `container:` prefix, as in the following example:

```
docker run -it --net=bridge myTomcat
docker run -it --net=container:myTomcat myPostgreSQL
```

In the previous example, we run the `myTomcat` image using the bridge network. The next command will run the `myPostgreSQL` image, using the same network as `myTomcat` uses. This is a very common scenario; your application will run on the same network as the database and this will allow them to communicate. Of course, the containers you launch into the same network must be run on the same Docker host. Each container in the network can directly communicate with other containers in the network. Though, the network itself isolates the containers from external networks, as seen in the following diagram:

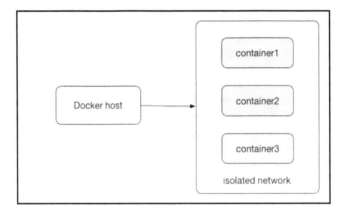

If you run your containers in a bridge, isolated network, we need to instruct Docker on how to map the ports of our containers to the host's ports. We are going to do this now.

# Exposing ports and mapping ports

A common scenario is usually when you want your containerized application to accept incoming connections, either from other containers or from outside of Docker. It can be an application server listening on port 80 or a database accepting incoming requests.

An image can expose ports. Exposing ports means that your containerized application will listen on an exposed port. As an example, the Tomcat application server will listen on the port 8080 by default. All containers running on the same host and on the same network can communicate with Tomcat on this port. Exposing a port can be done in two ways. It can be either in the Dockerfile with the EXPOSE instruction (we will do this in the chapter about creating images later) or in the docker run command using the --expose option. Take this official Tomcat image Dockerfile fragment (note that it has been shortened for clarity of the example):

```
FROM openjdk:8-jre-alpine
ENV CATALINA_HOME /usr/local/tomcat
ENV PATH $CATALINA_HOME/bin:$PATH
RUN mkdir -p "$CATALINA_HOME"
WORKDIR $CATALINA_HOME
EXPOSE 8080
CMD ["catalina.sh", "run"]
```

As you can see, there's an EXPOSE 8080 instruction near the end of the Dockerfile. It means that we could expect that the container, when run, will listen on port number 8080. Let's run the latest Tomcat image again. This time, we will also give our container a name, myTomcat. Start the application server using the following command:

```
docker run -it --name myTomcat --net=myNetwork tomcat
```

For the purpose of checking if containers on the same network can communicate, we will use another image, busybox. BusyBox is software that provides several stripped-down Unix tools in a single executable file. Let's run the following command in the separate shell or command prompt window:

```
docker run -it --net container:myTomcat busybox
```

As you can see, we have instructed Docker that we want our busybox container to use the same network as Tomcat uses. As an alternative, we could of course go with specifying a network name explicitly, using the --net myNetwork option.

Let's check if they indeed can communicate. Execute the following in the shell window with busybox running:

```
$ wget localhost:8080
```

The previous instruction will execute the `HTTP GET` request on port `8080`, on which Tomcat is listening in another container. After the successful download of Tomcat's `index.html`, we have proof that both containers can communicate:

```
Windows PowerShell                                               —   □   ×
/ # wget localhost:8080
Connecting to localhost:8080 (127.0.0.1:8080)
index.html           100% |*********************************************| 11230    0:00:00 ETA
/ #
```

So far so good, containers running on the same host and the same network can communicate with each other. But what about communicating with our container from the outside? Mapping ports comes in handy. We can map a port, exposed by the Docker container, into the port of the host machine, which will be a localhost in our case. The general idea is that we want the port on the host to be mapped to a specific port in the running container, the same as port number `8080` of the Tomcat container.

To bind a port (or group of ports) from a host to the container, we use the `-p` flag of the `docker run` command, as in the following example:

```
$ docker run -it --name myTomcat2 --net=myNetwork -p 8080:8080 tomcat
```

The previous command runs another Tomcat instance, also connected to the `myNetwork` network. This time, however, we map the container's port `8080` to the host's port of the same number. The syntax of the `-p` switch is quite straightforward: you just enter the host port number, a colon, and then a port number in the container you would like to be mapped:

```
$ docker run -p <hostPort>:<containerPort> <image ID or name>
```

The Docker image can expose a whole range of ports to other containers using either the `EXPOSE` instruction in a Dockerfile (the same as `EXPOSE 7000-8000`, for example) or the `docker run` command, for example:

```
$ docker run --expose=7000-8000 <container ID or name>
```

You can then map a whole range of ports from the host to the container by using the `docker run` command:

```
$ docker run -p 7000-8000:7000-8000 <container ID or name>
```

Let's verify if we can access the Tomcat container from outside of Docker. To do this, let's run Tomcat with mapped ports:

```
$ docker run -it --name myTomcat2 --net=myNetwork -p 8080:8080 tomcat
```

Then, we can simply enter the following address in our favorite web browser: http://localhost:8080.

As a result, we can see Tomcat's default welcome page, served straight from the Docker container running, as you can see in the following screenshot:

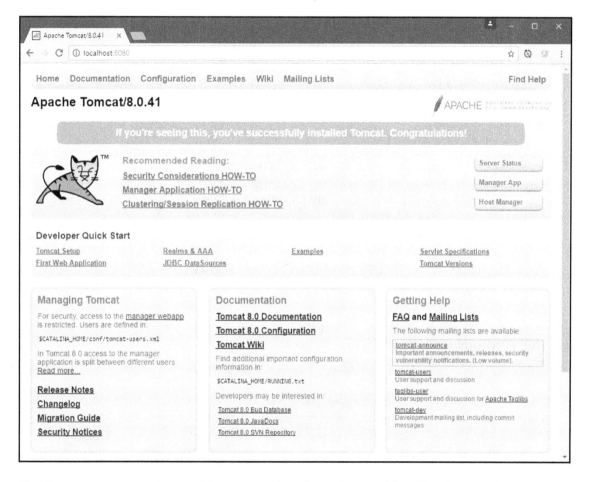

Good, we can communicate with our container from the outside of Docker. By the way, we now have two isolated Tomcats running on the host, without any port conflicts, resource conflicts, and so on. This is the power of containerization.

You may ask, what is the difference between exposing and mapping ports, that is, between --expose switch and –p switches? Well, the --expose will expose a port at runtime but will not create any mapping to the host. Exposed ports will be available only to another container running on the same network, on the same Docker host. The –p option, on the other hand, is the same as publish: it will create a port mapping rule, mapping a port on the container with the port on the host system. The mapped port will be available from outside Docker. Note that if you do –p, but there is no EXPOSE in the Dockerfile, Docker will do an implicit EXPOSE. This is because, if a port is open to the public, it is automatically also open to other Docker containers.

There is no way to create a port mapping in the Dockerfile. Mapping a port or ports is, just a runtime option. The reason for that is because port mapping configuration depends on the host. The Dockerfile needs to be host-independent and portable.

You can bind a port using –p in the runtime only.

There is yet one more option, which allows you to map all ports exposed in an image (that is; in the Dockerfile) at once, automatically during the container startup. The –P switch (capital P this time) will map a dynamically allocated random host port to all container ports that have been exposed in the Dockerfile by the EXPOSE instruction.

The –p option gives you more control than –P when mapping ports. Docker will not automatically pick any random port; it's up to you what ports on the host should be mapped to the container ports.

If you run the following command, Docker will map a random port on the host to Tomcat's exposed port number 8080:

```
$ docker run -it --name myTomcat3 --net=myNetwork -P tomcat
```

To check exactly which host port has been mapped, you can use the docker ps command. This is probably the quickest way of determining the current port mapping. The docker ps command is used to see the list of running containers. Execute the following from a separate shell console:

```
$ docker ps
```

In the output, Docker will list all running containers, showing which ports have been mapped in the PORTS column:

As you can see in the previous screenshot, our myTomcat3 container will have the 8080 port mapped to port number 32772 on the host. Again, executing the HTTP GET method on the http://localhost:32772 address will give us myTomcat3's welcome page. An alternative to the docker ps command is the docker port command, used with the container ID or with a name as a parameter (this will give you information about what ports have been mapped). In our case, this will be:

```
$ docker port myTomcat3
```

As a result, Docker will output the mapping, saying that port number 80 from the container has been mapped to port number 8080 on the host machine:

```
PS C:\Users\jarek> docker port myTomcat2
8080/tcp -> 0.0.0.0:8080
PS C:\Users\jarek>
```

Information about all the port mappings is also available in the result of the docker inspect command. Execute the following command, for example:

```
$ docker inspect myTomcat2
```

In the output of the docker inspect command, you will find the Ports section containing the information about mappings:

```
            "Ports": {
                "8080/tcp": [
                    {
                        "HostIp": "0.0.0.0",
                        "HostPort": "8080"
                    }
                ]
            },
            "SandboxKey": "/var/run/docker/netns/3f2438cdc982",
            "SecondaryIPAddresses": null,
            "SecondaryIPv6Addresses": null,
            "EndpointID": "",
            "Gateway": "",
            "GlobalIPv6Address": "",
            "GlobalIPv6PrefixLen": 0,
            "IPAddress": "",
            "IPPrefixLen": 0,
            "IPv6Gateway": "",
            "MacAddress": "",
```

Let's briefly summarize the options related to exposing and mapping ports in a table:

| Instruction | Meaning |
|---|---|
| `EXPOSE` | Signals that there is service available on the specified port. Used in the Dockerfile and makes exposed ports open for other containers. |
| `--expose` | The same as `EXPOSE` but used in the runtime, during the container startup. |
| `-p hostPort:containerPort` | Specify a port mapping rule, mapping the port on the container with the port on the host machine. Makes a port open from the outside of Docker. |
| `-P` | Map dynamically allocated random port (or ports) of the host to all ports exposed using `EXPOSE` or `--expose`. |

Mapping ports is a wonderful feature. It gives you flexible configuration possibilities to open your containers to the external world. In fact, it's indispensable if you want your containerized web server, database, or messaging server to be able to talk to others. If a default set of network drivers is not enough, you can always try to find a specific driver on the Internet or develop one yourself. Docker Engine network plugins extend Docker to support a wide range of networking technologies, such as IPVLAN, MACVLAN, or something completely different and exotic. Networking possibilities are almost endless in Docker. Let's focus now on another very important aspect of Docker container extensibility volumes.

# Persistent storage

As you remember from `Chapter 1`, *Introduction to Docker*, the Docker container filesystem is kind of temporary by default. If you start up a Docker image (that is, run the container), you'll end up with a read-write layer on top of the layers stack. You can create, modify, and delete files as you wish; if you commit the changes back into the image, they will become persisted. This is a great feature if you want to create a complete setup of your application in the image, altogether with all its environment. But, this is not very convenient when it comes to storing and retrieving data. The best option would be to separate the container life cycle and your application from the data. Ideally, you would probably want to keep these separate, so that the data generated (or being used) by your application is not destroyed or tied to the container life cycle and can thus be reused.

The perfect example would be a web application server: the Docker image contains web server software, the same as Tomcat for example, with your Java application deployed, configured, and ready to use. But, the data the server will be using should be separated from the image. This is done via volumes, which we will focus on in this part of the chapter. Volumes are not part of the union filesystem, and so the write operations are instant and as fast as possible, there is no need to commit any changes.

 Volumes live outside of the union filesystem and exist as normal directories and files on the host filesystem.

There are three main use cases for Docker data volumes:

- To share data between the host filesystem and the Docker container
- To keep data when a container is removed
- To share data with other Docker containers

Let's begin with a list of volume-related commands at our disposal.

# Volume-related commands

The basis of volume-related commands is docker volume. The commands are as follows:

- `$docker volume create`: Creates a volume
- `$ docker volume inspect`: Displays detailed information on one or more volumes
- `$docker volume ls`: Lists volumes
- `$ docker volume rm`: removes one or more volumes
- `$ docker volume prune`: removes all unused volumes, which is all volumes that are no longer mapped into any container

Similar to network-related commands, you can get the detailed description and all the possible options for each command if you execute it with the `-help` switch, for example: docker volume create `-help`. Let's begin with creating a volume.

# Creating a volume

As you remember from `Chapter 1`, *Introduction to Docker*, there's a settings screen in Docker for Windows or Docker for Mac, that allows us to specify which drives Docker can have access to. For a start, let's mark drive D in our Docker for Windows to make it available for Docker containers:

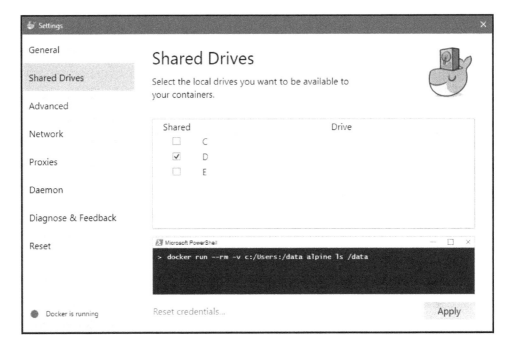

For the purpose of our volume examples, I've created a `docker_volumes/volume1` directory on my D drive and created an empty `data.txt` file inside:

```
Windows PowerShell                                                   —  □  ✕
PS D:\> mkdir docker_volumes\volume1


    Directory: D:\docker_volumes


Mode                LastWriteTime      Length Name
----                -------------      ------ ----
d-----        12.03.2017     10:23            volume1


PS D:\> cd .\docker_volumes\volume1\
PS D:\docker_volumes\volume1> touch data1.txt
PS D:\docker_volumes\volume1>
```

There are two ways to create volumes. The first one is to specify the `-v` option when running an image. Let's run the `busybox` image we already know and, at the same time, create a volume for our data:

```
$ docker run -v d:/docker_volumes/volume1:/volume -it busybox
```

In the previous command, we have created a volume using the `-v` switch and instructed Docker that the `host` directory `d:/docker_volumes/volume1` should be mapped into the `/volume` directory in the running container. If we now list the contents of the `/volume` directory in the running `busybox` container, we can see our empty `data1.txt` file, as you can see in the following screenshot:

```
Windows PowerShell                                                   —  □  ✕
PS C:\Users\jarek> docker run -v d:/docker_volumes/volume1:/volume -it busybox
/ # cd volume/
/volume # ls -la
total 4
drwxr-xr-x    2 root     root             0 Mar 12 09:24
drwxr-xr-x    1 root     root          4096 Mar 12 09:26
-rwxr-xr-x    1 root     root             0 Mar 12 09:24 data1.txt
/volume #
```

The parameters in the `-v` options are the directory on the host (your own operating system in this case, it is `d:/docker_volumes/volume1` in our example), a colon, and a path at which it will be available for the container, `/volume1` in our example. The volume created is a kind of mapped directory. It will be available for the container and also available from the host operating system. Any files already existing in the mapped directory (host's `d:/docker_volumes/volume1`) will be available inside the container; they will not be deleted during the mapping.

The $-v$ option can be used not only for directories but for a single file as well. This can be very useful if you want to have configuration files available in your container. The best example for this is the example from the official Docker documentation:

```
$ docker run -it -v ~/.bash_history:/root/.bash_history ubuntu
```

Executing the previous command will give you the same bash history between your local machine and a running Ubuntu container. And best of all, if you exit the container, the bash history on your own local machine will contain the bash commands you have been executing inside the container. Mapping files can be useful also for you, as a developer, when debugging or trying out your application configuration, for example.

 Mapping a single file from a host allows exposing a configuration of your application.

Apart from creating a volume when starting a container, there is a command to create a volume prior to starting a container. We will use it now.

The simplest form of creating a nameless volume will be just:

```
$ docker volume create
```

As the output, Docker will give you the volume identifier, which you can later use to refer to this volume. It's better to give a volume a meaningful name. To create a standalone, named volume, execute the following command:

```
$ docker volume create --name myVolume
```

To list the volumes we now have available, execute the `docker volume ls` command:

```
$ docker volume ls
```

The output will be simply the list of volumes we have created so far:

```
Windows PowerShell                                                          —   □   ×
PS C:\Users\jarek> docker volume ls
DRIVER              VOLUME NAME
local               ccaa9f93ef9d2d714c8bf00395283362ac4620fc9f434e5cb79b1fb19e111c6c
local               myVolume
PS C:\Users\jarek> _
```

Volumes created this way will not be mapped explicitly with a path on the host. If the container's base image contains data at the specified mount point (as a result of Dockerfile processing), this data will be copied into the new volume upon volume initialization. This is different in comparison to specifying a `host` directory explicitly. The idea behind it is that when creating your image, you should not care about the location of the volume on the host system, making the image portable between different hosts. Let's run another container and map the named volume into it:

```
$ docker run –it –v myVolume:/volume --name myBusybox3 busybox
```

Note that this time, we do not specify a path on the host. Instead, we instruct Docker to use the named volume we created in the previous step. The named volume will be available at the `/volume` path in the container. Let's create a text file on the volume:

```
PS C:\Users\jarek> docker run –it –v myVolume:/volume --name myBusybox3 busybox
/ # cd /volume/
/volume # echo "hello world" > data.txt
/volume # _
```

If we run another container now, specifying the same named volume, we will be able to access the same data we have available in our `myBusybox3` container which was created previously:

```
$ docker run –it –v myVolume:/volume --name myBusybox4 busybox
```

Our two containers share the single volume now, as you can see in the following screenshot:

```
PS C:\Users\jarek> docker run –it –v myVolume:/volume --name myBusybox4 busybox
/ # cd /volume/
/volume # more data.txt
hello world
/volume #
```

Docker named volumes are an easy way of sharing volumes between containers. They are also a great alternative to data-only containers that used to be a common practice in the old days of Docker. This is no longer the case—named volumes are way better. It's worth noting that you are not limited to just one volume per container, as that would be a serious limitation.

You can use the $-v$ multiple times to mount multiple data volumes.

Another option to share the volume between containers is the $-volumes-from$ switch. If one of your containers has volumes mounted already, by using this option we can instruct Docker to use the volume mapped in some other container, instead of providing the name of the volume. Consider this example:

```
$ docker run -it -volumes-from myBusybox4 --name myBusybox5 busybox
```

After running the `myBusybox5` container this way, again, if you enter the `/volume` directory in the `myBusybox5` container running, you will see the same `data.txt` file.

The `docker volume ls` command can take some filter parameters, which can be quite useful. For example, you can list volumes that are not being used by any container:

```
docker volume ls -f dangling=true
```

Volumes that are no longer used by any container can be easily removed by using the docker volumes prune command:

```
docker volume prune
```

To list volumes being created with a specific driver (we are going to cover drivers in a short while), you can filter a list using the driver filter, as in the following example:

```
docker volume ls -f driver=local
```

Last but not least, another way of creating a volume is the VOLUME CREATE instruction in a Dockerfile. We will be using it later in the book when creating an image from a Dockerfile. Creating volumes using the VOLUME CREATE instruction has one but very important difference in comparison to using the $-v$ option during the container startup: you cannot specify a `host` directory when using VOLUME CREATE. It's an analogy to exposing and mapping ports. You cannot map a port in a Dockerfile. Dockerfiles are meant to be portable, shareable, and host-independent. The `host` directory is 100% host-dependent and will break on any other machine, which is a little bit off from the Docker's idea. Because of this, it is only possible to use portable instructions within a Dockerfile.

 If you need to specify a `host` directory when creating a volume, you need to specify it at runtime.

# Removing a volume

The same as with creating volumes, there are two ways of removing a volume in Docker. Firstly, you can remove a volume by referencing a container's name and executing the docker `rm -v` command:

```
$ docker rm -v <containerName or ID>
```

Docker will not warn you, when removing a container without providing the `-v` option, to delete its volumes. As a result, you will have `dangling` volumes—volumes that are no longer referenced by a container. As you remember, they are easy to get rid of using the docker volume prune command.

Another option to remove the volume is by using the `docker volume rm` command:

```
$ docker volume rm <volumeName or ID>
```

If the volume happens to be in use by the container, Docker Engine will not allow you to delete it and will give you a warning message:

```
Windows PowerShell
Windows PowerShell
Copyright (C) 2016 Microsoft Corporation. All rights reserved.

PS C:\Users\jarek> docker volume rm myVolume2
Error response from daemon: Unable to remove volume, volume still in use: remove myVolume2: volume is in use - [f69
faf1a5f64cf33f9612dbcf602ed11d00a4b6633ed0353847840acd6bd055c]
PS C:\Users\jarek>
```

As you can see, creating, sharing, and removing volumes in Docker is not that tricky. It's very flexible and allows the creating a setup you will need for your applications. But there's more to this flexibility. When creating a volume, you can specify a `--driver` option (or `-d` for short), which may be useful if you need to map some external, not so standard storage. The volumes we have created so far were using the local filesystem driver (the files were being stored on the local drive of the host system); you can see the driver name when inspecting a volume using the `volume inspect` command. There are other options though—let's look at them now.

# Volume drivers

The same as with network driver plugins, volume plugins extend the capabilities of the Docker engine and enable integration with other types of storage. There are a ton of ready to use plugins available for free on the Internet; you can find a list on Docker's GitHub page. Some of them include:

- **Docker volume driver for Azure file storage**: This is a Docker volume driver which uses Azure file storage to mount file shares on the cloud to Docker containers as volumes. It uses the network file sharing (SMB/CIFS protocols) capabilities of Azure file storage. You can create Docker containers that can migrate from one host to another seamlessly or share volumes among multiple containers running on different hosts.
- **IPFS**: Open source volume plugin that allows the use of an IPFS filesystem as a volume. IPFS is a very interesting and promising storage system; it makes it possible to distribute high volumes of data with high efficiency. It provides deduplication, high performance, and clustered persistence, providing secure P2P content delivery, fast performance, and decentralized archiving. IPFS provides resilient access to data, independent of low latency or connectivity to the backbone.
- **Keywhiz**: You can use this driver to make your container talk to a remote Keywhiz server. Keywhiz is a system for managing and distributing secret data, the same as TLS certificates/keys, GPG keys, API tokens, and database credentials. Instead of putting this data in config files or copying files (which is similarly to be leaked or difficult to track), Keywhiz makes managing it easier and more secure: Keywhiz servers in a cluster centrally store secrets encrypted in a database. Clients use **mutually authenticated TLS** (**mTLS**) to retrieve secrets they have access to.

As you can see from the previous examples, they are quite interesting, sometimes even exotic. Because of the extendable nature of Docker and its plugin architecture, you can create very flexible setups. But, third-party drivers do not always introduce completely new storage types; sometimes, they just extend the existing drivers. An example of that can be the Local Persist Plugin, a volume plugin that extends the default local driver's functionality by allowing you to specify a mount point anywhere on the host, which enables the files to always persist, even if the volume is removed via the `docker volume rm` command.

If you need a volume plugin that is not yet available, you can just write your own. The process is very well documented on Docker's GitHub page, together with extensible examples.

We've now covered how to open our containers to the external world. We can use networking and mounted volumes to be able to share data between containers and other hosts. Let's summarize what we have learned so far in this chapter:

- We can use the network plugins to further extend the networking data exchange
- Volumes persist the data, even through container restarts
- Changes to files on the volume are made directly, but they will not be included when you update an image
- Data volumes persist even if the container itself is deleted
- Volumes allow of sharing data between the host filesystem and the Docker container, or between other Docker containers
- We can use the volume drivers to further extend the file exchange possibilities

 Containers from the same Docker host see each other automatically on the default bridge network.

# Summary

In this chapter, we have learned about Docker networking and storage volume features. We know how to differentiate between various network types, how to create a network, and expose and map network ports.

We've been through volume-related commands and can now create or remove a volume. In Chapter 3, *Working with Microservices*, we are going to focus on the software that we are going to deploy using Docker and Kubernetes, and later, Java microservices.

# 3
# Working with Microservices

After reading the previous two chapters, you should now have an understanding of the Docker architecture and its concepts. Before we go further on our Java, Docker, and Kubernetes journey, let's get to know the concept of microservices.

By reading this chapter, you will find out why a transition to microservices and cloud development is necessary and why monolithic architecture is not an option anymore. The microservices architecture is also where Docker and Kubernetes will be especially useful.

This chapter will cover the following topics:

- An introduction to microservices and comparison to a monolithic architecture
- How Docker and Kubernetes fits into the microservices world
- When to use microservices architecture

Before we actually create the Java microservice and deploy it using Docker and Kubernetes, let's start with an explanation of the microservices idea and compare it to the monolithic architecture.

## An introduction to microservices

By definition, microservices, also known as the **Microservice Architecture (MSA)**, is an architectural style and design pattern which says that an application should consist of a collection of loosely-coupled services. This architecture decomposes business domain models into smaller, consistent pieces implemented by services. In other words, each of the services will have its own responsibilities, independent of others, each one of them will provide a specific functionality.

These services should be isolated and autonomous. Yet, they of course need to communicate to provide some piece of business functionality. They usually communicate using REST exposures or by publishing and subscribing events in the publish/subscribe way.

The best way of explaining the reasoning behind the idea of microservices is to compare them with an old, traditional approach for building large applications, the monolithic design.

Take a look at the following diagram presenting the monolithic application and distributed application consisting of microservices:

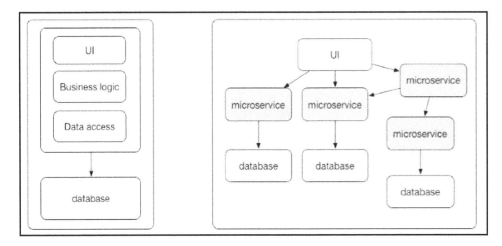

As you can see on the previous diagram, the monolithic application differs totally from an application created using the microservices architecture. Let's compare the two approaches and point out their advantages and flaws.

# Monolithic versus microservices

We begin the comparison by starting with the description of the monolithic architecture to present its characteristics.

# The monolithic architecture

In the past, we used to create applications as complete, massive, and uniform pieces of code. Let's take a web MVC application for example. A simplified architecture of such an application is presented in the following diagram:

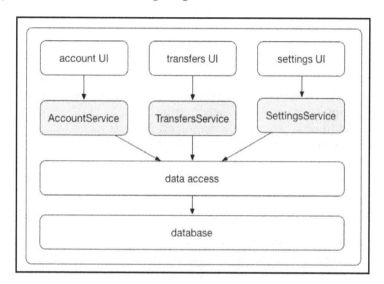

As you can see, the diagram presents the typical web application, a fragment of a banking system in this case. It's the **Model View Controller** (**MVC**) application, consisting of models, views, and controllers to serve up HTML content back to the client's browser. It could probably also accept and send the JSON content via the REST endpoints. This kind of an application is built as a single unit. As you can see, we have a couple of layers here. Enterprise Applications are built in three parts usually: a client-side user interface (consisting of HTML pages and JavaScript running in a browser), a server-side part handling the HTTP requests (probably constructed using some spring-like controllers), then we have a service layer, which could probably be implemented using EJBs or Spring services. The service layer executes the domain specific business logic, and retrieves/updates data in the database, eventually. This is a very typical web application which every one of us has probably created once in a while. The whole application is a monolith, a single logical executable. To make any changes to the system, we must build and deploy an updated version of the whole server-side application; this kind of application is packaged into single WAR or EAR archive, altogether with all the static content such as HTML and JavaScript files. When deployed, all the application code runs in the same machine. Scaling this kind of application usually requires deploying multiple copies of the exact same application code to multiple machines in a cluster, behind some load balancer perhaps.

This design wasn't too bad, we had our applications up and running, after all. But the world, especially when using Agile methodologies, changes fast. Businesses have started asking to release software faster than ever. ASAP has become a very common word in the IT development language dictionary. The specification fluctuates, so the code changes often and grows over time. If the team working on the application is large (and it probably will be in case of complex, huge applications) everyone must be very careful not to destroy each other's work. With every added feature, our applications become more and more complex. The compile and build times become longer, sooner or later it will become tricky to test the whole thing using unit or integration tests. Also, the point of entry for new members coming to the team can be daunting, they will need to checkout the whole project from the source code repository. Then they need to build it in their IDE (which is not always that easy in case of huge applications), and analyze and understand the component structure to get their job done. Additionally, people working on the user interface part will need to communicate with developers working on the middle-tier, with people modelling the database, DBAs, and so on. The team structure will often begin to mimic the application architecture over time. There's a risk that a developer working on the specific layer will tend to put as much logic into the layer he controls as he can. As a result, the code can become unmaintainable over time. We all have been there and done that, haven't we?

Also, the scaling of monolithic systems is not as easy as putting a WAR or EAR in another application server and then booting it. Because all the application code runs in the same process on the server, it's often almost impossible to scale individual portions of the application. Take this example: we have an application which integrates with the VOIP external service. We don't have many users of our application, but then there is a lot of events coming from the VOIP service we need to process. To handle the increasing load, we need to scale our application and, in the case of a monolithic system, we need to scale the whole system. That's because the application is a single, big, working unit. If just one of the application's services is CPU or resource hungry, the whole server must be provisioned with enough memory and CPU to handle the load. This can be expensive. Every server needs a fast CPU and enough RAM to be able to run the most demanding component of our application.

All monolithic applications have these characteristics:

- They are rather large, often involving a lot of people working on them. This can be a problem when loading your project into the IDE, despite having powerful machines and a great development environment, such as IntelliJ IDEA, for example. But it's not only about the hundreds, thousands, or millions of lines of code. It's about the complexity of the solution, such as communication problems between team members. Problems with communication could lead to multiple solutions for the same problem in different parts of the application. And this will make it even bigger, it can easily evolve into a big ball of mud where no one can understand the whole system any longer. Moreover, people can be afraid of introducing substantial changes to the system, because something at an opposite end could suddenly stop working. Too bad if this is reported by the users, on a production system.
- They have a long release cycle, we all know the process of release management, permissions, regression testing, and so on. It's almost impossible to create a continuous delivery flow having a huge, monolith application.
- They are difficult to scale; it typically takes a considerable amount of work to put in a new application instance in the cluster by the operations team. Scaling the specific feature is impossible, the only option you have is to multiply the instances of the whole system in the cluster. This makes scaling up and down a big challenge.
- In case of deployment failure, the whole system is unavailable.
- You are locked into the specific programming language or technology stack. Of course, with Java, parts of the system can be developed in one or more languages that run on JVM, such as Scala, Kotlin, or Groovy, but if you need to integrate with a `.net` library, here begins the trouble. This also means that you will not always be able to use the right tool for the job. Imagine a scenario in which you would like to store a lot of complex documents in the database. They often have different structures. MongoDB as a document database should be suitable, right? Yes, but our system is running on Oracle.
- It's not well suited well for agile development processes, where we need to implement changes all the time, release to production almost at once, and be ready for the next iteration.

As you can see, monolithic applications are only good for small scale teams and small projects. If you need something that has a larger scale and involves many teams, it's better to look at the alternative. But what to do with the existing monolithic system you may enjoy dealing with? You may realize that it can be handy to outsource some parts of the system outside, into small services. This will speed up the development process and increase testability. It will also make you application easier to scale. While the monolithic application still retains the core functionality, many pieces can be outsourced into small side services supporting the core module. This approach is presented in the following diagram:

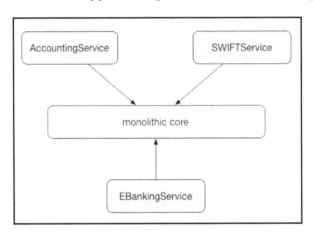

In this, let's say intermediary solution, the main business logic will stay in your application monolith. Things such as integrations, background jobs, or other small subsystems that can be triggered by messages, for example, can be moved to their own services. You can even put those services into the cloud, to limit the necessity for managing infrastructure around them even further. This approach allows you to gradually move your existing monolith application into a fully service-oriented architecture. Let's look at the microservices approach.

## The microservices architecture

The microservices architecture is designed to address the issues we've mentioned with monolithic applications. The main difference is that the services defined in the monolithic application are decomposed into individual services. Best of all, they are deployed separately from one another on separate hosts. Take a look at the following diagram:

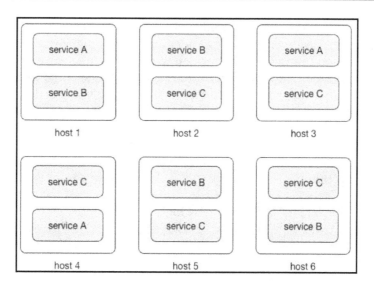

When creating an application using the microservices architecture, each microservice is responsible for a single, specific business function and contains only the implementation that is required to perform exactly that specific business logic. It's same as a **divide** and **conquer** way of creating a system. This may seem similar to the SOA-oriented architecture. In fact, traditional SOA and microservices architecture share some common features. Both organize fragments of the application into services and both define clear boundaries at which a service can be decoupled from the other. SOA, however, has its roots in the need to integrate monolithic applications with another one. This has been done, usually, using an API that was usually SOAP-based, using heavy XML messaging. In SOA, this integration was relying heavily on some kind of middleware in between, usually **Enterprise Service Bus (ESB)**. Microservices architecture can also utilize the message bus, with significant differences. In microservices architecture there is no logic in the messaging layer at all, it is purely used as a transport for messages from one service to another. This is a total contrast to ESB, which needed a lot of logic for message routing, schema validation, message translation, and so on. As a result, microservices architecture is less cumbersome than traditional SOA.

When it comes to scaling, there's a huge difference when comparing microservices to monolithic applications. The key advantage of microservices is that a single service can be scaled individually, depending on the resource requirements. That's because they are self-sufficient and independent. As a microservice is usually deployed on smaller (in terms of resources) host; the host needs to contain only resources that are required for a service to function properly. As the resource requirement grows, scaling is easy both ways, horizontally and vertically. To scale horizontally, you just deploy as many instances as you need to handle load on a specific component.

We will get back to this concept in the coming chapters, when we will be getting to know Kubernetes. Scaling vertically is also a lot easier and cheaper in comparison to the monolithic systems, you upgrade only a host on which your microservice is being deployed. Also, introducing new versions of the service is easy, you don't need to stop the whole system just to upgrade a piece of functionality. In fact, you can do it on the fly. When deployed, microservices improve the fault tolerance for the entire application. For example, if there is a memory leak in one service or some other problem, only this service will be affected and can then be fixed and upgraded without interfering with the rest of the system. This is not the case with monolithic architecture, where one faulty component can bring down the entire application.

From a developer's perspective, having your application split into separate pieces deployed individually gives a huge advantage. A developer skilled in server-side JavaScript can develop its piece node.js, while the rest of the system will be developed in Java. It's all related to the API exposed by each microservice; apart from this API, each microservice doesn't need to know anything about the rest of the services. This makes the development process a lot easier. Separate microservices can be developed and tested independently. Basically, the microservices approach dictates that instead of having one giant code base that all developers are working on, which often becomes tricky to manage, there are several smaller code bases managed by small and agile teams. The only dependency services have on one another is their exposed APIs. There's a difference in storing data as well. As we have said before, each microservice should be responsible for storing its own data, because again, it should be independent. This leads to another feature of the microservices architecture, a possibility to have a polyglot persistence. Microservices should own their data.

While microservices communicate and exchange data with other microservices using REST endpoints or events, they can store their own data in the form that is best suitable for the job. If the data is relational, the service will be using a traditional, relational database such as MySQL or PostgreSQL. If a document database is better suited for the job, a microservice can use MongoDB for example, or Neo4j if it's graph as data. That leads to another conclusion, by implementing the microservices architecture we can now only choose the programming language or framework that will be best suited for the job, this applies to the data storage as well. Of course, having its own data can lead to a challenge in the microservices architecture, data consistency. We are going to cover this subject in a while in this chapter.

Let's summarize the benefits of using the microservices architecture from the development process perspective:

- Services can be written using a variety of languages, frameworks, and their versions
- Each microservice is relatively small, easier to understand by the developer (which results in less bugs), easy to develop, and testable
- The deployment and start up time is fast, which makes developers more productive
- Each service can consist of multiple service instances for increased throughput and availability
- Each service can be deployed independently of other services, easier to deploy new versions of services frequently
- It is easier to organize the development process; each team owns and is responsible for one or more service and can develop, release, or scale their service independently of all of the other teams
- You can choose whatever programming language or framework you think is best for the job. There is no long-term commitment to a technology stack. If needed, the service can be rewritten in the new technology stack, and if there are no API changes, this will be transparent for the rest of the system
- It is better for continuous delivery as small units are easier to manage, test, and deploy. As long as each team maintains backwards and forward API compatibility, it can work in release cycles that are decoupled from other teams. There are some scenarios where these release cycles are coupled, but this is not the common case

# Maintaining data consistency

Services must be loosely coupled so that they can be developed, deployed, and scaled independently. They of course, need to communicate, but they are independent of each other. They, have well defined interfaces and encapsulate implementation details. But what about data? In the real world and in non-trivial applications (and microservice applications will probably be non-trivial), business transactions must often span multiple services. If you, for example, create a banking application, before you execute the customer's money transfer order, you need to ensure that it will not exceed his account balance. The single database that comes with a monolith application gives us a lot of convenience: atomic transactions, a single place to look for data, and so on.

On the other hand, in the microservices world, different services need to be independent. This also means that they can have different data storage requirements. For some services, it will be a relational database, others might need a document database such as MongoDB, which is good at storing complex, unstructured data.

So, when building microservices and thus splitting up our database into multiple smaller databases, how do we manage these challenges? We have also said that services should own their data. That is, every microservice should depend only on its own database. The service's database is effectively part of the implementation of that service. This leads to quite an interesting challenge when designing the microservices architecture. As Martin Fowler says in his `Microservice trade-offs` column: Maintaining strong consistency is extremely difficult for a distributed system, which means everyone has to manage eventual consistency. How do we deal with this? Well, it's all about boundaries.

Microservices should have clearly defined responsibilities and boundaries.

Microservices need to be grouped according to their business domain. Also, in practice, you will need to design your microservices in such a way that they cannot directly connect to a database owned by another service. The loose coupling means microservices should expose clear API interfaces that model the data and access patterns related to this data. They must stick to those interfaces, when changes are necessary, you will probably introduce a versioning mechanism and create another version of the microservice. You could use a publish/subscribe pattern to dispatch events from one microservice to be processed by others, as you can see in the following diagram:

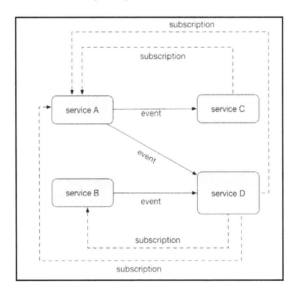

The publish/subscribe mechanism you would want to use should provide retry and rollback features for the event processing. In a publish/subscribe scenario, the service that modifies or generates the data allows other services to subscribe to events. The subscribed services receive the event saying that the data has been modified. It's often the case that the event contains the data that has been modified. Of course, the event publish/subscribe pattern can be used not only in relation to data changes, it can be used as a generic communication mechanism between services. This is a simple and effective approach but it has a downside, there is a possibility to lose an event.

When creating distributed applications, you may want to consider that there will be data inconsistency for some amount of time. When an application changes data items on one machine, that change needs to be propagated to the other replicas. Since the change propagation is not instant, there's a time interval during which some of the copies will have the most recent change, but others won't. However, the change will be propagated to all the copies, eventually. That's why this is called eventual consistency. Your services would need to assume that the data will be in an inconsistent state for a while and need to deal with the situation by using the data as is, postponing the operation, or even ignoring certain pieces of data.

As you can see, there are a lot of challenges, but also a lot of advantages behind using microservices architecture. You should be warned, though, there are more challenges we need to address. As services are independent of each other, they can be implemented in different programming languages. This means the deployment process of each may vary: it will be totally different for a Java web application and for a `node.js` application. This can make the deployment to a server complex. This is precisely the point where Docker comes to the rescue.

# The Docker role

As you remember from the previous chapters, Docker utilizes the concept of containerization. You simply put your application (in this context, the application will be a microservice) no matter what language and technology it uses, into a single, deployable and runnable piece of software, called the image. We are going to cover the process of packaging a Java application into the image in detail in the Chapter 4, *Creating Java Microservices*. The Docker image will contain everything our service needs to work, it can be a Java Virtual Machine with all required libraries and an application server, or it can also be a `node.js` application packaged together with the `node.js` runtime with all the needed `node.js` modules, such as `express.js` or whatever the `node.js` service needs to run. A microservice might consist of two containers, one running the service code and another running a database to keep the service's own data.

Docker isolates containers to one process or service. In effect, all the pieces of our application will just be a bunch of black boxes, packaged and ready to use Docker images. Containers operate as fully isolated sandboxes, with only the minimal kernel of the operating system present for each container. Docker uses the Linux kernel and makes use of kernel interfaces such as cnames and namespaces, which allow multiple containers to share the same kernel while running in complete isolation from one another.

Because the system resources of the underlying system are shared, you can run your services at optimal performance, the footprint is substantially smaller in comparison to traditional virtual machines. Because containers are portable, as we have said in Chapter 2, *Networking and Persistent Storage*, they can run everywhere the Docker engine can run. This makes the process of deployment of microservices easy. To deploy a new version of a service running on a given host, the running container can simply be stopped and a new container started that is based on a Docker image using the latest version of the service code. We are going to cover the process of creating new versions of the image later in this book. Of course, all the other containers running on the host will not be affected by this change.

As microservices need to communicate using the REST protocol, our Docker containers (or, to be more precise, your Java microservices packaged and running from within the Docker container) also need to communicate using the network. As you remember from Chapter 2, *Networking and Persistent Storage*, about networking, it's very easy to expose and map a network port for the Docker container. It seems that Docker containerization is ideal for the purposes of microservice architecture. You can package the microservice into a portable box and expose the needed network ports, enabling it to communicate to the outside world. When needed, you can run as many of those boxes as you want.

Let's summarize the Docker features that are useful when dealing with microservices:

- It is easy to scale up and scale down a service, you just change the running container instances count
- The container hides the details of the technology behind each of the services. All containers with our services are started and stopped in exactly the same way, no matter what technology stack they use
- Each service instance is isolated
- You can limit the runtime constraints on the CPU and memory consumed by a container
- Containers are fast to build and start. As you remember from Chapter 1, *Introduction to Docker*, there's minimal overhead in comparison to traditional virtualization

- Docker image layers are cached, this gives you another speed boost when creating a new version of the service

Doesn't it fit perfectly for the definition of the microservices architecture? Sure it does, but there's one problem. Because our microservices are spread out across multiple hosts, it can be difficult to track which hosts are running certain services and also monitor which of them need more resources or, in the worst case, are dead and not functioning properly. Also, we need to group services that belong to the specific application or feature. This is the missing element in our puzzle: container management and orchestration. A lot of frameworks emerged for the sole purpose of handling more complex scenarios: managing single services in a cluster or multiple instances in a service across hosts, or how to coordinate between multiple services on a deployment and management level. One of these tools is Kubernetes.

# Kubernetes' role

While Docker provides the lifecycle management of containers, Kubernetes takes it to the next level by providing orchestration and managing clusters of containers. As you know, your application created using the microservice architecture will contain a couple of separated, independent services. How do we orchestrate and manage them? Kubernetes is an open-source tool that's perfect for this scenario. It defines a set of building blocks which provide mechanisms for deploying, maintaining, and scaling applications. The basic scheduling unit in Kubernetes is called a pod. Containers in a pod run on the same host, share the same IP address, and find each other via localhost. They can also communicate with each other using standard inter-process communications, such as shared memory or semaphores. A pod adds another level of abstraction to containerized components. A pod consists of one or more containers that are guaranteed to be co-located on the host machine and can share resources. It's same as a logical collection of containers that belong to an application.

For traditional services, such as a REST endpoint together with the corresponding database (our complete microservice, in fact), Kubernetes provides a concept of service. A service defines a logical group of pods and also enforces rules for accessing such logical groups from the outside world. Kubernetes uses the concept of Labels for pods and other resources (services, deployments, and so on). These are simple the key-value pairs that can be attached to resources at creation time and then added and modified at any time. We will be using labels later on, to organize and to select subsets of resources (pods, for example) to manage them as one entity.

Kubernetes can place your container or a group of containers in the specific host automatically. To find a suitable host (the one with the smallest workload), it will analyze the current workload of the hosts and different colocation and availability constraints. Of course, you will be able to specify the host manually, but having this automatic feature can make the best of the processing power and resources available. Kubernetes can monitor the resource usage (CPU and RAM) at the container, pod, and cluster level. The resource usage and performance analysis agent runs on each node, auto-discovers containers on the node, and collects CPU, memory, filesystem, and network usage statistics.

Kubernetes also manages the lifecycle of your container instances. If there are too many of them, some of them will be stopped. If the workload increases, new containers will be started automatically. This feature is called container auto-scaling. It will automatically change the number of running containers, based on memory, CPU utilization, or other metrics you define for your services, as the number of queries per second, for example.

As you remember from `Chapter 2`, *Networking and Persistent Storage*, Docker operates volumes to persist your application data. Kubernetes also supports two kinds of volume: regular which has the same lifecycle as the pod, and persistent with a lifecycle independent of any pod. Volume types are implemented the same way as in Docker in the form of plugins. This extensible design enables you to have almost any type of volume you need. It currently contains storage plugins such as Google Cloud Platform volume, AWS elastic block storage volume, and others.

Kubernetes can monitor the health of your services, it can do it by executing a specified `HTTP` method (the same as `GET` for example) for the specified URL and analyzing the `HTTP` status code given back in response. Also, a TCP probe can check if a specified port is open which can also be used to monitor the health of your service. Last, but not least, you can specify the command that can be executed in the container, and some actions that could be taken based on the command's response. If the specified probe method signals that something is wrong with the container, it can be automatically restarted. When you need to update your software, Kubernetes supports rolling updates. This feature allows you to update a deployed, containerized application with minimal downtime. The rolling update feature lets you specify the number of old replicas that may be down while they are being updated. Upgrading containerized software with Docker is especially easy, as you already know, it will just be a new image version for the container. I guess you are now getting the complete picture. Deployments can be updated, rolled out, or rolled back. Load balancing, service discovery, all the features you would probably need when orchestrating and managing your herd of microservices running from within Docker containers are available in Kubernetes. Initially made by Google for big scale, Kubernetes is nowadays widely used by organizations of various sizes to run containers in production.

# When to use the microservice architecture

The microservice architecture is a new way to think about structuring applications At the beginning, when you begin creating a system and it's relatively small, there will probably be no need to use the microservices approach. Of course, it's nothing wrong with the basic web application. When doing basic web applications for the people in your office, going with the microservice architecture may be overkill. On the other hand, if you plan to develop a new, super internet service that will be used by millions of mobile clients, I would consider going with microservices from the start. Joking aside, you get the picture, always try to pick the best tool for the job. In the end, the goal is to provide business value.

However, you should keep in mind the whole picture of your system after some time. If your application is growing larger in features and functionality than you expected, or you know that from the beginning, you may want to start breaking features off into microservices. You should try to do the functional decomposition and point out the fragments of your systems that have clear boundaries and which would need scaling, and separate deployments in the future. If there's a lot of people working on a project, having them developing the separate, independent pieces of an application will give the development process a huge boost. There can be a mix of technology stacks used each service can be implemented in a different programming language or framework and store its own data in the most suitable data storage. It's all about API and the way services communicate with each other. Having this architecture will result in a faster time to market the build, test, and deployment time is highly reduced in comparison to a monolith architecture. If you need to scale only the service that needs to handle higher workload. Having Docker and Kubernetes available, there is no reason not to go into the microservice architecture; it will pay off in the future, for sure.

The microservice architecture is not just a new trendy buzzword, it's generally accepted as a better way to build applications today. The birth of the microservice idea has been driven by the need to make better use of compute resources and the need to maintain more and more complex web-based applications.

Java is an excellent choice when building microservices. You can create a microservice as a single executable JAR, self-contained Spring Boot application, or fully featured web application deployed on an application server such as Wildfly or Tomcat. Depending on your use case and the responsibilities and features of your microservices, any of the previous will do. Docker Repository contains a lot of useful images you can use freely as a base for your microservice. Many images present in The Docker Hub are created by private individuals, some extending official images and customizing them to their needs, but others are entire platform configurations customized from base images. The base image can be as simple as pure JDK or it can be a fully configured Wildfly ready to run. This gives a serious development performance boost.

# Summary

In this chapter, we have compared monolithic and microservices architectures. I hope you see the advantages of using the latter. We have also learned how Docker and Kubernetes fits into the whole picture when deploying containerized applications, making this process a lot more easy and pleasant. Java is a proven ecosystem for implementing microservices. The software you are going to create will consist of small, highly testable, and efficient modules. In fact, in `Chapter 4`, *Creating Java Microservices*, we are going to get our hands dirty and create such a microservice.

# 4
# Creating Java Microservices

We've seen a lot of theory behind microservice architecture in `Chapter 3`, *Working with Microservices*. It's time to do some hands-on practice; we are going to implement our own microservice. This will be a simple REST service, accepting `HTTP` methods such as `GET` and `POST` to retrieve and update entities. There are a couple of choices when developing microservices in Java. In this chapter, we are going to get an overview about two main approaches, probably the most popular will be JEE7, and Spring Boot. We will briefly see how we can code a microservice using JEE JAX-RS. We will also create a microservice running on Spring Boot. In fact, in `Chapter 5`, *Creating Images with Java Applications*, we are going to run our Spring Boot microservice from within a Docker container. As we have said in `Chapter 3`, *Working with Microservices*, microservices usually communicate with the outside world using REST. Our REST microservice will be as simple as possible; we just need to have something to deploy using Docker and Kubernetes. We will not focus on advanced microservice features such as authentication, security, filters, and so on, as this is outside the scope of this book. The purpose of our examples is to give you an idea of how to develop REST services and then deploy them using Docker and Kubernetes. This chapter will cover the following topics:

- Introduction to REST
- Creating a REST service in Java using Java EE7 annotations
- Creating a REST service using Spring Boot
- Running the service and then calling it with different HTTP clients

At the end of the chapter, we will become familiar with some useful tools- we will use some code generation tools such as Spring Initialzr to quickly bootstrap a Spring Boot service project. Before we start coding our own microservice, let's explain briefly what REST is.

# Introduction to REST

The REST acronym stands for Representational State Transfer. It's an architectural style and a design for network-based software. It describes how one system can communicate a state with another. This fits perfectly well into the microservice world. As you will remember from `Chapter 3`, *Working with Microservices*, the software applications based on the microservices architecture is a bunch of separated, independent services talking to each other.

There are some concepts in REST that we need to understand, before we go further:

- `resource`: This is the main concept in the REST architecture. Any information can be a resource. A bank account, a person, an image, a book. A representation of a resource must be **stateless**
- `representation`: A specific way a resource can be represented. For example, a bank account resource can be represented using JSON, XML, or HTML. Different clients might request different representations of the resource, one can accept JSON, while others will be expecting XML
- `server`: A service provider. It exposes services which can be consumed by clients
- `client`: A service consumer. This could be another microservice, application, or just a user's web browser running an Angular application, for example

As the definition says, REST is being used to transport those resource representations over the network. The representation itself is being created via some media type. Media types can be different. Some examples of media types include JSON, XML, or RDF. The JSON media type is widely accepted and probably the most often used. In our examples, we will also use JSON to communicate with our service. Of course, REST is not the only option for microservices communication; there are others, such as Google's very good gRPC, for example, which brings a lot of advantages such as HTTP/2 and protobuff. In the REST architecture, resources are manipulated by components. In fact, these components are our microservices. Components request and manipulate resources via a standard uniform interface. REST is not tied to any specific protocol; however, REST calls are most often being made using the most popular `HTTP` or `HTTPS` protocol. In the case of `HTTP`, this uniform interface consists of standard HTTP methods such as `GET`, `PUT`, `POST`, and `DELETE`.

 REST is not tied to any specific protocol.

Before we start implementing our service that will respond to HTTP calls, it's worth knowing about the HTTP methods we are going to use. We are going to focus on them a little bit closer now.

# HTTP methods

The REST-based architecture uses standard HTTP methods: PUT, GET, POST, and DELETE. The following list gives an explanation of these operations:

- GET gives a read access to the resource. Calling GET should not create any side-effects. It means that the GET operation is idempotent. The resource is never changed via a GET request; for example, the request has no side effects. It means it's idempotent
- PUT creates a new resource. Similar to GET, it should also be idempotent
- DELETE removes the resource or resources. The DELETE operation should not give different results when called repeatedly
- POST will update an existing resource or create a new one

A RESTful web service is simply a web service that is based on the REST resource concept and usage of HTTP methods. It should define the base URI for the exposed methods, the MIME-types supported, such as XML, text, or JSON, and the set of operations (POST, GET, PUT, and DELETE) which the service handles. HTTP is simple and very natural for REST, according to RESTful principles. These principles are a set of constraints that ensure that clients (service consumers, other services or browsers, for example) can communicate with servers in a flexible way. Let's look at them now.

In REST principles client-server communication, all applications built in the RESTful style must also be client-server in principle. There should be a server (service provider) and a client (service consumer). Having this enables loose coupling and independent evolution of server and client. This fits very well to the concept of a microservice. As you will remember from Chapter 3, *Working with Microservices*, they must be independent:

- **Stateless**: Each client request to the server requires that its state be fully represented. The server must be able to completely understand the client request without using any server context or server session state. In other words, all states must be managed on the client side. Each REST service should be **stateless**. Subsequent requests should not depend on some data from a previous request being temporarily stored. Messages should be self-descriptive.

- **Cacheable**: Response data could be marked as cacheable or non-cacheable. Any data marked as cacheable may be reused as the response to the same subsequent request. Each response should indicate if it is cacheable.
- **Uniform interface**: All components must interact through a single uniform interface. Because all component interactions occur via this interface, interaction with different services is very simple.
- **Layered system**: A consumer of the service should not assume direct connection to the service provider. In other words, at any time the client cannot tell if it is connected to the end server or to an intermediate. The intermediate layer helps to enforce the security policies and improve the system scalability by enabling load-balancing. Since requests can be cached, the client might be getting the cached response from a middle layer.
- **Manipulation of resources through representations**: A resource can have multiple representations. It should be possible to modify the resource through a message with any of these representations.
- **Hypermedia As The Engine Of Application State (HATEOAS)**: A consumer of a RESTful application should know about only one fixed service URL. All subsequent resources should be discoverable from the links included in the resource representations.

The previous concepts represent defining characteristics of REST and differentiate the REST architecture from other architectures such as web services. It is useful to note that a REST service is a web service, but a web service is not necessarily a REST service. The REST microservice should represent the state of an entity. Let our entity be a book, for example (altogether with its properties such as ID, title, and an author), represented as XML, JSON, or plain text. The most basic way of thinking about REST is as a way of formatting the URLs of your service. For example, having our `book` resource, we could imagine having the following operations defined in the service:

- `/books` would allow access of all the books
- `/books/:id` would be an operation for viewing an individual book, retrieved based on its unique ID
- sending a `POST` request to `/books` would be how you would actually create a new book and store it in a database
- sending a `PUT` request to `/books/:id` would be how you would update the attributes of a given book, again identified by its unique ID
- sending a `DELETE` request to `/books/:id` would be how you would delete a specific book, again identified by its unique ID

It's worth trying to understand that REST is not HTTP. It often uses HTTP because in its most general form, REST is about mapping the concept of a verb against an arbitrary collection of nouns and fits well with HTTP methods. HTTP contains a useful set of generic verbs (`GET`, `POST`, `PUT`, `PATCH`, and so on). In REST, we do not transfer an actual object but a representation of it in a specific form, such as XML, text, or JSON. REST as an architectural style means it is just a concept. How it's implemented, is up to you. Java is suited well for developing REST services. Let's see how can we do it.

# REST in Java

When developing a REST service in Java, we have at least a couple of options for the framework we could use. The most popular will be pure JEE7 with JAX-RS or Spring Framework with its Spring Boot. You can use either of them or mix them together. Let's look at those two now in more detail, starting with JAX-RS.

# Java EE7 - JAX-RS with Jersey

JAX-RS was born as a result of **Java Specification Request (JSR)** 311. As the official definition says, the JAX-RS is the Java API for RESTful web services. It's a specification that provides support in creating web services according to the REST architectural pattern. JAX-RS uses Java annotations, introduced in Java SE 5, to simplify the development and deployment of web service clients and endpoints. From version 1.1 on, JAX-RS is an official part of Java EE. A notable feature of being an official part of Java EE is that no configuration is necessary to start using JAX-RS.

Java EE 7 with JAX-RS 2.0 brings several useful features, which further simplify the development of microservices. One of the most important new features of JAX-RS 2.0 is the support for hypermedia following the HATEOAS principle of REST. `Jersey`, a library from Oracle, is probably the most widely known library, which implements this specification.

Jersey is the reference implementation for the JSR 311 specification.

The Jersey implementation provides a library to implement RESTful web services in a Java servlet container. On the server-side, Jersey provides a servlet implementation which scans predefined classes to identify RESTful resources. Jersey makes it a lot easier to write RESTful services. It abstracts away a lot of the low level coding you will need to do yourself otherwise. Using Jersey, you do it in a declarative way. The servlet, registered in your web.xml file, analyzes the incoming HTTP request and selects the correct class and method to respond to this request. It finds the proper method to execute by looking at the class and method level annotations. Annotated classes can reside in different packages, but you can instruct a Jersey servlet via the web.xml to scan certain packages for annotated classes.

JAX-RS supports the creation of XML and JSON via the **Java Architecture for XML Binding** (**JAXB**). The Jersey implementation also provides a client library to communicate with a RESTful web service.

As we have said before, we develop JAX-RS applications using Java annotations. It's easy and pleasant to work with. Let's describe those annotations now.

# JAX-RS annotations

The most important annotations in JAX-RS are listed in the following table:

| Annotation | Meaning |
| --- | --- |
| @PATH | Sets the path to base URL + /your_path. The base URL is based on your application name, the servlet, and the URL pattern from the web.xml configuration file. |
| @POST | Indicates that the following method will answer to an HTTP POST request. |
| @GET | Indicates that the following method will answer to an HTTP GET request. |
| @PUT | Indicates that the following method will answer to an HTTP PUT request. |
| @DELETE | Indicates that the following method will answer to an HTTP DELETE request. |
| @Produces | Defines which MIME type is delivered by a method annotated with @GET. It can be "text/plain", "application/xml", or "application/json" for example. |
| @Consumes | Defines which MIME type is consumed by this method. |

| @PathParam | Used to extract (inject) values from the URL into a method parameter. This way you inject, for example, the ID of a resource into the method to get the correct object. |
|---|---|
| @QueryParam | Used to extract (inject) the URI query parameter coming with the request. The **Uniform Resource Identifier** (**URI**) is a string of characters used to identify a name or a resource on the Internet. |
| @DefaultValue | Specifies a default value. Useful for optional parameters. |
| @CookieParam | Annotation that allows you to inject cookies sent by a client request into your JAX-RS resource methods. |
| @Provider | The @Provider annotation is used for anything that is of interest to the JAX-RS runtime, such as MessageBodyReader and MessageBodyWriter. For HTTP requests, MessageBodyReader is used to map an HTTP request entity body to method parameters. On the response side, a return value is mapped to an HTTP response entity body by using MessageBodyWriter. If the application needs to supply additional metadata, such as HTTP headers or a different status code, a method can return a response that wraps the entity and that can be built using Response.ResponseBuilder. |
| @ApplicationPath | The @ApplicationPath annotation is used to define the URL mapping for the application. The path specified by @ApplicationPath is the base URI for all resource URIs specified by @Path annotations in the resource class. You may only apply @ApplicationPath to a subclass of javax.ws.rs.core.Application. |

The annotation names might not be clear or self-explanatory at first glance. Let's look at the sample REST endpoint implementation, and it will become a lot clearer. The application itself is marked with the @ApplicationPath annotation. By default, during start-up of the JEE compliant server, JAX-RS will scan all the resources in a Java application archive to find the exposed endpoints. We can override the getClasses() method to manually register the resource classes in the application with the JAX-RS runtime. You can see it in the following example:

```
package pl.finsys.jaxrs_example
@ApplicationPath("/myApp")
public class MyApplication extends Application {
    @Override
    public Set<Class<?>> getClasses() {
        final Set<Class<?>> classes = new HashSet<>();
```

```
        classes.add(MyBeansExposure.class);
        return classes;
    }
}
```

In the previous example, we just register a REST application, giving it the /myApp base URI
path. There is only one REST method handler (endpoint), the MyBeansExposure class,
which we register within the REST application. The simplified REST endpoint,
implemented in the separate Java class can look same as this:

```
package pl.finsys.jaxrs_example
import javax.annotation.PostConstruct;
import javax.enterprise.context.ApplicationScoped;
import javax.ws.rs.DELETE;
import javax.ws.rs.GET;
import javax.ws.rs.POST;
import javax.ws.rs.Path;
import javax.ws.rs.PathParam;
import javax.ws.rs.container.ResourceContext;
import javax.ws.rs.core.Context;
import javax.ws.rs.core.Response;

@ApplicationScoped
@Path("beans")
public class MyBeansExposure {
    @Context ResourceContext rc;
    private Map<String, Bean> myBeans;

    @GET
    @Produces("application/json")
    public Collection<Bean> allBeans() {
        return Response.status(200).entity(myBeans.values()).build();
    }

    @GET
    @Produces("application/json")
    @Path("{id}")
    public Bean singleBean(@PathParam("id") String id) {
        return Response.status(200).entity(myBeans.get(id)).build();
    }

    @POST
    @Consumes("application/json")
    public Response add(Bean bean) {
        if (bean != null) {
            myBeans.put(bean.getName(), bean);
        }
        final URI id = URI.create(bean.getName());
```

```
        return Response.created(id).build();
    }

    @DELETE
    @Path("{id}")
    public void remove(@PathParam("id") String id) {
        myBeans.remove(id);
    }
}
```

As you can see in the previous example, we have class-level `@Path` annotation. Every method marked with `@GET`, `@PUT`, `@DELETE`, or `@POST` annotations will respond to a call to the URI starting with the base `@Path`. Additionally, we can use the `@Path` annotation on a method level; it will, kind of, extend the URI path that the specific method responds to. In our example, the HTTP GET executed with a URI path `myApp/beans` will call the `allBeans()` method, returning the collection of beans in JSON format. The GET method executed using the `myApp/beans/12` URI path will call the `singleBean()` method, and the `{id}` parameter will be transferred to the method because of the `@PathParam` annotation. Calling the HTTP DELETE method on the `myApp|beans|12` URI will execute the `remove()` method with an `id` parameter value 12. To give you almost infinite flexibility, the `@Path` annotation supports regular expressions. Consider the following example:

```
package pl.finsys.jaxrs_example
import javax.ws.rs.GET;
import javax.ws.rs.Path;
import javax.ws.rs.PathParam;
import javax.ws.rs.core.Response;

@Stateless
@Path("/books")
public class BookResource {
    @GET
    @Path("{title : [a-zA-Z][a-zA-Z_0-9]}")
     public Response getBookByTitle(@PathParam("title") String title) {
        return Response.status(200).entity("getBookByTitle is called, title :
" + title).build();
    }

    @GET
    @Path("{isbn : \\d+}")
    public Response getBookByISBN(@PathParam("isbn") String isbn) {
        return Response.status(200).entity("getBookByISBN is called, isbn : "
+ isbn).build();
    }
}
```

In the previous example, we have two `@GET` mappings, each with the same `/books/` path mapped. The first one, with the `/{title : [a-zA-Z][a-zA-Z_0-9]}` parameter, will react only to letters and numbers. The second one, with the `/{isbn : \\d+}` parameter, will be executed only if you provide a number when calling the URI. As you can see, we have mapped two identical paths, but each one will react to a different type of incoming path parameter.

Apart from using `@PathParam`, we can also use `@QueryParams` to supply parameters using the request parameters. Take a look at the following example:

```java
package pl.finsys.jaxrs_example
import java.util.List;
import javax.ws.rs.GET;
import javax.ws.rs.Path;
import javax.ws.rs.core.Context;
import javax.ws.rs.core.Response;
import javax.ws.rs.core.UriInfo;

@Stateless
@Path("/users")
public class UserResource {
    @EJB private UserService userService;
    @GET
    @Path("/query")
    @Produces("application/json")
    public Response getUsers(
        @QueryParam("from") int from,
        @QueryParam("to") int to,
        @QueryParam("orderBy") List<String> orderBy)) {
        List<User> users = userService.getUsers(from, to, orderBy);
        return Response.status(200).entity(users).build();
    }
}
```

In the previous example, when calling `HTTP GET` on the `/users/query?from=1&to=100&orderBy=name` JAX-RS will pass the URI parameters into the `getUsers()` method parameter and call the injected `userService` to get the data (for example, from a database).

To package the JAX-RS application, we will need a Maven `pom.xml` file, of course. In its simplest form, it can look the same as the following:

```xml
<?xml version="1.0" encoding="UTF-8"?>
<project xmlns="http://maven.apache.org/POM/4.0.0"
         xmlns:xsi="http://www.w3.org/2001/XMLSchema-instance"
         xsi:schemaLocation="http://maven.apache.org/POM/4.0.0
```

```
http://maven.apache.org/xsd/maven-4.0.0.xsd">
    <modelVersion>4.0.0</modelVersion>

    <groupId>pl.finsys</groupId>
    <artifactId>jee7-rest</artifactId>
    <packaging>war</packaging>
    <version>1.0-SNAPSHOT</version>

    <dependencies>
        <dependency>
            <groupId>javax</groupId>
            <artifactId>javaee-api</artifactId>
            <version>7.0</version>
            <scope>provided</scope>
        </dependency>
    </dependencies>
    <build>
        <finalName>jee7-rest</finalName>
    </build>

    <properties>
        <maven.compiler.source>1.8</maven.compiler.source>
        <maven.compiler.target>1.8</maven.compiler.target>
        <failOnMissingWebXml>false</failOnMissingWebXml>
    </properties>
</project>
```

Creating JEE7 REST services is quite straightforward, isn't it? By building the project and deploying it to a JEE compliant application server, we have a couple of endpoints ready and waiting to be called over HTTP. But there's an even more simple and faster approach. In the era of microservices, we would want to create individual components faster with a minimal overhead, after all. Here comes Spring Boot. Let's look at it now.

# Spring Boot

Spring itself is a very popular Java-based framework for building web and enterprise applications. It's not only the Spring Core, which focuses on dependency injection. Spring Framework provides a lot of features that can make a developer's life easier out of the box and allows you to deliver needed features faster. The list is long; here are just a few examples:

- **Spring data**: Simplifies data access from relational and NoSQL data stores
- **Spring batch**: Provides a powerful batch processing framework

- **Spring security**: Provides numerous ways to secure applications
- **Spring social**: Supports integration with social networking sites such as Twitter, Facebook, GitHub, and so on
- **Spring integration**: An implementation of enterprise integration patterns to facilitate integration with other enterprise applications using lightweight messaging and declarative adapters

But why did Spring become so popular? There are several reasons for that:

- It uses the dependency injection approach, which encourages writing testable, loosely coupled code
- It's easy to include database transaction management capabilities
- The integration with other popular Java frameworks such as JPA/Hibernate, for example
- It includes a state of the art MVC framework for building web applications faster, separating the view from the business logic

Configuring beans in the Spring framework can be done in multiple ways such as the XML definition file, Java annotations, and code configuration. This can be a tedious process. Also, we often do a lot of boilerplate configuration all the time, for different applications. Spring Boot was born to address the complexity of configuration. We can use Spring Boot for our own purposes, and develop small, independent services that can just be run. It can be a single runnable fat JAR file, with all the Java dependencies needed to run your application. There's no need for an application server or the complicated deployment descriptor configuration. In fact, behind the scenes, Spring Boot will boot up an embedded server for you. Of course, you are not forced to use the embedded application server. You can always build a WAR file to deploy it on your own Tomcat or Wildfly, for example. It's worth knowing, that even though most things will happen automatically when running a Spring Boot application, it's not a code generation framework.

Does all of this remind you about the simplicity and portability of Docker containers? Sure it does, but on the application level. As we discussed in `Chapter 3`, *Working with Microservices*, we are moving towards architectures with smaller, independently deployable microservices. This means we will need to be able to quickly get off the ground and get running with new components. We get a lot of features out of the box when using Spring Boot. These features are delivered in the form of Maven artifacts, which you can just include in your Maven `pom.xml` file.

The following table shows some of the important starter projects provided by Spring Boot we will be using:

| Project | Description |
| --- | --- |
| `spring-boot-starter` | Base starter for Spring Boot applications. Provides support for auto-configuration and logging. |
| `spring-boot-starter-web` | Starter project for building Spring MVC based web applications or RESTful applications. This uses Tomcat as the default embedded servlet container. |
| `spring-boot-starter-data-jpa` | Provides support for Spring Data JPA. Default implementation is Hibernate. |
| `spring-boot-starter-validation` | Provides support for Java Bean Validation API. Default implementation is Hibernate Validator. |
| `spring-boot-starter-test` | Provides support for various unit testing frameworks, such as JUnit, Mockito, and Hamcrest matchers |

There are a lot more projects, which can be useful for you. We are not going to use them, but let's look at what else is available:

| | |
| --- | --- |
| `spring-boot-starter-web-services` | Starter project for developing XML based web services |
| `spring-boot-starter-activemq` | Supports message based communication using JMS on ActiveMQ |
| `spring-boot-starter-integration` | Supports Spring Integration, framework that provides implementations for Enterprise Integration Patterns |
| `spring-boot-starter-jdbc` | Provides support for using Spring JDBC. Configures a Tomcat JDBC connection pool by default. |
| `spring-boot-starter-hateoas` | HATEOAS stands for Hypermedia as the Engine of Application State. RESTful services that use HATEOAS return links to additional resources that are related to the current context in addition to data. |

| `spring-boot-starter-jersey` | JAX-RS is the Java EE standard for developing REST APIs. Jersey is the default implementation. This starter project provides support for building JAX-RS based REST APIs. |
|---|---|
| `spring-boot-starter-websocket` | `HTTP` is stateless. Web sockets allow maintaining connection between server and browser. This starter project provides support for Spring WebSockets. |
| `spring-boot-starter-aop` | Provides support for Aspect oriented programming. Also provides support for AspectJ for advanced Aspect oriented programming. |
| `spring-boot-starter-amqp` | With default as `RabbitMQ`, this starter project provides message passing with AMQP. |
| `spring-boot-starter-security` | This starter project enables auto-configuration for Spring Security. |
| `spring-boot-starter-batch` | Provides support for developing batch applications using Spring Batch. |
| `spring-boot-starter-cache` | Basic support for caching using Spring Framework. |
| `spring-boot-starter-data-rest` | Support for exposing REST services using Spring Data REST. |

Let's use some of these goodies to code our own Spring Boot microservice.

# Coding the Spring Boot microservice

We know that we have some starters available, so let's make use of them to save some time. The service that we are going to create will be the simple REST microservice for storing and retrieving entities from a database: books, in our case. We are not going to implement authentication and security features, just to make it as clean and simple as possible. Books will be stored in an in-memory relational H2 database. We are going to build and run our bookstore with Maven, so let's begin with the pom.xml build file.

# Maven build file

As you will see, the parent project for our own service is spring-boot-starter-parent. Spring this is the parent project providing dependency and plugin management for Spring Boot-based applications. This gives us a lot of features to start with. We also include two starters:

- `spring-boot-starter-web`: This is because we are going to create our request mappings (similar to `@GET` or `@POST` mappings with the `@Path` annotation we did previously using JEE7 JAX-RS
- `spring-boot-starter-data-jpa`: Because we are going to save our books in the in-memory H2 database

Starters are simplified dependency descriptors customized for different purposes. For example, `spring-boot-starter-web` is the starter for building web and RESTful, applications using Spring MVC. It uses Tomcat as the default embedded container. We also include the Spring Boot Maven plugin, which allows us to run the applications in place without building a JAR or a WAR, or preparing a JAR or WAR file for future deployment. Our complete `pom.xml` should look the same as this:

```xml
<?xml version="1.0" encoding="UTF-8"?>
<project xmlns="http://maven.apache.org/POM/4.0.0"
xmlns:xsi="http://www.w3.org/2001/XMLSchema-instance"
         xsi:schemaLocation="http://maven.apache.org/POM/4.0.0
http://maven.apache.org/xsd/maven-4.0.0.xsd">
    <modelVersion>4.0.0</modelVersion>

    <groupId>pl.finsys</groupId>
    <artifactId>rest-example</artifactId>
    <version>0.1.0</version>

    <parent>
        <groupId>org.springframework.boot</groupId>
        <artifactId>spring-boot-starter-
         parent</artifactId>
        <version>1.5.2.RELEASE</version>
    </parent>

    <dependencies>
        <dependency>
            <groupId>org.springframework.boot</groupId>
            <artifactId>spring-boot-starter-
              web</artifactId>
        </dependency>
        <dependency>
            <groupId>org.springframework.boot</groupId>
```

```
            <artifactId>spring-boot-starter-data-
             jpa</artifactId>
        </dependency>
        <dependency>
            <groupId>org.hibernate</groupId>
            <artifactId>hibernate-validator</artifactId>
        </dependency>
        <dependency>
            <groupId>org.hsqldb</groupId>
            <artifactId>hsqldb</artifactId>
            <scope>runtime</scope>
        </dependency>

        <!--test dependencies-->
        <dependency>
            <groupId>org.springframework.boot</groupId>
            <artifactId>spring-boot-starter-test</artifactId>
            <scope>test</scope>
        </dependency>
        <dependency>
            <groupId>com.jayway.jsonpath</groupId>
            <artifactId>json-path</artifactId>
            <scope>test</scope>
        </dependency>
    </dependencies>

<properties>
    <java.version>1.8</java.version>
</properties>

<build>
    <plugins>
        <plugin>
            <groupId>org.springframework.boot</groupId>
            <artifactId>spring-boot-maven-plugin</artifactId>
        </plugin>
    </plugins>
</build>

<repositories>
    <repository>
        <id>spring-releases</id>
        <url>https://repo.spring.io/libs-release</url>
    </repository>
</repositories>
<pluginRepositories>
    <pluginRepository>
        <id>spring-releases</id>
```

```
        <url>https://repo.spring.io/libs-release</url>
    </pluginRepository>
  </pluginRepositories>
</project>
```

First, in the pom.xml file, we define the parent Maven artifact. As our application is the Spring Boot application, we inherit our pom.xml from the spring-boot-starter-parent artifact. This gives us all the Spring Boot goodies out of the box, such as the startup mechanism, dependency injection, and so on. By adding spring-boot-starter-data-jpa as a dependency, we will be able to use all the database-related features, such as JDBC transaction management, JPA annotations for the entity classes, and so on. Having the pom.xml ready, let's continue and define the entry point for our microservice.

# Application entry point

Our application entry point will be named BookStoreApplication and will be BookstoreApplication.java:

```
package pl.finsys.example;

import org.springframework.boot.SpringApplication;
import org.springframework.boot.autoconfigure.SpringBootApplication;

@SpringBootApplication
public class BookstoreApplication {

    public static void main(final String[] args) {
        SpringApplication.run(BookstoreApplication.class, args);
    }
}
```

That's it. The whole nine lines of code, not counting blank lines. It could not be more concise. The @SpringBootApplication is a kind of shortcut annotation, which is very convenient. It replaces all of the following annotations:

- @Configuration: A class marked with this annotation becomes a source of bean definitions for the application context
- @EnableAutoConfiguration: This annotation makes Spring Boot add beans based on classpath settings, other beans, and various property settings

- `@EnableWebMvc`: Normally you would add `this` one for a Spring MVC application, but Spring Boot adds it automatically when it sees `spring-webmvc` on the classpath. This marks the application as a web application, which in turn will activate key behaviors such as setting up a `DispatcherServlet`
- `@ComponentScan`: Tells Spring to look for other components, configurations, and services, allowing it to find the controllers

So far so good. We need some models for our service. We are going to save some entities in the database; this is where the `spring-boot-starter-data-jpa` starter will come in handy. We will be able to use JPA (implemented with Hibernate) and `javax.transaction-api` without even declaring it explicitly. We need an entity model for our bookstore.

# Domain model and a repository

A domain model in our service will be a `Book` class, defined in the `Book.java` file:

```
package pl.finsys.example.domain;

import javax.persistence.Column;
import javax.persistence.Entity;
import javax.persistence.Id;
import javax.validation.constraints.NotNull;
import javax.validation.constraints.Size;

@Entity
public class Book {

    @Id
    @NotNull
    @Column(name = "id", nullable = false, updatable = false)
    private Long id;

    @NotNull
    @Size(max = 64)
    @Column(name = "author", nullable = false)
    private String author;

    @NotNull
    @Size(max = 64)
    @Column(name = "title", nullable = false)
    private String title;

    public Book() {
```

```
    }

    public Book(final Long id, final String author, final String title) {
        this.id = id;
        this.title = title;
        this.author = author;
    }

    public Long getId() {
        return id;
    }

    public String getAuthor() {
        return author;
    }

    public String getTitle() {
        return title;
    }

    public void setTitle(String title) {
        this.title = title;
    }
    @Override
    public String toString() {
        return "Book{" +
                "id=" + id +
                ", author='" + author + '\'' +
                ", title='" + title + '\'' +
                '}';
    }
}
```

As you can see on the previous listing, the Book class is a simple POJO with some annotations, properties, and getters and setters. The @Entity annotations come from the javax.persistence package and marks the POJO as a database entity, to enable JPA to store or retrieve it from the H2 database. @Column annotations specify the names of database columns where the corresponding book properties will be stored. The @NotNull and @Size annotations will make sure that our entity has proper values filled in, before it goes into the database.

We have our entity defined; it's now time to have a mechanism to read and store it in the database. We will use Spring's JpaRepository for this purpose. The name of our repository will be BookRepository in the BookRepository.java file:

```
package pl.finsys.example.repository;

import pl.finsys.example.domain.Book;
import org.springframework.data.jpa.repository.JpaRepository;

public interface BookRepository extends JpaRepository<Book, Long> {
}
```

The Spring Data JPA provides a repository programming model that starts with an interface per managed domain object. Defining this interface serves two purposes. First, by extending the JPARepository interfaces, we get a bunch of generic CRUD methods into our type that allows saving our entities, deleting them, and so on. For example, the following methods are available (declared in the JPARepository interfaces we are extending):

- List<T> findAll();
- List<T> findAll(Sort sort);
- List<T> findAll(Iterable<ID> ids);
- <S extends T> List<S> save(Iterable<S> entities);
- T getOne(ID id);
- <S extends T> S save(S entity);
- <S extends T> Iterable<S> save(Iterable<S> entities);
- T findOne(ID id);
- boolean exists(ID id);
- Iterable<T> findAll();
- Iterable<T> findAll(Iterable<ID> ids);
- long count();
- void delete(ID id);
- void delete(T entity);
- void delete(Iterable<? extends T> entities);
- void deleteAll();

No SQL coding, no JPA-QL queries, nothing. Simply by extending the Spring `JPARepository` interface, all those methods are at our disposal. Of course, we are not limited to those. We can declare our own methods in our interface, as `findByTitle(String title)`, for example. It will be picked up by Spring at runtime and will find us a book by its title. I highly recommend reading the Spring Data project documentation and experimenting further; it's very convenient to use. Using the `entity` repository straight from the controller is usually not very good practice, so it's time to have a book service. It will be a `BookService` interface, defined in the `BookService.java`:

```
package pl.finsys.example.service;

import pl.finsys.example.domain.Book;
import javax.validation.Valid;
import javax.validation.constraints.NotNull;
import java.util.List;

public interface BookService {
    Book saveBook(@NotNull @Valid final Book book);
    List<Book> getList();
    Book getBook(Long bookId);
    void deleteBook(final Long bookId);
}
```

The implementation, in the `BookServiceImpl.java`, can look the same as following:

```
package pl.finsys.example.service;

import org.springframework.beans.factory.annotation.Autowired;
import pl.finsys.example.domain.Book;
import pl.finsys.example.repository.BookRepository;
import pl.finsys.example.service.exception.BookAlreadyExistsException;
import org.slf4j.Logger;
import org.slf4j.LoggerFactory;
import org.springframework.stereotype.Service;
import org.springframework.transaction.annotation.Transactional;
import org.springframework.validation.annotation.Validated;

import javax.validation.Valid;
import javax.validation.constraints.NotNull;
import java.util.List;

@Service
@Validated
public class BookServiceImpl implements BookService {

    private static final Logger LOGGER =
LoggerFactory.getLogger(BookServiceImpl.class);
```

```
        private final BookRepository repository;

        @Autowired
        public BookServiceImpl(final BookRepository repository) {
            this.repository = repository;
        }

        @Override
        @Transactional
        public Book saveBook(@NotNull @Valid final Book book) {
            LOGGER.debug("Creating {}", book);
            Book existing = repository.findOne(book.getId());
            if (existing != null) {
                throw new BookAlreadyExistsException(
                        String.format("There already exists a book with id=%s",
book.getId()));
            }
            return repository.save(book);
        }

        @Override
        @Transactional(readOnly = true)
        public List<Book> getList() {
            LOGGER.debug("Retrieving the list of all users");
            return repository.findAll();
        }

        @Override
        public Book getBook(Long bookId) {
            return repository.findOne(bookId);
        }

        @Override
        @Transactional
        public void deleteBook(final Long bookId) {
            LOGGER.debug("deleting {}", bookId);
            repository.delete(bookId);
        }

    }
```

The previous listing presents the `BookService` implementation. Note that we have injected the `BookRepository` in the constructor. All the implementation methods, such as `saveBook()`, `getBook()`, `deleteBook()`, and `getList()` will use the injected `BookRepository` to operate on the book entities in the database. It's time for the last class, the actual controller that will wire all the previous classes together.

# REST controller

The REST controller defines URI paths that the service is going to respond to. It declares paths and corresponding `HTTP` methods that each controller method should react to. We define all of these using annotations. This approach is very similar to JAX-RS with Jersey. Our service has just one, single `book` resource, so we will have just a single controller for starters. It will be `BookController` class, defined in the `BookController.java`:

```java
package pl.finsys.example.controller;

import org.springframework.beans.factory.annotation.Autowired;
import pl.finsys.example.domain.Book;
import pl.finsys.example.service.BookService;
import pl.finsys.example.service.exception.BookAlreadyExistsException;
import org.slf4j.Logger;
import org.slf4j.LoggerFactory;
import org.springframework.http.HttpStatus;
import org.springframework.web.bind.annotation.*;

import javax.validation.Valid;
import java.util.List;

@RestController
public class BookController {

    private static final Logger LOGGER =
LoggerFactory.getLogger(BookController.class);
private final BookService bookService;

    @Autowired
    public BookController(final BookService bookService) {
        this.bookService = bookService;
    }

@RequestMapping(value = "/books", method = RequestMethod.POST,
consumes={"application/json"})
    public Book saveBook(@RequestBody @Valid final Book book) {
        LOGGER.debug("Received request to create the {}", book);
        return bookService.saveBook(book);
    }

@RequestMapping(value = "/books", method = RequestMethod.GET,
produces={"application/json"})
    public List<Book> listBooks() {
        LOGGER.debug("Received request to list all books");
        return bookService.getList();
    }
```

```
@RequestMapping(value = "/books/{id}", method = RequestMethod.GET,
produces={"application/json"})
    public Book singleBook(@PathVariable Long id) {
        LOGGER.debug("Received request to list a specific book");
        return bookService.getBook(id);
    }

@RequestMapping(value = "/books/{id}", method = RequestMethod.DELETE)
    public void deleteBook(@PathVariable Long id) {
        LOGGER.debug("Received request to delete a specific book");
        bookService.deleteBook(id);
    }
    @ExceptionHandler
    @ResponseStatus(HttpStatus.CONFLICT)
    public String
handleUserAlreadyExistsException(BookAlreadyExistsException e) {
        return e.getMessage();
    }
}
```

As you can see in the previous example, the class is annotated with the `@RestController` annotation. This is what makes it a controller, actually. In fact, it's a convenient annotation that is itself annotated with `@Controller` and `@ResponseBody` annotations. `@Controller` indicates that an annotated class is a controller (a web controller), also allowing for implementation classes to be autodetected through Spring's classpath scanning. Every method in a controller that should respond to a call to a specific URI is mapped with the `@RequestMapping` annotation. `@RequestMapping` takes parameters, the most important ones are:

- `value` : It will specify the URI path
- `method` : Specifyies the `HTTP` method to handle
- `headers` : The headers of the mapped request, in a format `myHeader=myValue`. A request will be handled by the method using the headers parameter, only if the incoming request header is found to have the given value
- `consumes` : Specifies the media types the mapped request can consume, such as `"text/plain"` or `"application/json"`. This can be a list of media types, for example: `{"text/plain", "application/json"}`
- `produces` : Specifies the media types the mapped request can produce, such as `"text/plain"` or `"application/json"`. This again can be a list of media types, for example: `{"text/plain", "application/json"}`

Similar to JAX-RS `@PathParam` and `@QueryParam` to specify the controller method's input parameters, now we have `@PathVariable` and `@RequestParam` in Spring. If you need to have your method parameter come in the request body (as a whole JSON object that you want to save, the same as in our `saveBook()` method), you will need to map the parameter using the `@RequestBody` annotation. As for the output, the `@ResponseBody` annotation can tell our controller that the method return value should be bound to the web response body.

In a real-world service, you will probably have a lot of controllers with a lot of paths mapped. When exposing such a service to the world, it's usually a good practice to document the API of the service. This API documentation is the service contract. Doing this manually could be a tedious process. Also, if you make changes, it's good to have the API documentation in sync. There is a tool that can make it a lot easier, Swagger.

# Documenting the API

Before a client can consume a service, it would need a service contract. A service contract defines all the details about a service; for example, how the service can be called, the URI of the service, and what the request and response formats are. Your clients will need to know how to interact with your API. Swagger is gaining a lot of ground with support from major vendors in the last couple of years. Swagger's specification presents all the details of your service resources and operations in a JSON format. The format of the specification is known as the OpenAPI specification (Swagger RESTful API documentation specification). It's human and machine readable, easy for parsing, transferring, and using in integration. The `SpringFox` library can be used to generate Swagger documentation from the RESTful services code. What's more, there is a wonderful tool called Swagger UI, which when integrated into the application, provides human readable documentation. In this section, we will generate Swagger documentation for our services. The `SpringFox` library, available on GitHub at `http://springfox.github.io/springfox/` and in the Maven central, is a tool to automatically build JSON API documentation for APIs built with Spring. Even better, the library provides the Swagger UI tool. The tool will be deployed together with your service and can be used, browse the generated API documentation in a very convenient way. Let's introduce Swagger to our service. We begin with adding the needed dependencies to our service `pom.xml` file:

```xml
<dependency>
    <groupId>io.springfox</groupId>
    <artifactId>springfox-swagger2</artifactId>
    <version>2.6.1</version>
</dependency>

<dependency>
```

```
        <groupId>io.springfox</groupId>
        <artifactId>springfox-swagger-ui</artifactId>
        <version>2.5.0</version>
    </dependency>
```

Having the library available in a classpath of our application, we need to turn it on. The next step will be then be adding the configuration class to enable and generate the Swagger documentation. We do it by creating a class annotated with the Spring `@Configuration` annotation, the same as in the following example:

```java
package pl.finsys.example.configuration;

import org.springframework.context.annotation.Bean;
import org.springframework.context.annotation.Configuration;
import springfox.documentation.builders.PathSelectors;
import springfox.documentation.builders.RequestHandlerSelectors;
import springfox.documentation.spi.DocumentationType;
import springfox.documentation.spring.web.plugins.Docket;
import springfox.documentation.swagger2.annotations.EnableSwagger2;

@Configuration
@EnableSwagger2
public class SwaggerConfig {
    @Bean
    public Docket api() {
        return new Docket(DocumentationType.SWAGGER_2)
                .select()
                .apis(RequestHandlerSelectors.any())
                .paths(PathSelectors.any()).build();
    }
}
```

A couple of words of explanation here. `@Configuration` means that the annotated class is defining a Spring configuration, `@EnableSwagger2` turns off the Swagger support. The `Docket` is a builder class to configure the generation of Swagger documentation, configured with `DocumentationType.SWAGGER_2` to generate Swagger 2 compatible API documentation. The `select()` method called on the `Docket` bean instance returns an `ApiSelectorBuilder`, which provides the `apis()` and `paths()` methods to filter the controllers and methods being documented using string predicates. In our example, we want all controllers and all mapped paths to be documented; that's why we use `.apis(RequestHandlerSelectors.any()).paths(PathSelectors.any())`

You could also use the `regex` parameter passed to `paths()` to provide an additional filter to generate documentation only for the path matching the regex expression.

That's it; it's the simplest form of generating a documentation for your API. If you now run the service (we are going to do this in a short while), two endpoints will be available:

- `http://localhost:8080/v2/api-docs`
- `http://localhost:8080/swagger-ui.html`

The first one contains the Swagger 2 compatible documentation, in a JSON format, as you can see in the following screenshot:

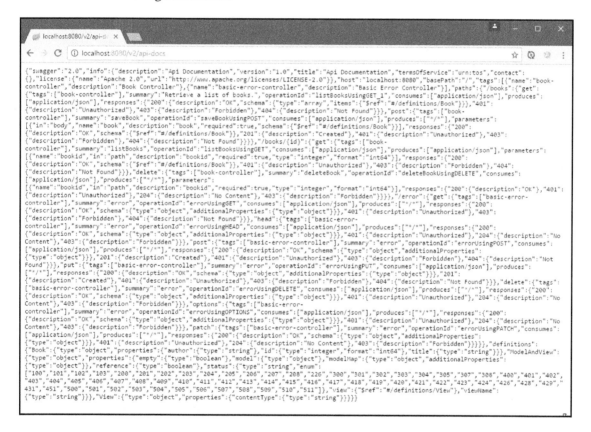

To browse the API documentation in a lot more useful form, point your browser to the second URL. You will be presented with the Swagger UI tool interface:

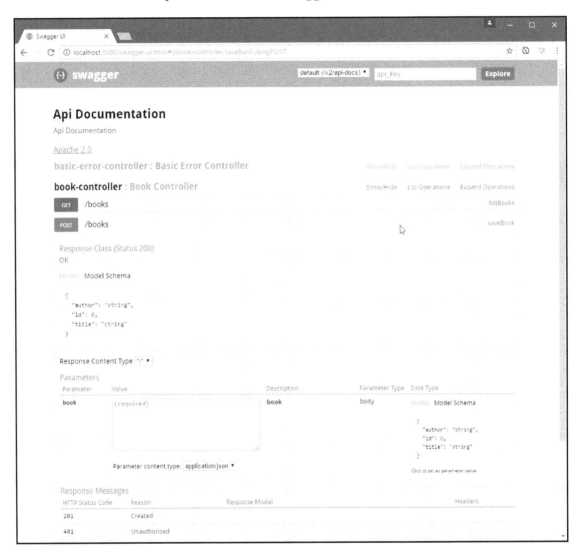

The Swagger UI is a collection of HTML, JavaScript, and CSS assets that dynamically generate beautiful documentation from a Swagger-compliant API. It lists your service operations, and its request and response formats. Best of all, you can test your service using this tool, by executing specific requests. In fact, it's a great tool to quickly test your service. Our documentation is not very descriptive. Of course, we have a listing of our exposed endpoints with their input and output description. It would be nice if we could enhance the documentation with some more specific details. We CAN do it, there are Java annotations we can use in the service's code to enhance the generated documentation. The annotations come from the Swagger-annotation package, which will be available if you use the `springfox-swagger2` library in your project. For example, consider the following code snippet:

```
@ApiOperation(value = "Retrieve a list of books.",
responseContainer = "List")
@RequestMapping(value = "/books", method = RequestMethod.GET, produces =
{"application/json"})
public List<Book> listBooks() {
LOGGER.debug("Received request to list all books");
return bookService.getList();
}
```

In the previous code, we use the `@ApiOperation` annotation to provide a more detailed description of what the operation does. There's a lot more: `@ApiImplicitParam` for describing parameters, `@Authorization` to provide a name of the authorization scheme to be used on this resource/operation, `@License` to provide information about the license, and so on. All of those annotations will be picked up by `springfox-swagger2` and used to enhance the generated documentation. I highly recommend looking at the swagger-annotations JavaDoc; you will be able to document your API in a detailed, professional way.

I guess our little service is ready; it's time to bring it to life.

# Running the application

Because we have defined the Spring Boot plugin in our `pom.xml` build file, we can now start the application using Maven. All you need to have is Maven present on the system path, but you probably have this already as a Java developer. To run the application, execute the following from the command shell (terminal on MacOS or `cmd.exe` on Windows):

```
$ mvn spring-boot:run
```

After a while, the Spring splash log will show up in the console and your microservice will be ready to accept HTTP requests. Soon, in Chapter 5, *Creating Images with Java Applications*, our goal will be to see the same coming from the Docker container:

```
cmd - mvn spring-boot:run                                                                    —  □  ×

[INFO] --- maven-resources-plugin:2.6:resources (default-resources) @ rest-example ---
[INFO] Using 'UTF-8' encoding to copy filtered resources.
[INFO] Copying 1 resource
[INFO] Copying 1 resource
[INFO]
[INFO] --- maven-compiler-plugin:3.1:compile (default-compile) @ rest-example ---
[INFO] Nothing to compile - all classes are up to date
[INFO]
[INFO] --- maven-resources-plugin:2.6:testResources (default-testResources) @ rest-example ---
[INFO] Using 'UTF-8' encoding to copy filtered resources.
[INFO] skip non existing resourceDirectory C:\Users\jarek\projects\rest-example\src\test\resources
[INFO]
[INFO] --- maven-compiler-plugin:3.1:testCompile (default-testCompile) @ rest-example ---
[INFO] Nothing to compile - all classes are up to date
[INFO]
[INFO] <<< spring-boot-maven-plugin:1.5.2.RELEASE:run (default-cli) < test-compile @ rest-example <<<
[INFO]
[INFO] --- spring-boot-maven-plugin:1.5.2.RELEASE:run (default-cli) @ rest-example ---

  /\\ / ___'_ __ _ _(_)_ __  __ _ \ \ \ \
 ( ( )\___ | '_ | '_| | '_ \/ _` | \ \ \ \
  \\/  ___)| |_)| | | | | || (_| |  ) ) ) )
   '  |____| .__|_| |_|_| |_\__, | / / / /
  =========|_|==============|___/=/_/_/_/
  :: Spring Boot ::        (v1.5.2.RELEASE)

2017-04-09 15:04:20 INFO  p.f.e.BookstoreApplication:48 - Starting BookstoreApplication on DESKTOP-RI2V0UU with PID 16884 (C:\Us
ers\jarek\projects\rest-example\target\classes started by jarek in C:\Users\jarek\projects\rest-example)
2017-04-09 15:04:20 DEBUG p.f.e.BookstoreApplication:51 - Running with Spring Boot v1.5.2.RELEASE, Spring v4.3.7.RELEASE
2017-04-09 15:04:20 INFO  p.f.e.BookstoreApplication:641 - The following profiles are active: dev
2017-04-09 15:04:22 INFO  p.f.e.BookstoreApplication:57 - Started BookstoreApplication in 2.88 seconds (JVM running for 4.846)

java.exe                                                      Search
```

If you want to, you can also run the application straight from the IDE, be it IntelliJ IDEA, Eclipse, or Netbeans. Our BookstoreApplication class has a main() method; you will just need to create a runtime configuration in your IDE and run it. This is different from the JEE7 JAX-RS service. It that case, you would need to deploy the service in a JEE compliant application server to be able to run it. Having the main() method defined is very convenient when debugging your service. Just start a debugging session with BookstoreApplication as the entry point. There is no need to create a remote debugging session. Having our service running, it's time to make some calls to its exposed endpoints.

# Making calls

Making a call to the operation exposed from the service can be done using any tool or library that can execute the HTTP requests. The first obvious choice would be just a web browser. But a web browser is convenient only for executing GET requests (as for getting a list of books from our bookstore service). If you need to execute other methods such as POST or PUT or provide additional request parameters, header values, and so on, you will need to use some alternatives. The first choice could be cURL, a command-line tool for transferring data using various protocols. Let's look at other options we have.

# Spring RestTemplate

If you need to call a service from another service, you will need a HTTP client. Spring provides the very useful RestTemplate class. It gives you a synchronous client-side HTTP access, simplifies communication with HTTP servers, and enforces RESTful principles. It handles HTTP connections, leaving application code to provide URLs (with possible template variables) and extracts results. By default, RestTemplate relies on standard JDK facilities to establish HTTP connections. You can switch to a different HTTP library of your choice, such as Apache HttpComponents, Netty, and OkHttp through its setRequestFactory() method. Calling the REST resource to get a book with ID = 1 can be as simple as follows:

```
package pl.finsys.example.client;

import org.springframework.http.ResponseEntity;
import org.springframework.web.client.RestTemplate;
import pl.finsys.example.domain.Book;

public class ExampleClient {
    public static void main(String[] args) {
        try {
            RestTemplate restTemplate = new RestTemplate();
            ResponseEntity<Book> response =
restTemplate.getForEntity("http://localhost:8080/books/1", Book.class);
            System.out.println(response.getBody());
        } catch (Exception e) {
            e.printStackTrace();
        }
    }
}
```

Of course, this is just a simplified client example, to present you the idea. You can use `RestTemplate` to create more sophisticated client calls to the REST resources.

# HTTPie

A great command-line alternative to cURL is HTTPie, available at `https://httpie.org`. It's a command-line `HTTP` client. Luckily, the *ie* in the name doesn't come from Internet Explorer. If you prefer to work from the shell or command line, `HTTPie` is a just a single command which adds the following features to cUrl: sensible defaults, expressive and intuitive command syntax, colorized and formatted terminal output, built-in JSON support, persistent sessions, forms and file uploads, proxies and authentication support, and support for arbitrary request data and headers. It's written in Python and works on Linux, macOSX, and Windows.

# Postman

Postman is a tool of choice for many developers. It's available as the Chrome plugin or a standalone utility at `https://www.getpostman.com`. Postman is very convenient for use. It's a powerful GUI platform to make your API development faster and easier, from building API requests through testing, documentation, and sharing. You can save your `HTTP` requests for later use and organize them in collections. If you work in multiple environments, for example your localhost, when developing the service and a production environment later on, Postman introduces the concept of environments. Environments give you the ability to customize your requests using variables. This way you can easily switch between different setups without changing your requests. Each environment is represented as a set of key-value pairs. This makes working with multiple environments easy. It also has a very handy UI for editing your `HTTP` requests:

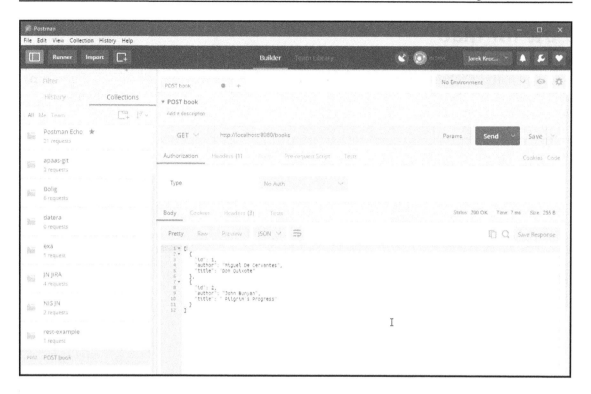

You can define request headers, cookies, and body. If your service supports authentication, Postman contains a lot of authentication helpers: it can be basic Auth, digest Auth, and OAuth. The response body can be viewed in one of three views: pretty, raw, and preview. The pretty mode formats JSON or XML responses so that they are easier to look at and headers are displayed as key/value pairs in the header tab. It's a really powerful and pleasant to use tool. If you work on macOS, there's something even better.

# Paw for Mac

**Paw** is a full-featured HTTP client that lets you test the APIs you build or consume. It has a beautiful native OS X interface to compose requests, inspect server responses, and generate client code out of the box. As you can see in the following screenshot, it also contains a powerful editor to compose your requests:

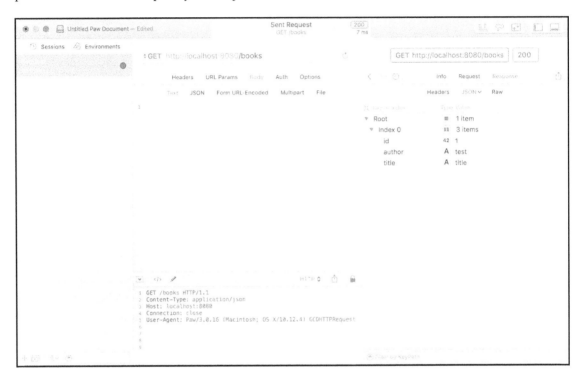

It also supports a lot of authentication schemas including OAuth 1 and 2, Basic Auth, Digest Auth, Hawk, AWS Signature Version 4, and Amazon S3. Similar to Postman, Paw also allows you to organize your requests in folders. You can also define and switch different environments quickly. The interesting feature is that Paw can generate client code to execute your requests. It can generate code for cURL, HTTPie, Objective-C, Python, JavaScript, Ruby, PHP, Java, Go, and many others. And guess what? Paw can also import the Swagger documentation we have been talking about. You can use this feature to test the service you were given the documentation for.

If you need to quickly start with your new service, there are a couple of tools that may come in handy. One of them is **Initializr**.

# Spring Initializr

Spring Initializr is a web-based tool available at `https://start.spring.io`. It's a quick start generator for Spring projects. Spring Initializr can be used as follows:

- From the web browser at `https://start.spring.io`
- In your IDE (IntelliJ IDEA Ultimate or NetBeans, using plugins)
- From the command line with the Spring Boot CLI or simply with cURL or HTTPie

Using the web application is very convenient; all you need to do is provide details about your application Maven archetype, such as group, artifact name, description, and so on:

In the **Dependencies** section, you can enter the keywords of the features you would like to have included, such as JPA, web, and so on. You can also switch the UI to an advanced view, to have all the features listed and ready to be selected:

---

### Core

☐ Security
Secure your application via spring-security

☐ AOP
Aspect-oriented programming including spring-aop and AspectJ

☐ Atomikos (JTA)
JTA distributed transactions via Atomikos

☐ Bitronix (JTA)
JTA distributed transactions via Bitronix

☐ Narayana (JTA)
JTA distributed transactions via Narayana

☐ Cache
Spring's Cache abstraction

☐ DevTools
Spring Boot Development Tools

☐ Configuration Processor
Generate metadata for your custom configuration keys

☐ Validation
JSR-303 validation infrastructure (already included with web)

☐ Session
API and implementations for managing a user's session information

☐ Retry
Provide declarative retry support via spring-retry

☐ Lombok
Java annotation library which helps to reduce boilerplate code and code faster

### Web

☐ Web
Full-stack web development with Tomcat and Spring MVC

☐ Reactive Web
Reactive web development with Netty and Spring WebFlux
requires Spring Boot >=2.0.0.BUILD-SNAPSHOT

☐ Websocket
Websocket development with SockJS and STOMP

☐ Web Services
Contract-first SOAP service development with Spring Web Services

☐ Jersey (JAX-RS)
RESTful Web Services framework

☐ Ratpack
Spring Boot integration for the Ratpack framework

☐ Vaadin
Vaadin java web application framework

☐ Rest Repositories
Exposing Spring Data repositories over REST via spring-data-rest-webmvc

☐ HATEOAS
HATEOAS-based RESTful services

☐ Rest Repositories HAL Browser
Browsing Spring Data REST repositories in your browser

☐ Mobile
Simplify the development of mobile web applications with spring-mobile

☐ REST Docs
Document RESTful services by combining hand-written and auto-generated documentation

☐ Stormpath
Stormpath default starter including Spring MVC, Thymeleaf and Spring Security

### Template Engines

### SQL

---

As the output, Spring Initializr will create a ZIP archive with the base Maven project you want to start with. The project created by Spring Initializr is a Maven project and follows the standard `Maven` directory layout. This really saves a lot of time when creating new Spring projects. You no longer need to search for specific Maven archetypes and look for their versions. Initializr will generate the `pom.xml` for you, automatically. The presence of the dependencies in the `pom.xml` is important because Spring Boot will make decisions on what to create automatically when certain things are found on the classpath. For example, if the dependency for the H2 database is present and exists on the classpath when the application is run, Spring Boot will automatically create a data connection and an embedded H2 database.

# Summary

As you can see, developing Java microservices is not as tricky as it may sound. You can choose between JEE7 JAX-RS or Spring Boot, wire some classes, and a basic service is ready. You are not limited to using Spring MVC for creating your REST endpoints. If you are more familiar with the Java EE JAX-RS specification, you can easily integrate JAX-RS into Spring applications, especially Spring Boot applications. You can then take what is best for you from both.

Of course, in the real world you would probably want to include some more advanced features such as authentication and security. Having Spring Initializr available can give you a serious speed boost when developing your own service. In Chapter 5, *Creating Images with Java Applications*, we are going to package our bookstore service into a Docker image and run it using Docker Engine.

# 5

# Creating Images with Java Applications

Now that we have a simple, but functional Java microservice based on Spring Bootstrap, we can go further. Before we deploy it using Kubernetes, let's package it as a Docker image. In this chapter, we will create a Docker image containing our application, and we will dockerize a Spring Boot application to run it in an isolated environment, a container.

Topics covered in this chapter will be:

- Creating a Dockerfile
- Dockerfile instructions
- Building the image
- Creating and removing images

Let's begin with the definition of a `Dockerfile`, which will be the definition of our container.

## Dockerfile

As you will remember from `Chapter 1`, *Introduction to Docker*, the `Dockerfile` is kind of a recipe to build an image. It's a plain text file containing instructions which are executed by Docker in the order they are placed. Each `Dockerfile` has a base image that the Docker engine will use to build upon. A resulting image will be a specific state of a file system: a read-only, frozen immutable snapshot of a live container, composed of layers representing changes in the filesystem at various points in time.

The image creation flow in Docker is pretty straightforward and consists basically of two steps:

1. First, you prepare a text file named `Dockerfile`, which contains a series of instructions on how to build the image. The set of instructions you can use in the `Dockerfile` is not very broad, but sufficient to fully instruct Docker how to create an image.

2. Next, you execute the `docker build` command to create a Docker image based on the `Dockerfile` that you have just created. The `docker build` command runs within the context. The build's context is the files at a specified location, which can be a `PATH` or a URL. The `PATH` is a directory on your local filesystem and the URL is a Git repository location. A context is processed recursively. `PATH` will include any subdirectories. The URL will include the repository and its submodules.

If you create an image containing a Java application, you can also skip the second step and utilize one of the Docker Maven plugins available. After we learn how to build images using the `docker build` command, we will also create our image using Maven. When building using Maven, the context to the `docker build` command (or a build process, in this case) will be provided automatically by Maven itself. Actually, there is no need for the `Dockerfile` at all, it will be created automatically during the build process. We will get to this in a short while.

The standard name for a `Dockerfile` is just `Dockerfile`. It's just a plain text file. Depending on the IDE you use, there are plugins to provide Dockerfile syntax highlighting and autocompletion, which makes editing them a breeze. Dockerfile instructions use simple and clear syntax which makes them quite easy to understand, create, and use. They are designed to be self-explanatory, especially because they allow commenting just as properly written application source code. Let's get to know the `Dockerfile` instructions now.

# Dockerfile instructions

We will begin with the instruction that every Dockerfile must have at the top, the `FROM` instruction.

# FROM

This is the first instruction in the Dockerfile. It sets the base image for every subsequent instruction coming next in the file. The syntax for the FROM instruction is straightforward. It's just:

```
FROM <image>, or FROM <image>:<tag>, or FROM <image>@<digest>
```

The FROM instruction takes a tag or digest as a parameter. If you decide to skip them, Docker will assume you want to build your image from the latest tag. Be aware that latest will not always be the latest version of the image you want to build upon. The latest tag is kind of a special one. Also, it may not work as you may expect. Well, to cut a long story short, it doesn't mean anything special unless the image creator (openjdk or fabric8, for example) has a specific build, tag, and push pattern. The latest tag assigned to an image simply means that it's the image that was last built and executed without a specific tag provided. It's easy to understand that it may be confusing, pulling the image tagged latest will not fetch the latest version of the software.

 Docker will not take care of checking if you are getting the newest version of the software when pulling the image tagged latest.

Docker will throw an error during the build if it cannot find a tag or digest you provide. You should choose the base image wisely. My recommendation would be to always prefer the official repositories that can be found on Docker Hub. By choosing an official image you can be pretty sure it will be of high quality, tested, supported, and maintained.

For containerizing a Java application, we have two options. The first one is to use a base Linux image and install Java using the RUN instruction (we will cover RUN in a while). The second option will be to pull an image containing the Java runtime already installed. Here you have a lot more to choose from. For example:

- openjdk: An official repository containing an open-source implementation of the Java platform, Standard Edition. The tag latest, which will be used if you do not specify any tag, points to the 8u121-alpine OpenJDK release, as of the time of writing this book
- fabric8/java-alpine-openjdk8-jdk: This base image is actually also being used by the fabric8 Maven plugin

- `frolvlad/alpine-oraclejdk8`: There are three tags you can choose from: full (only src tarballs get removed), cleaned (desktop parts get cleaned), slim, everything but the compiler and JVM is removed. The tag latest points to the cleaned one
- `jeanblanchard/java`: A repository containing images based on Alpine Linux to keep the size minimal (about 25% of an Ubuntu-based image). The tag `latest` points to Oracle Java 8 (Server JRE)

By registering and creating your account on the Docker Hub at `https://hub.docker.com`, you will get access to the Docker Store. It's available at `https://store.docker.com`. Try searching the Docker Store for Java-related images. You will find a lot of useful images to choose from, and one of them is the official Oracle Java 8 SE (Server JRE) image. This Docker image provides the Server JRE, a runtime environment specifically targeted for deploying Java in server environments. The Server JRE includes tools for JVM monitoring and tools commonly required for server applications. You can get this official Java Docker image by buying it on the Docker Store. Click Get Content, it's priced $0.00, so it will be available for your development purposes free of charge.

 Take note that images coming from the Docker Store are bound to your Docker Hub account. Before you pull them or build your own images having them as the base image, you will need to the authenticate to Docker Store using the `docker login` command and your Docker Hub credentials.

For our purposes, let's choose `jeanblanchard/java`. It's the official Oracle Java running on top of the Alpine Linux distribution. The base image is small and fast to download. Our FROM instruction will look the same as this:

```
FROM jeanblanchard/java:8
```

If a FROM image is not found on your Docker host (on your local machine, for example), Docker will try to find and pull it out from the Docker Hub (or your private repository if you have it set up). All subsequent instructions in the `Dockerfile` will use the image specified in the FROM as a base starting point. That's why it's mandatory; a valid `Dockerfile` must have it at the top.

# MAINTAINER

By using the `MAINTAINER` instruction, you set the `Author` field of the generated image. This can be your name, username, or whatever you would like as an author of the image that will be created by using the `Dockerfile` you are writing. This command can be placed anywhere in a `Dockerfile`, but good practice is to place it on the top of the file, just after the `FROM` instruction. This is a so-called, non-executing command, meaning that it will not make any changes to the generated image. The syntax, again, is very simple:

```
MAINTAINER authors_name
```

# WORKDIR

The `WORKDIR` instruction adds a working directory for any `CMD`, `RUN`, `ENTRYPOINT`, `COPY`, and `ADD` instructions that comes after it in the Dockerfile. The syntax for the instruction is `WORKDIR /PATH`. You can have multiple `WORKDIR` instructions in one Dockerfile, if the relative path is provided; it will be relative to the path of the previous `WORKDIR` instruction.

# ADD

What `ADD` basically does is copy the files from the source into the container's own filesystem at the desired destination. It takes two arguments: the source (`<source path or URL>`) and a destination (`<destination path>`):

```
ADD <source path or URL> <destination path >
```

The source can have two forms: it can be a path to a file, a directory, or the URL. The path is relative to the directory in which the build process is going to be started (the build context we have mentioned earlier). This means you cannot have, for example `"../../config.json"` placed as a source path parameter of the `ADD` instruction.

The source and destination paths can contain wildcards. Those are the same as in a conventional file system: `*` for any text string, or `?` for any single character.

For example, `ADD target/*.jar /` will add all files ending with `.jar` into the root directory in the image's file system.

If you need, you can specify multiple source paths, and separate them with a comma. All of them must be relative to the build context, the same as if you have just a single source path. If your source or destination paths contain spaces, you will need to use a special syntax, adding the square brackets around:

```
ADD ["<source path or URL>" "<destination path>"]
```

If the source path doesn't end with a trailing slash, it will be considered a single file and just copied into the destination. If the source path ends with a trailing slash, it will be considered a directory: its whole contents will then be copied into the destination path, but the directory itself will not be created at the destination path. So, as you can see, a trailing slash / is quite important when adding files or directories to an image. If the source path points to the compressed archive in one of the common formats such as ZIP, TAR, and so on, it will be decompressed into the destination path. Docker doesn't recognize an archive by the filename, it checks the contents of the file.

> If the archive is damaged or unreadable by Docker in any other way, it will not be extracted and you will not be given an error message. The file will just be copied into the destination path.

The same trailing slash rules apply to the destination path; if it ends with a trailing slash, it means that it's a directory. Otherwise, it will be considered a single file. This gives you great flexibility when constructing the file system content of your image; you can add files into directories, add files as single files (with the same or different names), or just add whole directories.

The ADD command is not only about copying files from the local file system, you can use it to get the file from the network. If the source is a URL then the contents of the URL will be automatically downloaded and placed at the destination. Note that file archives that were downloaded from the network will not be decompressed. Again, the trailing slash is important when downloading files; if the destination path ends with a slash, the file will be downloaded into the directory. Otherwise, the downloaded file will just be saved under the name you provided as the destination path.

The <destination directory> is either an absolute path or a path which is relative to the directory specific by the WORKDIR instruction (we will cover it in a while). The source (or multiple sources) will just be copied into the destination specified. For example:

- ADD config.json projectRoot/ will add the config.json file to <WORKDIR>/projectRoot/
- ADD config.json /absoluteDirectory/ will add the config.json file to the /absoluteDirectory/

When it comes to the ownership of the files created in the image, they will always be created with the user ID (UID) 0 and group ID (GID) 0. Permissions will be the same as in the source file, unless it's a file downloaded from the remote URL: in this case, it will get permissions value 600 (only the owner can read and write the file). If you need to change these values (ownership or permissions), you will need to provide more instructions in your Dockerfile, after the ADD instruction.

> If the files that you need to add to the image are placed on the URL that needs authentication, the ADD instruction will not work. You will need to use a shell command to download the file, such as wget or curl.

Note that ADD shouldn't be used if you don't need its special features, such as unpacking archives, you should use COPY instead.

# COPY

The COPY instruction will copy new files or directories from <source path> and add them to the file system of the container at the path <destination path>.

It's very similar to the ADD instruction, even the syntax is no different:

```
COPY <source path or URL> <destination path >
```

The same rules from ADD apply to COPY: all source paths must be relative to the context of the build. Again the presence of the trailing slash at the end of the source and destination path is important: if it's present, the path will be considered a file; otherwise, it will be treated as a directory.

Of course, as in ADD, you can have multiple source paths. If source or destination paths contain spaces, you will need to wrap them in square brackets:

```
COPY ["<source path or URL>" "<destination path>"]
```

The <destination path> is an absolute path (if begins with a slash), or a path relative to the path specified by the WORKDIR instruction.

As you can see, the functionality of COPY is almost the same as the ADD instruction, with one difference. COPY supports only the basic copying of local files into the container. On the other hand, ADD gives some more features, such as archive extraction, downloading files through URL, and so on. Docker's best practices say that you should prefer COPY if you do not need those additional features of ADD. The Dockerfile will be cleaner and easier to understand thanks to the transparency of the COPY command.

There is one common, important aspect for both ADD and COPY instructions, a cache. Basically, Docker caches the files that go into the image during the build. The contents of the file or files in the image are examined and a checksum is calculated for each file. During the cache lookup, the checksum is compared against the checksum in the existing images. If anything has changed in the file(s), such as the contents and metadata, then the cache is being invalidated. Otherwise, if the source file has not changed, an existing image layer is being reused.

 If you have multiple Dockerfile steps that use different files from your context, COPY them individually, rather than all at once. This will ensure that each step's build cache is only invalidated (forcing the step to be re-run) if the specifically required files change.

As you can see, the COPY instruction has almost identical syntax and behavior to the ADD instruction, but their feature set is somehow different. For files and directories that do not require the ADD feature of archive unpacking or fetching from the URL, you should always use COPY.

# RUN

The RUN instruction is the central executing instruction for the Dockerfile. In essence, the RUN instruction will execute a command (or commands) in a new layer on top of the current image and then commit the results. The resulting committed image will be used as a base for the next instruction in the Dockerfile. As you will remember from Chapter 1, *Introduction to Docker*, layering is the core concept in Docker. RUN, takes a command as its argument and runs it to create the new layer.

This also means that COPY and ENTRYPOINT set parameters can be overridden at runtime, so if you don't change anything after starting your container, the result will always be the same. RUN however, will be executed at build time and no matter what you do at runtime, its effects will be here.

To make your Dockerfile more readable and easier to maintain, you can split long or complex RUN statements on multiple lines separating them with a backslash.

The RUN commands from the `Dockerfile` will be executed in the order they appear in it.

Each RUN instruction creates a new layer in the image.

As you already know from `Chapter 1`, *Introduction to Docker,* layers are being cached and reused by Docker. The cache for RUN instructions isn't invalidated automatically during the next build. For example, the cache for an instruction the same as RUN `apt-get upgrade -y` will be reused during the next build. What makes the cache important? For the most part, the cache is exceptionally helpful and can save you a tremendous amount of time while building your image. It makes building a new container really, really fast. However, there is a word of warning. There are times when the caching can be dangerous and provide unexpected results. The cache is used pretty heavily during the build process and this may cause issues when you want the updated output of a RUN command to make it into the new container. If the RUN command doesn't change between two builds, Docker's cache will not get invalidated. In effect, Docker will reuse the previous results from the cache. This is clearly harmful. Imagine a case when you use the RUN command for pulling source code from the Git repository, by using the `git clone` as the first step of building the image.

Be aware when the Docker cache needs to be invalidated, otherwise you will get unexpected results with your image builds.

That's why it's good to know how to selectively invalidate the cache. In the Docker world, this is called cache busting.

Consider the following example. Probably the most common usecase for RUN is an application of `apt-get`, which is a package manager command for downloading packages on Ubuntu. Let's say we have the following Dockerfile, installing Java runtime:

```
FROM ubuntu
RUN apt-get update
RUN apt-get install -y openjdk-8-jre
```

If we build an image from this `Dockerfile`, all layers from two `RUN` instructions will be put into the layers cache. But, after a while you decide you want the `node.js` package in your image, so now the Dockerfile looks the same as this:

```
FROM ubuntu
RUN apt-get update
RUN apt-get install -y openjdk-8-jre
RUN apt-get install -y nodejs
```

If you run the `docker build` for the second time, Docker will reuse the layers by taking them from the cache. As a result, the `apt-get update` will not be executed, because the cached version will be used. In effect, your newly created image will potentially have an outdated version of the `java` and `node.js` packages. You should always have the cache concept in mind when creating `RUN` instructions. In our example, we should always combine `RUN apt-get update` with `apt-get install` in the same `RUN` statement, which will create just a single layer; for example:

```
RUN apt-get update \
&& apt-get install -y openjdk-8-jre \
&& apt-get install -y nodejs \
&& apt-get clean
```

Better than this, you can also use a technique called "version pinning" to avoid cache problems. It's nothing more than just providing a specific, concrete version for the package you want to install.

# CMD

The purpose of a `CMD` instruction is to provide defaults for an executing container. You can think of the `CMD` instruction as a starting point of your image, when the container is being run later on. This can be an executable, or, if you specify the `ENTRYPOINT` instruction (we are going to explain it next), you can omit the executable and provide the default parameters only. The `CMD` instruction syntax can have two forms:

- `CMD ["executable","parameter1","parameter2"]`: This is a so called `exec` form. It's also the preferred and recommended form. The parameters are JSON array, and they need to be enclosed in square brackets. The important note is that the `exec` form does not invoke a command shell when the container is run. It just runs the executable provided as the first parameter. If the `ENTRYPOINT` instruction is present in the `Dockerfile`, `CMD` provides a default set of parameters for the `ENTRYPOINT` instruction.

- `CMD command parameter1 parameter2`: This a shell form of the instruction. This time, the shell (if present in the image) will be processing the provided command. The specified binary will be executed with an invocation of the shell using `/bin/sh -c`. It means that if you display the container's hostname, for example, using `CMD echo $HOSTNAME`, you should use the shell form of the instruction.

We have said before that the recommended form of `CMD` instruction is the `exec` form. Here's why: everything started through the shell will be started as a subcommand of `/bin/sh -c`, which does not pass signals. This means that the executable will not be the container's PID 1, and will not receive Unix signals, so your executable will not receive a `SIGTERM` from `docker stop <container>`. There is another drawback: you will need a shell in your container. If you're building a minimal image, it doesn't need to contain a shell binary. The `CMD` instruction using the shell form will simply fail.

When Docker is executing the command, it doesn't check if the shell is available inside the container. If there is no `/bin/sh` in the image, the container will fail to start.

On the other hand, if we change the `CMD` to the `exec` form, Docker will be looking for an executable named `echo`, which, of course, will fail, because `echo` is a shell command.

Because `CMD` is the same as a starting point for the Docker engine when running a container, there can only be one single `CMD` instruction in a Dockerfile.

If there are more than one `CMD` instruction in a Dockerfile, only the last one will take effect.

You may notice that the `CMD` instruction is very similar to `RUN`. They both can run any command (or application). There is a key important difference: the time of execution. The command supplied through the `RUN` instruction is executed during the build time, whereas the command specified through the `CMD` instruction is executed when the container is launched by executing `docker run` on the newly created image. Unlike `CMD`, the `RUN` instruction is actually used to build the image, by creating a new layer on top of the previous one which is committed.

RUN is a build-time instruction, the CMD is a runtime instruction.

Believe it or not, we can now have our REST example microservice containerized. Let's check if it builds by executing the mvn clean install on the pom.xml file created in Chapter 4, *Creating Java Microservices*. After the successful build, we should have a target directory with the rest-example-0.1.0.jar file created. The Spring Boot application JAR in the target directory is an executable, fat JAR. We are going to run it from within the Docker container. Let's write the basic Dockerfile using the command we already know and place it in the root of our project (this will be the context for our docker build command):

```
FROM jeanblanchard/java:8
COPY target/rest-example-0.1.0.jar rest-example-0.1.0.jar
CMD java -jar rest-example-0.1.0.jar
```

We can now run the docker build command, using rest-example as the image name, omitting the tag (as you will remember, omitting a tag when building an image will result in creating the latest tag):

```
$ docker build . -t rest-example
```

The dot as the first parameter specifies the context for the docker build command. In our case, it will be just a root directory of our little microservice. During the build process, Docker will output all the steps and layer IDs. Notice that almost every Dockerfile instruction creates a new layer. If you remember from Chapter 1, *Introduction to Docker*, Docker utilizes the layer cache. If a specific layer can be reused, it will be taken from the cache. It greatly improves the build process performance. At the end, Docker will output the ID of the newly created image, as you can see in the following screenshot:

```
C:\Users\jarek\projects\rest-example (master)
λ docker build . -t rest-example
Sending build context to Docker daemon 32.18 MB
Step 1/3 : FROM jeanblanchard/java:8
 ---> a418f9766777
Step 2/3 : COPY target/rest-example-0.1.0.jar rest-example-0.1.0.jar
 ---> Using cache
 ---> e3e9fe4ee75c
Step 3/3 : CMD java -jar rest-example-0.1.0.jar
 ---> Using cache
 ---> 2b0e4cbaed0a
Successfully built 2b0e4cbaed0a
SECURITY WARNING: You are building a Docker image from Windows against a non-Windows Docker host. All files and directories
added to build context will have '-rwxr-xr-x' permissions. It is recommended to double check and reset permissions for sensi
tive files and directories.

C:\Users\jarek\projects\rest-example (master)
λ
```

An image has been created, so it should be present on the images available to run. To list images, execute the following Docker command:

```
$ docker image ls
```

As you can see in the following screenshot, our `rest-example` image is present and ready to be run:

```
C:\Users\jarek\projects\rest-example (master)
λ docker image ls
REPOSITORY               TAG        IMAGE ID            CREATED            SIZE
rest-example             latest     2b0e4cbaed0a        21 minutes ago     194 MB
jeanblanchard/java       8          a418f9766777        3 days ago         162 MB
store/oracle/serverjre   8          ca8d7b60ea60        5 days ago         274 MB

C:\Users\jarek\projects\rest-example (master)
λ
```

So far, so good. We have a basic form of our image built. Although the process of running images is the topic for Chapter 6, *Running Containers with Java Applications*, let's quickly run it now to prove it's working. To run the image, execute the following:

```
$ docker run -it rest-example
```

After a while, you should see the familiar Spring Boot banner as a sign that our service is running from inside the Docker container:

That wasn't very tricky, right? The basic `Dockerfile` contains just three lines, the base image definition using `FROM`, `COPY` to transfer the executable jar into the image's filesystem, and a `CMD` instruction to run the service.

Building an application jar archive using Maven and then copying it using a Dockerfile `COPY` instruction simply works. What about delegating the build process to the Docker daemon itself? Well, we can do it, using the `Dockerfile` instructions we already know. The drawback of building a Java app using the Docker daemon is that the image will contain all of the JDK (including the Java compiler), Maven binaries, and our application source code. I would recommend building a single artifact (a JAR or WAR file), testing it thoroughly (using a release-oriented QA cycle), and deploying the sole artifact (with its dependencies of course) onto the target machine. However, to have an idea what's possible with a `Dockerfile`, take a look at the following example, assuming that our application code in the `/app` folder on the local disk:

```
FROM java:8
RUN apt-get update
RUN apt-get install -y maven
WORKDIR /app
COPY pom.xml /app/pom.xml
COPY src /app/src
RUN ["mvn", "package"]
CMD ["/usr/lib/jvm/java-8-openjdk-amd64/bin/java",
"-jar", "target/ rest-example-0.1.0.jar"]
```

In the previous example, the Maven build process will be executed by Docker. We just run the `apt-get` command to install Maven, add our application source code to the image, execute the Maven `package` command, and then run our service. It will behave exactly the same as if we just copy the already-built artifact into the image's file system.

There's a Dockerfile instruction which is kind of related to CMD instruction: the ENTRYPOINT. Let's look at it now.

# The ENTRYPOINT

The official Docker documentation says that the ENTRYPOINT instruction allows you to configure a container that will run as an executable. It's not very clear, at least for the first time. The ENTRYPOINT instruction is related to the CMD instruction. In fact, it can be confusing at the beginning. The reason for that is simple: CMD was developed first, then ENTRYPOINT was developed for more customization, and some functionality overlaps between those two instructions. Let's explain it a bit. The ENTRYPOINT specifies a command that will always be executed when the container starts. The CMD, on the other hand, specifies the arguments that will be fed to the ENTRYPOINT. Docker has a default ENTRYPOINT which is /bin/sh -c but does not have a default CMD. For example, consider this Docker command:

```
docker run ubuntu "echo" "hello world"
```

In this case, the image will be the latest ubuntu, the ENTRYPOINT will be the default /bin/sh -c, and the command passed to the ENTRYPOINT will be echo "hello world".

The syntax for the ENTRYPOINT instruction can have two forms, similar to CMD.

ENTRYPOINT ["executable", "parameter1", "parameter2"] is the exec form, preferred and recommended. Exactly the same as the exec form of the CMD instruction, this will not invoke a command shell. This means that the normal shell processing will not happen. For example, ENTRYPOINT [ "echo", "$HOSTNAME" ] will not do variable substitution on the $HOSTNAME variable. If you want shell processing then you need either to use the shell form or execute a shell directly. For example:

```
ENTRYPOINT [ "sh", "-c", "echo $HOSTNAME" ]
```

Variables that are defined in the Dockerfile using ENV (we are going to cover this in a while), will be substituted by the Dockerfile parser.

ENTRYPOINT command parameter1 parameter2 is a a shell form. Normal shell processing will occur. This form will also ignore any CMD or docker run command line arguments. Also, your command will not be PID 1, because it will be executed by the shell. As a result, if you then run docker stop <container>, the container will not exit cleanly, and the stop command will be forced to send a SIGKILL after the timeout.

Exactly the same as with the CMD instruction, only the last ENTRYPOINT instruction in the Dockerfile will have an effect. Overriding the ENTRYPOINT in the Dockerfile allows you to have a different command processing your arguments when the container is run. If you need to change the default shell in your image, you can do this by changing an ENTRYPOINT:

```
FROM ubuntu
ENTRYPOINT ["/bin/bash"]
```

From now on, all parameters from CMD, or provided when starting the container using docker run, will be processed by the Bash shell instead of the default /bin/sh -c.

Consider this simple Dockerfile based on BusyBox. BusyBox is software that provides several stripped-down Unix tools in a single executable file. To demonstrate ENTRYPOINT, we are going to use a ping command from BusyBox:

```
FROM busybox
ENTRYPOINT ["/bin/ping"]
CMD ["localhost"]
```

Let's build the image using the previous Dockerfile, by executing the command:

```
$ docker build -t ping-example .
```

If you now run the container using the ping image, the ENTRYPOINT instruction will be processing arguments from the supplied CMD argument: it will be localhost by default in our case. Let's run it, using the following command:

```
$ docker run ping-example
```

As a result, you will have a `/bin/ping localhost` command-line response, as you can see in the following screenshot:

```
C:\Users\jarek\projects\busybox
λ docker run ping-example
PING localhost (127.0.0.1): 56 data bytes
64 bytes from 127.0.0.1: seq=0 ttl=64 time=0.033 ms
64 bytes from 127.0.0.1: seq=1 ttl=64 time=0.084 ms
64 bytes from 127.0.0.1: seq=2 ttl=64 time=0.097 ms
64 bytes from 127.0.0.1: seq=3 ttl=64 time=0.084 ms
64 bytes from 127.0.0.1: seq=4 ttl=64 time=0.097 ms

C:\Users\jarek\projects\busybox
λ
```

The CMD instruction, as you will remember from its description, sets the default command and/or parameters, which can be overwritten from the command line when you run the container. The ENTRYPOINT is different, its command and parameters cannot be overwritten using the command line. Instead, all command line arguments will be appended after the ENTRYPOINT parameters. This way you can, kind of, lock the command that will be executed always during the container start.

> Unlike the CMD parameters, the ENTRYPOINT command and parameters are not ignored when a Docker container runs with command-line parameters.

Because the command-line parameter will be appended to the ENTRYPOINT parameters, we can run our ping image with different parameters passed to the ENTRYPOINT. Let's try it, by running our ping example with different input:

```
$ docker run ping-example www.google.com
```

This time it will behave differently. The provided argument value `www.google.com` will be appended to the `ENTRYPOINT`, instead of the default `CMD` value provided in the Dockerfile. The total command line that will be executed will be `/bin/ping www.google.com`, as you can see in the following screenshot:

```
C:\Users\jarek\projects\busybox
λ docker run ping-example www.google.com
PING www.google.com (172.217.20.100): 56 data bytes
64 bytes from 172.217.20.100: seq=0 ttl=37 time=0.598 ms
64 bytes from 172.217.20.100: seq=1 ttl=37 time=0.975 ms
64 bytes from 172.217.20.100: seq=2 ttl=37 time=0.935 ms
64 bytes from 172.217.20.100: seq=3 ttl=37 time=1.006 ms
64 bytes from 172.217.20.100: seq=4 ttl=37 time=0.732 ms
64 bytes from 172.217.20.100: seq=5 ttl=37 time=0.960 ms
64 bytes from 172.217.20.100: seq=6 ttl=37 time=0.988 ms

C:\Users\jarek\projects\busybox
λ
```

> You can use the `exec` form of `ENTRYPOINT` to set fairly stable default commands and arguments and then use either form of `CMD` to set additional defaults that are more likely to be changed.

Having the `ENTRYPOINT` instruction gives us a lot of flexibility. And, last but not least, an `ENTRYPOINT` can be also overridden when starting the container using the `--entrypoint` parameter for the `docker run` command. Note that you can override the `ENTRYPOINT` setting using `--entrypoint`, but this can only set the binary to execute (no `sh -c` will be used). As you can see, both `CMD` and `ENTRYPOINT` instructions define what command gets executed when running a container. Let's summarize what we have learned about the differences and their cooperation:

- A Dockerfile should specify at least one `CMD` or `ENTRYPOINT` instruction
- Only the last `CMD` and `ENTRYPOINT` in a Dockerfile will be used
- `ENTRYPOINT` should be defined when using the container as an executable
- You should use the `CMD` instruction as a way of defining default arguments for the command defined as `ENTRYPOINT` or for executing an `ad-hoc` command in a container
- `CMD` will be overridden when running the container with alternative arguments
- `ENTRYPOINT` sets the concrete default application that is used every time a container is created using the image

- If you couple `ENTRYPOINT` with `CMD`, you can remove an executable from `CMD` and just leave its arguments which will be passed to `ENTRYPOINT`
- The best use for `ENTRYPOINT` is to set the image's main command, allowing that image to be run as though it was that command (and then use `CMD` as the default flags)

Well, our service is running fine, but it's not very useful. First, it involves a lot of manual steps to get it running, that's why we are going to automate it later in this chapter using Maven. Second, as you will remember, our service listens for `HTTP` requests incoming on port number `8080`. Our basic image runs, but doesn't expose any network ports so no one and nothing can access the service. Let's continue learning about the remaining Dockerfile instructions to fix it.

# EXPOSE

The `EXPOSE` instruction informs Docker that the container listens on the specified network ports at runtime. We have already mentioned the `EXPOSE` instruction in Chapter 2, *Networking and Persistent Storage*. As you will remember, `EXPOSE` in a Dockerfile is the equivalent to the `--expose` command-line option. Docker uses the `EXPOSE` command followed by a port number to allow incoming traffic to the container. We already know that `EXPOSE` does not make the ports of the container automatically accessible on the host. To do that, you must use either the `-p` flag to publish a range of ports or the `-P` flag to publish all of the exposed ports at once.

Let's get back to our `Dockerfile` and expose a port:

```
FROM jeanblanchard/java:8
COPY target/rest-example-0.1.0.jar rest-example-0.1.0.jar
CMD java -jar rest-example-0.1.0.jar
EXPOSE 8080
```

If you now re-build the image using the same command, `docker build . -t rest-example`, you'll notice that Docker outputs the fourth layer, saying that port `8080` has been exposed. Exposed ports will be available for the other containers on this Docker host, and, if you map them during runtime, also for the external world. Well, let's try it, using the following `docker run` command:

```
$ docker run -p 8080:8080 -it rest-example
```

If you now call the localhost with a HTTP request such as POST (for saving our book entities) or GET (for getting the list of books or a single book) as we have done in Chapter 4, *Creating Java Microservices*, using any of the HTTP tools such as HTTPie or Postman, it will respond the same as before. This time, however, from with the Docker container. Now, this is something. Let's get to know the remaining important Dockerfile instructions.

# VOLUME

As you will remember from Chapter 1, *Introduction to Docker*, container file systems are kind of temporary by default. If you start a Docker image up (that is, run the container), you'll end up with a read-write layer on top of the layer's stack. You can create, modify, and delete files as you wish, then commit the layer to persist the changes. In Chapter 2, *Networking and Persistent Storage*, we have learned how to create volumes, which is a great way of storing and retrieving data from the Docker container. We can do the same in the Dockerfile, using the VOLUME instruction.

The syntax couldn't be simpler: it's just VOLUME ["/volumeName"].

The parameter for VOLUME can be a JSON array, a plain string with one or more arguments. For example:

```
VOLUME ["/var/lib/tomcat8/webapps/"]
VOLUME /var/log/mongodb /var/log/tomcat
```

The VOLUME instruction creates a mount point with the specified name and marks it as holding externally mounted volumes from a native host or other containers.

The VOLUME command will mount a directory inside your container and store any files created or edited inside that directory on your host's disk outside the container file structure. Using VOLUME in the Dockerfile let's Docker know that a certain directory contains permanent data. Docker will create a volume for that data and never delete it, even if you remove all the containers that use it. It also bypasses the union file system, so that the volume is in fact an actual directory that gets mounted, either read-write or read-only, in the right place, in all the containers that share it (if they are started with the --volumes-from option, for example). To understand VOLUME, let's look at the simple Dockerfile:

```
FROM ubuntu
VOLUME /var/myVolume
```

If you now run your container and save some files in the /var/myVolume, they will be available for other containers for sharing.

Basically, VOLUME and -v are almost equal. The difference between VOLUME and -v is that you can use -v dynamically and mount your host directory on your container when starting it by executing docker run. The reason for that is Dockerfiles are meant to be portable and shared. The host directory volume is 100% host dependent and will break on any other machine, which is a little bit off the Docker idea. Because of this, it is only possible to use portable instructions within a Dockerfile.

> The fundamental difference between VOLUME and -v is this: -v will mount existing files from your operating system inside your Docker container and VOLUME will create a new, empty volume on your host and mount it inside your container.

# LABEL

To add the metadata to our image, we use the LABEL instruction. A single label is a key-value pair. If you need to have spaces in the label value, you will need to wrap it in a pair of quotes. Labels are additive, they include all labels taken from an image that is the base of your own image (the one from the FROM instruction). If Docker encounters a label that already exists, it will override the label having the same key with the new value. There are some rules that you must stick to when defining labels: keys can only consist of lowercase alphanumeric characters, dots, and dashes, and must begin and end with alphanumeric characters. To prevent naming conflicts, Docker recommends using namespaces to label keys using reverse domain notation. On the other hand, keys without namespaces (dots) are reserved for command-line use.

The syntax of the LABEL instruction is straightforward:

```
LABEL "key"="value"
```

To have a multiline value, separate the lines with backslashes; for example:

```
LABEL description="This is my \
multiline description of the software."
```

You can have multiple labels in a single image. Provide them separated with a space or a backslash; for example:

```
LABEL key1="value1" key2="value2" key3="value3"
LABEL key1="value1" \
key2="value2" \
key3="value3"
```

Actually, if you need to have multiple labels in your image, it's recommended to use the multi-label form of the LABEL instruction, because it will result in just one additional layer in the image.

Each LABEL instruction creates a new layer. If your image has many labels, use the multiple form of the single LABEL instruction.

If you want to inspect what labels an image has, use the `docker inspect` command you already know about from the previous chapters.

# ENV

ENV is a `Dockerfile` instruction that sets the environment variable <key> to the value <value>. You have two options for using ENV:

- The first one, ENV <key> <value>, will set a single variable to a value. The entire string after the first space will be treated as the <value>. This will include any character, and also spaces and quotes. For example:

    **ENV JAVA_HOME /var/lib/java8**

- The second one, with an equal sign, is ENV <key>=<value>. This form allows setting multiple environment variables at once. If you need to provide spaces in the values, you will need to use quotes. If you need quotes in the values, use backslashes:

    **ENV CONFIG_TYPE=file CONFIG_LOCATION="home/Jarek/my \app/config.json"**

Note that you can use ENV to update the PATH environment variable, and then CMD parameters will be aware of that setting. This will result in a cleaner form of CMD parameters in the `Dockerfile`. For example, set the following:

**ENV PATH /var/lib/tomcat8/bin:$PATH**

This will ensure that `CMD ["startup.sh"]` will work, because it will find the `startup.sh` file in the system `PATH`. You can also use `ENV` to set the often-modified version numbers so that upgrades are easier to handle, as seen in the following example:

```
ENV TOMCAT_VERSION_MAJOR 8
ENV TOMCAT_VERSION 8.5.4
RUN curl -SL
http://apache.uib.no/tomcat/tomcat-$TOMCAT_VERSION_MAJOR/v$TOMCAT_VERSION/b
in/apache-tomcat-$TOMCAT_VERSION.tar.gz | tar zxvf apache-tomcat-
$TOMCAT_VERSION.tar.gz -c /usr/Jarek/apache-tomcat-$TOMCAT_VERSION
ENV PATH /usr/Jarek/apache-tomcat-$TOMCAT_VERSION/bin:$PATH
```

In the previous example, Docker will download the version of Tomcat specified in the `ENV` variable, extract it to the new directory with that version in its name, and also set up the system `PATH` to make it available for running.

The environment variables set using `ENV` will persist when a container is run from the resulting image. The same as with labels created with `LABEL`, you can view the `ENV` values using the `docker inspect` command. The `ENV` values can also be overridden just before the start of the container, using `docker run --env <key>=<value>`.

# USER

The `USER` instruction sets the username or UID to use when running the image. It will affect the user for any `RUN`, `CMD`, and `ENTRYPOINT` instructions that will come next in the `Dockerfile`.

The syntax of the instruction is just `USER <user name or UID>`; for example:

```
USER tomcat
```

You can use the `USER` command if an executable can be run without privileges. The Dockerfile can contain the user and group creation instruction the same as this one:

```
RUN groupadd -r tomcat && useradd -r -g tomcat tomcat
```

Switching USER back and forth frequently will increase the number of layers in the resulting image and also will make the Dockerfile more complex.

# ARG

The ARG instruction is being used to pass an argument to the Docker daemon during the docker build command. An ARG variable definition comes into effect from the line on which it is defined in the Dockerfile. By using the --build-arg switch, you can assign a value to the defined variable:

```
$ docker build --build-arg <variable name>=<value> .
```

The value from the --build-arg will be passed to the daemon building the image. You can specify multiple arguments using multiple ARG instructions. If you specify a build time argument that is not defined using ARG, the build will fail with an error, but the default value can be specified in the Dockerfile . You specify the default argument value this way:

```
FROM ubuntu
ARG user=jarek
```

If no argument will be specified before starting the build, the default value will be used:

 It is not recommended to use ARG for passing secrets as GitHub keys, user credentials, passwords, and so on, as all of them will be visible to any user of the image by using the docker history command!

# ONBUILD

The ONBUILD instruction specifies an additional instruction which will be triggered when some other image is built by using this image as its base image. In other words, the ONBUILD instruction is an instruction the parent Dockerfile gives to the child Dockerfile (downstream build). Any build instruction can be registered as a trigger and those instructions will be triggered immediately after the FROM instruction in the Dockerfile.

The syntax of the ONBUILD instruction is as follows:

```
ONBUILD <INSTRUCTION>
```

Within this, <INSTRUCTION> is another Dockerfile build instruction, which will be triggered later when the child image is going to be built. There are some limitations: the ONBUILD instruction does not allow the chaining of another ONBUILD instruction and it does not allow the FROM and MAINTAINER instructions as ONBUILD triggers.

This is useful if you are building an image which will be used as a base to build other images. For example, an application build environment or a daemon which may be customized with a user-specific configuration. The ONBUILD instruction is very useful (https://docs.docker.com/engine/reference/builder/#onbuild and https://docs.docker.com/engine/reference/builder/#maintainer-deprecated), for automating the build of your chosen software stack. Consider the following example with Maven and building Java applications (yes, Maven is also available as a Docker container). Basically, all your project's Dockerfile needs to do is reference the base container containing the ONBUILD instructions:

```
FROM maven:3.3-jdk-8-onbuild
CMD ["java","-jar","/usr/src/app/target/app-1.0-SNAPSHOT-jar-with-
dependencies.jar"]
```

There's no magic, and everything becomes clear if you look into the parent's Dockerfile. In our case, it will be a docker-maven Dockerfile available on GitHub:

```
FROM maven:3-jdk-8
RUN mkdir -p /usr/src/app
WORKDIR /usr/src/app
ONBUILD ADD . /usr/src/app
ONBUILD RUN mvn install
```

There's a base image that has both Java and Maven installed and a series of instructions to copy files and run Maven.

The ONBUILD instruction adds to the image a trigger instruction to be executed at a later time, when the image is used as the base for another build. The trigger will be executed in the context of the child build, as if it had been inserted immediately after the FROM instruction in the child Dockerfile.

When Docker encounters an ONBUILD instruction during the build process, the builder adds a kind of trigger to the metadata of the image being built. But this is the only way this image is being affected. At the end of the build, a list of all triggers is stored in the image manifest, under the key OnBuild. You can see them using the docker inspect command, which we already know.

Later the image may be used as a base for a new build, using the FROM instruction. As part of processing the FROM instruction, the Docker builder looks for ONBUILD triggers, and executes them in the same order they were registered. If any of the triggers fail, the FROM instruction is aborted which will make the build fail. If all triggers succeed, the FROM instruction completes and the build resumes.

# STOPSIGNAL

To specify what system call signal should be sent to the container to exit, use the STOPSIGNAL instruction. This signal can be a valid unsigned number that matches a position in the kernel's syscall table: for instance 9, or a signal name in the format SIGNAME, for instance SIGKILL.

# HEALTHCHECK

The HEALTHCHECK instruction can be used to inform Docker how to test a container to check that it is still working. This can be checking if our rest service responds to HTTP calls or just listens on a specified port.

A container can have several statuses which can be listed using the docker ps command. These can be created, restarting, running, paused, exited, or dead. But sometimes this is not enough; a container may be still alive from Docker's point of view, but the application can hang or fail in some other way. An additional checking for the application status can be useful and HEALTHCHECK comes in handy.

The HEALTHCHECK status is initially starting. Whenever a health check passes, it becomes healthy (whatever state it was previously in). After a certain number of consecutive failures, it becomes unhealthy.

The syntax for a HEALTHCHECK instruction is as follows:

```
HEALTHCHECK --interval=<interval> --timeout=<timeout> CMD <command>
```

The <interval> (the default value is 30 seconds) and <timeout> (again, the default is 30 seconds) are time values, specifying the checking interval and timeout accordingly. The <command> is the command actually being used to check if the application is still running. The exit code of the <command> is being used by Docker to determine if a health check failed or succeeded. The values can be 0, meaning the container is healthy and ready for use and 1 meaning that something is wrong and the container is not working correctly. The Java microservice healthcheck implementation could be just a simple /ping REST endpoint, returning whatever (as a timestamp) or even returning an empty response with HTTP 200 status code proving it's alive. Our HEALTHCHECK could execute a GET method on this endpoint, checking if the service is responding:

```
HEALTHCHECK --interval=5m --timeout=2s --retries=3 CMD curl -f
http://localhost/ping || exit 1
```

In the previous example, the command `curl -f http://localhost/ping` will be executed every 5 minutes, for the maximum timeout of 2 seconds. If a single run of the check takes longer than 2 seconds then the check is considered to have failed. If three consecutive retries fail, the container will get the `unhealthy` status.

> There can only be one `HEALTHCHECK` instruction in a Dockerfile. If you list more than one then only the last `HEALTHCHECK` will take effect.

The `HEALTCHECK` instruction gives you the possibility to fine tune the container monitoring, and thus be sure that your container is working fine. It's better than just `running`, `exited` or `dead` standard Docker status.

Now that we have an understanding of `Dockerfile` instructions, we are ready to prepare our images. Let's automate things a bit. We are going to create and run our image using Maven.

# Creating an image using Maven

Naturally, we could build our Docker image using Docker itself. But this is not a typical use case for Spring developers. A typical use case for us would be to use Maven. This can be especially useful, if you have continuous integration flow set up, using Jenkins for example. Delegating the image build process to Maven gives you a lot of flexibility and also saves a lot of time. There is at least a couple of Docker Maven plugins available for free on GitHub, such as:

- `https://github.com/spotify/docker-maven-plugin`: A Maven plugin for building and pushing Docker images by Spotify.
- `https://github.com/alexec/docker-maven-plugin`.

  `https://github.com/fabric8io/docker-maven-plugin`: This is the one I find to be most useful and configurable. Of all the Maven plugins for Docker at the time of writing, Fabric8 seems to be the most robust. Fabric8 is an integrated open source DevOps and integration platform which works out of the box on any Kubernetes or OpenShift environment and provides continuous delivery, management, ChatOps, and a Chaos Monkey. We are going to use this one for the rest of the chapter.

Our use case will be using Maven to package the Spring Boot executable JAR, and then have that build artifact copied into the Docker image. Using the Maven plugin for Docker focuses on two major aspects:

- Building and pushing Docker images which contain build artifacts
- Starting and stopping Docker containers for integration testing and development. This is what we are going to focus on in `Chapter 6`, *Running Containers with Java Applications*

Let's focus on creating an image now starting with the plugin goals and possible configuration options.

The fabric8 Docker plugin provides a couple of Maven goals:

- `docker:build`: This uses the assembly descriptor format from the maven-assembly-plugin to specify the content which will be added from a sub-directory in the image (`/maven` by default)
- `docker:push`: Images that are built with this plugin can be pushed to public or private Docker registries
- `docker:start` and `docker:stop`: For or starting and stopping the container
- `docker:watch`: This will execute `docker:build` and `docker:run` sequentially. It can run forever in the background (separate console), unless you stop it with CTRL+C. It can watch for assembly files changing and re-run the build. It saves a lot of time
- `docker:remove`: This is for cleaning up the images and containers
- `docker:logs`: This prints out the output of the running containers
- `docker:volume-create` and `docker:volume-remove`: For creating and removing volumes, respectively. We will get back to these later in this chapter

Before we can run these targets, we need to instruct the plugin how it should behave. We do it in the plugin configuration in the project's `pom.xml` file:

- Maven Docker plugin configuration

The important part in the plugin definition is the `<configuration>` element. This is where you set up the plugin's behavior. There are two main elements in the `<configuration>`:

- A `<build>`configuration specifying how images are built
- A `<run>`configuration describing how containers should be created and started

Here is a simplest example of the configuration for the `fabric8` Maven plugin for Docker:

```
<plugin>
  <groupId>io.fabric8</groupId>
  <artifactId>docker-maven-plugin</artifactId>
  <version>0.20.1</version>
  <configuration>
   <dockerHost>http://127.0.0.1:2375</dockerHost>
   <verbose>true</verbose>
  <images>
    <image>
     <name>rest-example:${project.version}</name>
     <build>
     <dockerFile>Dockerfile</dockerFile>
     <assembly>
       <descriptorRef>artifact</descriptorRef>
     </assembly>
     </build>
    </image>
  </images>
  </configuration>
</plugin>
```

The `<dockerHost>` specifies the IP address and the port of the running Docker engine, so of course, to make it build you will need to have Docker running first. In the previous case, if you run the `mvn clean package docker:build` command from the shell, the Fabric8 Docker plugin will build the image using the `Dockerfile` you provide. But there is another way of building the image, using no `Dockerfile` at all, at least not defined explicitly. To do this, we need to change the plugin configuration a bit. Take a look at the modified configuration:

```
<configuration>
  <images>
    <image>
     <name>rest-example:${project.version}</name>
     <alias>rest-example</alias>
     <build>
      <from>jeanblanchard/java:8</from>
      <assembly>
        <descriptorRef>artifact</descriptorRef>
      </assembly>
      <cmd>java -jar
       maven/${project.name}-${project.version}.jar</cmd>
     </build>
    </image>
  </images>
</configuration>
```

As you can see, we no longer deliver a `Dockerfile`. Instead, we just provide the `Dockerfile` instructions as plugin configuration elements. It's very convenient because we no longer need to hardcode an executable jar name, version, and so on. It will be taken from the Maven build scope. For example, the name of the jar will be provided for the `<cmd>` element. It will result in the generation of a valid `CMD` instruction in the `Dockerfile` automatically. If we now build the project using the `mvn clean package docker:build` command, Docker will build an image with our application. Let's list the configuration elements available for us, alphabetically:

| Element | Description |
|---------|-------------|
| assembly | The `<assembly>` element defines how to build artifacts and other files that can enter the Docker image. You can use `targetDir` element to provide a directory under which the files and artifacts contained in the assembly will be copied into the image. The default value for this is `/maven`. In our example, we will use `<descriptorRef>` to provide one of the predefined assembly descriptors. The `<descriptorRef>` is kind of a handy shortcut, which can take the following values:<br>• `artifact-with-dependencies`: Attaches a project's artifact and all its dependencies. Also, when a classpath file exists in the target directory, this will be added to.<br>• `artifact`: Attaches only the project's artifact but no dependencies.<br>• `project`: Attaches the whole Maven project but without the `target/` directory.<br>• `rootWar`: Copies the artifact as `ROOT.war` to the `exposed` directory. For example, Tomcat can then deploy the war under `root` context. |
| buildArgs | Allows for providing a map specifying the value of Docker `buildArgs`, which should be used when building the image with an external Dockerfile which uses build arguments. The key-value syntax is the same as when defining Maven properties (or `labels` or `env`). |
| buildOptions | A map specifying the build options to provide to the Docker daemon when building the image. |
| cleanup | This is useful to clean up untagged images after each build (including any containers created from them). The default value is `try` which tries to remove the old image, but doesn't fail the build if this is not possible because, for example, the image is still used by a running container. |
| cmd | This is equivalent to the `CMD` instruction we already know about, for providing a command to execute by default. |

| | |
|---|---|
| compression | Can take none (which is the default), gzip, or bzip2 values. It allows us to specify the compression mode and how the build archive is transmitted to the Docker daemon (docker:build). |
| entryPoint | Equivalent to ENTRYPOINT in a Dockerfile. |
| env | Equivalent to ENV in a Dockerfile. |
| from | Equivalent to FROM in a Dockerfile, for specifying a base image. |
| healthCheck | Equivalent to HEALTHCHECK in a Dockerfile. |
| labels | For defining labels, the same as LABEL in a Dockerfile. |
| maintainer | Equivalent to MAINTAINER in a Dockerfile. |
| nocache | Used to disable Docker's build layer cache. This can be overwritten by setting a system property docker.nocache, when running a Maven command. |
| optimize | If set to true then it will compress all the runCmds into a single RUN directive. Highly recommended to minimize the number of image layers created. |
| ports | The equivalent of EXPOSE in a Dockerfile. This is a list of \<port> elements, one for each port to expose. The format can be either pure numerical as "8080" or with the protocol attached, as "8080/tcp". |
| runCmds | Equivalent to RUN, commands to be run during the build process. It contains \<run> elements which will be passed to the shell. |
| tags | Can contain a list of \<tag> elements to provide additional tags which an image is to be tagged with after the build. |
| user | Equivalent to USER in a Dockerfile, it specifies the user to which the Dockerfile should switch. |
| volumes | Contains a list of VOLUME equivalents, a list of \<volume> elements to create a container volume. |
| workdir | Equivalent to WORKDIR from a Dockerfile, a directory to change into when starting the container. |

As you can see, the plugin configuration is very flexible, it contains a complete set of equivalents for Dockerfile instructions. Let's see how our `pom.xml` can look with the proper configuration.

The complete `pom.xml`.

If you have been following our project from the beginning, the complete Maven POM is the same as the following:

```xml
<?xml version="1.0" encoding="UTF-8"?>
<project xmlns="http://maven.apache.org/POM/4.0.0"
xmlns:xsi="http://www.w3.org/2001/XMLSchema-instance"
xsi:schemaLocation="http://maven.apache.org/POM/4.0.0
http://maven.apache.org/xsd/maven-4.0.0.xsd">
    <modelVersion>4.0.0</modelVersion>
    <groupId>pl.finsys</groupId>
    <artifactId>rest-example</artifactId>
    <version>0.1.0</version>
    <parent>
      <groupId>org.springframework.boot</groupId>
      <artifactId>spring-boot-starter-
       parent</artifactId>
      <version>1.5.2.RELEASE</version>
    </parent>
    <dependencies>
      <dependency>
        <groupId>org.springframework.boot</groupId>
        <artifactId>spring-boot-starter-web</artifactId>
      </dependency>
      <dependency>
        <groupId>org.springframework.boot</groupId>
        <artifactId>spring-boot-starter-data-
         jpa</artifactId>
      </dependency>
      <dependency>
        <groupId>org.hibernate</groupId>
        <artifactId>hibernate-validator</artifactId>
      </dependency>
      <dependency>
        <groupId>org.hsqldb</groupId>
        <artifactId>hsqldb</artifactId>
        <scope>runtime</scope>
      </dependency>
      <dependency>
        <groupId>io.springfox</groupId>
        <artifactId>springfox-swagger2</artifactId>
        <version>2.6.1</version>
```

```
      </dependency>
      <dependency>
        <groupId>io.springfox</groupId>
        <artifactId>springfox-swagger-ui</artifactId>
        <version>2.5.0</version>
      </dependency>
      <!--test dependencies-->
      <dependency>
        <groupId>org.springframework.boot</groupId>
        <artifactId>spring-boot-starter-
         test</artifactId>
        <scope>test</scope>
      </dependency>
      <dependency>
        <groupId>org.springframework.boot</groupId>
        <artifactId>spring-boot-starter-
         test</artifactId>
        <scope>test</scope>
      </dependency>
      <dependency>
        <groupId>com.jayway.jsonpath</groupId>
        <artifactId>json-path</artifactId>
        <scope>test</scope>
      </dependency>
    </dependencies>
    <properties>
      <java.version>1.8</java.version>
    </properties>
    <build>
      <plugins>
        <plugin>
          <groupId>org.springframework.boot</groupId>
          <artifactId>spring-boot-maven-
           plugin</artifactId>
        </plugin>
        <plugin>
          <groupId>org.springframework.boot</groupId>
          <artifactId>spring-boot-maven-
          plugin</artifactId>
        </plugin>
        <plugin>
          <groupId>io.fabric8</groupId>
          <artifactId>docker-maven-plugin</artifactId>
          <version>0.20.1</version>
          <configuration>
            <images>
              <image>
                <name>rest-example:${project.version}
```

```
                   </name>
                   <alias>rest-example</alias>
                   <build>
                     <from>openjdk:latest</from>
                     <assembly>
                       <descriptorRef>artifact</descriptorRef>
                     </assembly>
                     <cmd>java -jar maven/${project.name}-
${project.version}.jar</cmd>
                   </build>
                   <run>
                     <wait>
                       <log>Hello World!</log>
                     </wait>
                   </run>
                 </image>
               </images>
             </configuration>
           </plugin>
         </plugins>
       </build>
       <repositories>
         <repository>
           <id>spring-releases</id>
           <url>https://repo.spring.io/libs-release</url>
         </repository>
       </repositories>
       <pluginRepositories>
         <pluginRepository>
           <id>spring-releases</id>
           <url>https://repo.spring.io/libs-release</url>
         </pluginRepository>
       </pluginRepositories>
     </project>
```

# Building the image

To build the Docker image with our Spring Boot artifact, run this command:

```
$ mvn clean package docker:build
```

The `clean` tells Maven to delete the `target` directory. Maven will always compile your classes with the `package` command. It is very important to run the `package` command with the `docker:build` command. You'll encounter errors if you try to run these in two separate steps. While the Docker image is building, you will see the following output in the console:

```
rget\docker\rest-example\0.1.0\build\maven
[INFO] Building tar: C:\Users\jarek\projects\rest-example\target\docker\rest-example\0.1.0\tmp\docker-build.tar
[INFO] DOCKER> [rest-example:0.1.0] "rest-example": Created docker-build.tar in 1 second
[INFO] DOCKER> [rest-example:0.1.0] "rest-example": Built image sha256:b9b47
[INFO] ------------------------------------------------------------------------
[INFO] BUILD SUCCESS
[INFO] ------------------------------------------------------------------------
[INFO] Total time: 6.888 s
[INFO] Finished at: 2017-04-27T11:42:37+02:00
[INFO] Final Memory: 46M/869M
[INFO] ------------------------------------------------------------------------

C:\Users\jarek\projects\rest-example (master)
λ |
```

The ID of a new image will be presented in the console output. If you wonder how the automatically generated Dockerfile looks the same as, you will find it in the `target/docker/rest-example/0.1.0/build` directory in your project. The first time you build this Docker image, it will take longer since all the layers are being downloaded. But every build will be a lot faster thanks to layer caching.

# Creating and removing volumes

The Fabric8 Maven Docker plugin couldn't be a complete solution without the possibility of managing volumes. Indeed, it provides two ways to handle volumes: `docker:volume-create` and `docker:volume-remove`. As you probably remember from Chapter 2, *Networking and Persistent Storage*, Docker uses a plugin-like architecture when handling volumes and their drivers. The `fabric8` plugin can be configured to pass a specific volume driver and its parameters to the Docker daemon. Consider the following fragment of the plugin configuration:

```
<plugin>
    <configuration>
    [...]
    <volumes>
      <volume>
        <name>myVolume</name>
        <driver>local</driver>
        <opts>
          <type>tmpfs</type>
          <device>tmpfs</device>
```

```
              <o>size=100m,uid=1000</o>
          </opts>
          <labels>
            <volatileData>true</volatileData>
          </labels>
        </volume>
      </volumes>
    </configuration>
</plugin>
```

In the previous example, we create a named volume using the local filesystem driver. It can be mounted during the startup of the container, as specified in the <run> section of the pom.xml file.

# Summary

In this chapter, we looked at how to get started with Docker containers and packaging Java applications. We can do it manually by hand using the docker build command and a Dockerfile or we can use Maven to automate things. For Java developers, Docker helps isolate our apps in a clean environment. Isolation is important because it reduces the complexity of the software environment we're using. The Fabric8 Maven Docker plugin is a great tool which we can use to automate our image builds using Maven, especially when dealing with Java applications. No more writing Dockerfiles by hand, we just configure the plugin using the extensive set of options and we are done. Additionally, having this working with Maven allows us to easily incorporate Docker builds into our existing development flows, as continuous delivery using Jenkins, for example. In Chapter 6, *Running Containers with Java Applications*, we will go into more detail about running our Java applications from within a container. Of course, we will use Maven for this, as well.

# 6
# Running Containers with Java Applications

In `Chapter 5`, *Creating Images with Java Applications*, we learned about the structure of a Dockerfile and how to build our images. At this point, you should be able to create your own Docker image and start using it. Actually, we did run the containers several times, but without getting much into details. We built the image manually, using a Dockerfile, and then issuing a `docker build` command. We have also been using Maven to automate the build process. The image we have created contains our simple REST Java service. We've already been running it for the purpose of checking if it really works. This time, however, we are going into some more detail about running the containers from our images. This chapter will include the following concepts:

- Starting and stopping containers
- Container running modes
- Monitoring containers
- Container restart policies
- Runtime constraints on resources
- Running containers using Maven

## Starting and stopping containers

Let's go back a little and begin with the basics: how to run and stop the Docker container manually, from the shell or the command line.

# Starting

As you have seen in the previous chapters, to spin-up the container from the image, we use the `docker run` command. The running container will have its own file system, networking stack, and isolated process tree separate from the host. As you will remember from `Chapter 5`, *Creating Images with Java Applications*, every single `docker run` command creates a new container and executes a command specified in the Dockerfile, `CMD`, or `ENTRYPOINT`.

The syntax of the `docker run` command is as follows:

```
$ docker run [OPTIONS] IMAGE[:TAG|@DIGEST] [COMMAND] [ARG...]
```

The command takes the image name, with the optional `TAG` or `DIGEST`. If you skip the `TAG` and `DIGEST` command parameters, Docker will run the container based on the image tagged `latest`. The `docker run` command also takes a set of possible options you may find useful, such as the runtime mode, detached or foreground, network settings, or runtime restrictions on CPU and memory. We are going to cover these later in this chapter. Of course, you can execute the `docker run` command without almost any arguments except the image name. It will run and take the default options defined in the image. Specifying options gives you the chance to override the options specified by the author of the image and also runtime defaults of the Docker engine.

The `COMMAND` parameter is not mandatory, the author of the image may have already provided a default `COMMAND` using the `CMD` instruction in the `Dockerfile`. The `CMD` occurs only once in a Dockerfile and it's usually the last instruction. When starting the container from an image, we can override the `CMD` instruction, simply by providing our own command or parameters as the `COMMAND` parameter for the `docker run`. Anything that appears after the image name in the `docker run` command will be passed to the container and treated as `CMD` arguments. If the image also specifies an `ENTRYPOINT` then the `CMD` or `COMMAND` gets appended as an argument to the `ENTRYPOINT`. But guess what, we can override the `ENTRYPOINT` as well, using the `--entrypoint` option for the `docker run` command.

# Stopping

To stop one or more running Docker containers we use the `docker stop` command. The syntax is simple:

```
$ docker stop [OPTIONS] CONTAINER [CONTAINER...]
```

You can specify one or more container to stop. The only option for `docker stop` is `-t` (`--time`) which allows us to specify a time to wait before stopping a container. 10 seconds is the default value, which is supposed to be enough for the container to gracefully stop. To stop the container in a more brutal way, you can execute the following command:

```
$ docker kill  CONTAINER [CONTAINER...]
```

What's the difference between `docker stop` and `docker kill`? They will both stop a running container. There's an important difference though:

- `docker stop`: The main process inside the container will first receive a SIGTERM, and after a grace period, a SIGKILL
- `docker kill`: The main process inside the container will be sent SIGKILL (by default) or any signal specified with option `--signal`

In other words, `docker stop` attempts to trigger a graceful shutdown by sending the standard POSIX signal SIGTERM, whereas `docker kill` just brutally kills the process and, therefore, shuts down the container.

# Listing the running containers

To list the running containers, simply execute the `docker ps` command:

```
$ docker ps
```

To include all containers present on your Docker host, include the `-a` option:

```
$ docker ps -a
```

You can also filter the list using `-f` option to specify a filter. The filter needs to be provided as a `key=value` format. Currently available filters include:

- `id`: Filters by the container's id
- `label`: Filters by label
- `name`: Filters by the container's name

- `exited`: Filters by the container's exit code
- `status`: Filters by status, which can be created, restarting, running, removing, paused, exited or dead
- `volume`: When specified with volume name or mount point will include containers that mount specified volumes
- `network`: When specified with network id or name, will include containers connected to the specified network

Consider the following example, which will take all containers present on the Docker host and filter them out by running status:

```
$ docker ps -a -f status=running
```

# Removing the containers

To remove the container from the host, we use the `docker rm` command. The syntax is as follows:

```
$ docker rm [OPTIONS] CONTAINER [CONTAINER...]
```

You can specify a single container or more containers at once. If you are running short-term foreground processes over and over many times, these file systems can grow rapidly in size. There's a solution for that: instead of cleaning manually by hand, tell Docker to automatically clean up the container and remove the file system when the container exits. You do this by adding the `--rm` flag, so that the container data is removed automatically after the process has finished.

> `--rm` flag will make Docker remove container after it has been shut down.

For example, use the `run` command as in the following example:

```
$ docker run --rm -it Ubuntu /bin/bash
```

The preceding command tells Docker to remove the container if it's shut down.

When starting a Docker container, you can decide if you want to run the container in the default mode, in the foreground, or in the background, in the so called detached mode. Let's explain what the difference is.

# Container running modes

Docker has two container running modes, foreground and detached. Let's begin with the default one, the foreground mode.

# Foreground

In the foreground mode, the console you are using to execute `docker run` will be attached to standard input, output, and error streams. This is the default; Docker will attach `STDIN`, `STDOUT` and `STDERR` streams to your shell console. If you need to, you can change this behavior and use the `-a` switch for the `docker run` command. As a parameter for the `-a` switch, you use the name of the stream you want to attach to the console. For example:

```
$ docker run -a stdin -a stdout -i -t centos /bin/bash
```

The preceding command will attach both `stdin` and `stdout` streams to your console.

The useful `docker run` options are the `-i` or `--interactive` (for keeping `STDIN` stream open, even if not attached) and `-t` or `-tty` (for attaching a `pseudo-tty`) switches, commonly used together as `-it` which you will need to use to allocate a `pseudo-tty` console for the process running in the container. Actually, we used this option in Chapter 5, *Creating Images with Java Applications*, when we were running our REST service:

```
$ docker run -it rest-example
```

Simply speaking, the `-it` is used combined to attach the command line to the container after it has started. This way you can see what's going on in the running container in your shell console and interact with the container, if needed.

# Detached

You can start a Docker container in detached mode with a `-d` option. It's the opposite of the foreground mode. The container starts up and runs in background, the same as a daemon or a service. Let's try to run our rest-example in the background, executing the following command:

```
$ docker run -d -p 8080:8080 rest-example
```

After the container starts, you will be given a control and can use a shell or command line for executing other commands. Docker will just output the container ID, as you can see on the following screenshot:

```
C:\Users\jarek\projects\rest-example (master)
λ docker run -d -p 8080:8080 rest-example
5687bd611f84b53716424fd826984f551251bc95f3db49715fc7211a6bb23840

C:\Users\jarek\projects\rest-example (master)
λ |
```

You can use the container ID to reference the container in other docker commands, for example, if you need to stop the container or attach to it. Our service, while sitting in the background, still works: the Spring Boot application listens on port 8080 for HTTP GET or POST requests. Take note that containers started in detached mode stop when the root process used to run the container exits. Understanding this is important, even if you have some process running in the background (started from the instruction in the Dockerfile), Docker will stop the container if the command that started the container finishes. In our case, Spring Boot application is running and listening, and, at the same time, prevents Docker from shutting down the container. To bring the container back from the background into the foreground of your console, you will need to attach to it.

# Attaching to running containers

To retain control over a detached container, use `docker attach` command. The syntax for `docker attach` is quite simple:

```
$ docker attach [OPTIONS] <container ID or name>
```

In our case this would be the ID we were given, when the container was started:

```
$ docker attach
5687bd611f84b53716424fd826984f551251bc95f3db49715fc7211a6bb23840
```

At this time, if there is something that gets printed out, such as another log line from our running REST service, you will see it on the console. As you can see, the `docker attach` command can come in handy if you need to see what is written to the `stdout` stream in real time. It will basically *reattach* your console to the process running in the container. In other words, it will stream the `stdout` into your screen and map the `stdin` to your keyboard, allowing you to enter the commands and see their output. Note that pressing the *CTRL + C* keyboard sequence while being attached to the container would kill the running process of the container, not detach from the console. To detach from the process use the default *CTRL+P* and *CTRL+Q* keyboard sequence. If the *CTRL + P* and *CTRL + Q* sequence clashes with your existing keyboard shortcuts, you can provide your own detach sequence by setting the `--detach-keys` option for the `docker attach` command. If you would like to be able to detach using *CTRL + C*, you may tell Docker not to send `sig-term` to the process running in the container by using the `sig-proxy` parameter set to `false`:

```
$ docker attach --sig-proxy=false [container-name or ID]
```

If the container is running in the background, it would be nice to be able to monitor its behavior. Docker provides a set of features for doing that. Let's see how we can monitor running containers.

# Monitoring containers

There are some ways of monitoring running Docker containers. It can be viewing the log files, looking at the container events and statistics, and also inspecting container properties. Let's begin with the powerful logging features Docker has. Access to the log entries is crucial, especially if you have your container running in the detached runtime mode. Let's see what Docker can offer when it comes to a logging mechanism.

# Viewing logs

Most applications output their log entries to the standard `stdout` stream. If the container is being run in the foreground mode, you will just see it in the console. However, when running a container in detached mode, you will see nothing but the container ID on the console. However, the Docker engine collects all the `stdout` output from a running container in a history file on the host. You can display it by using the `docker logs` command. The syntax of the command is as follows:

```
$ docker logs -f <container name or ID>
```

The `docker logs` command will output just a few last lines of the log into the console. As the container still works in the background (in detached mode), you will be given the prompt back immediately, as you can see on the following screenshot, presenting a fragment of the logfile from our REST service:

The `-f` flag acts as the same flag in Linux `tail` command, it will continuously display new log entries on the console. When you are done, hit *CTRL + C* to stop displaying log files on the console. Note that this is different from hitting *CTRL + C* when attached to the container, where *CTRL + C* would kill the process running within the container. This time, it will just stop displaying the log file and it's safe.

The log file is permanent and available even after the container stops, as long as its file system is still present on disk (until it is removed with the `docker rm` command). By default, the log entries are stored in a JSON file located in the `/var/lib/docker` directory. You can see the complete path of the log file using the `docker inspect` command and using a template to extract the `LogPath` (we are going to cover `inspect` and templates in a while).

We have said that, by default, the log entries will go to the JSON file. But this can be easily changed, because Docker utilizes the concept of logging drivers. By using different drivers, you can pick other storage for your containers log. The default driver is the `json-file` driver, which just writes out the entries into the JSON file. Each driver can take additional parameters. The JSON driver accepts, for example:

```
--log-opt max-size=[0-9+][k|m|g]
--log-opt max-file=[0-9+]
```

As you may have guessed, it's similar to a rolling file in our Java applications. The `max-size` specifies the maximum file size that can be created; after reaching the specified size, Docker will create a new file. You can use the size suffixes k, m, or g, where k will be for kilobytes, m for megabytes and g for gigabytes. Splitting a log into separate files makes it easier to transfer, archive, and so on. Also, searching through the log file is a lot more convenient if the file is smaller.

> The `docker log` command only displays log entries from the latest log file.

There are some other log drivers available. The list includes:

- `none`: It will just switch off logging completely
- `syslog`: It's a `syslog` logging driver for Docker. It will write log messages to the system `syslog`
- `journald`: Will log messages to `journald`. `systemd-journald` is a daemon responsible for event logging, with append-only binary files serving as its logfiles
- `splunk`: Provides the writing of log messages to Splunk using `Event Http` Collector. Splunk can be used as an enterprise-grade log analyzer. You can read more about it at `https://www.splunk.com`
- `gelf`: Will write log entries into a GELF endpoint such as Graylog or Logstash. Graylog, available at `https://www.graylog.org`, is an open source log management, supporting search, analysis, and alerting across all of your log files. Logstash, which you can find at `https://www.elastic.co/products/logstash`, is a pipeline for processing any data (including log data) from any source
- `fluentd`: Writes log messages to `fluentd`. Fluentd is an open source data collector for a unified logging layer. The main feature of Fluentd is that it separates data sources from backend systems by providing a unified logging layer in between. It's small, fast and has hundreds of plugins that make a very flexible solution out of it. You can read more about `fluentd` on its website at `https://www.fluentd.org`
- `gcplogs`: Will send the log entries to Google Cloud logging
- `awslogs`: This driver will write log messages to the Amazon CloudWatch logs.

As you can see, again, the Docker's pluggable architecture gives you almost infinite flexibility when running the container. To switch to the other log driver, use the `--log-driver` option for the `docker run` command. To store log entries in the `syslog` for example, execute the following:

```
$ docker run --log-driver=syslog rest-example
```

Note that the `docker logs` command works only for the `json-file` and `journald` drivers. To access logs written to another log engine, you will need to use the tool matching the driver you have chosen. It will often be more convenient to use the specialized tool for browsing log entries; actually, this is often the reason you choose another logging driver. For example, searching and browsing the logs in Logstash or Splunk is way faster than digging though the text files full of JSON entries.

Looking at the log entries is the convenient way of monitoring how our application behaves on the host. Sometimes, it could be also nice to see the properties of the running containers, as the mapped network port or volume being mapped and so on. To display the container properties, we use the `docker inspect` command, which is extremely useful.

## Inspecting a container

The `docker ps` command we have been using to list the running containers gives us a lot of information about containers, such as their IDs, uptime, mapped ports, and so on. To display more details about the running container, we can user `docker inspect`. The syntax of the command is as follows:

```
$ docker inspect [OPTIONS] CONTAINER|IMAGE|TASK [CONTAINER|IMAGE|TASK...]
```

By default, the `docker inspect` command will output information about the container or image in a JSON array format. Because there are many properties, it may not be very readable. If we know what we are looking for, we can provide a template for processing the output, using the `-f` (or `--format`) option. The template uses the template format coming from the Go language (Docker itself is written in Go, by the way). The simplest and the most often used template for the `docker inspect` command is just a short template to extract exactly the information you need, for example:

```
$ docker inspect -f '{{.State.ExitCode}}' jboss/wildfly
```

As the `inspect` command accepts the Go template to form the output of the container or image metadata, this feature gives you almost infinite possibilities for processing and transforming the results. The Go templating engine is quite powerful, so, instead of piping the output through grep, which is quick but messy, you can use the template engine to further process the result.

The argument to `--format` is a just a template that we want to apply to the metadata of the container. In this template, we can use conditional statements, loops, and other Go language features. For example, the following will find the names of all containers with a non-zero exit code:

```
$ docker inspect -f '{{if ne 0.0 .State.ExitCode }}{{.Name}}
{{.State.ExitCode}}{{ end }}' $(docker ps -aq)
```

Note that we provide `$(docker ps -aq)` instead of the container ID or name. As a result, all of the running containers' IDs will be piped to the `docker inspect` command, which can be quite a handy shortcut. The curly brackets `{{}}` mean Go template directives, anything outside of them will be printed out literally. The dot (`.`) in Go templates means context. Most of the time the current context will be whole data structure for the metadata, but it can be rebound when needed, including using the `with` action. For example, these two `inspect` commands will print out exactly the same result:

```
$ docker inspect -f '{{.State.ExitCode}}' wildfly
$ docker inspect -f '{{with .State}} {{.ExitCode}} {{end}}' wildfly
```

If you are inside the bound context, the dollar sign (`$`) will always get you the `root` context. We can execute this command:

```
$ docker inspect -f '{{with .State}} {{$.Name}} exited with {{.ExitCode}}
exit code \ {{end}}' wildfly
```

It will then output:

```
/wildfly exited with 0 exit code.
```

The template engine supports logical functions, such as `and`, `or` and `not`; they will return a boolean result. Also, the comparison functions are supported, such as `eq` (equals), `ne` (not equals), `lt` (less than), `le` (less than or equal to), `gt` (greater than), and `ge` (greater than or equal to). Comparison functions can compare strings, floats or integers. Together with the conditional functions such as `if`, all of these can be very useful when creating some more sophisticated output from the `inspect` command:

```
$ docker inspect -f '{{if eq .State.ExitCode 0.0}} \
Normal Exit \
{{else if eq .State.ExitCode 1.0}} \
```

```
Not a Normal Exit \
{{else}} \
Still Not a Normal Exit \
{{end}}' wildfly
```

Sometimes the huge output of the `docker inspect` command can be quite confusing. Since the output comes in JSON format, the `jq` tool can be used to get an overview of the output and pick out interesting parts.

The `jq` tool is available for free at `https://stedolan.github.io/jq/`. It's a lightweight and flexible command-line JSON processor, such as `sed` command for the JSON data. For example, let's extract the container IP address from the metadata:

```
$ docker inspect <containerID> | jq -r '.[0].NetworkSettings.IPAddress'
```

As you can see, the `docker inspect` command provides useful information about Docker containers. Combined with the Go template features and optionally with the `jq` tool, it gives you a powerful tool to get the information about your containers and can be used further in scripting. But there's another source of valuable information apart from the metadata. It's runtime statistics, which we are going to focus on now.

# Statistics

To see the CPU, memory, disk i/o and network i/o statistics for containers, use the `docker stats` command. The syntax for the command is as follows:

```
docker stats [OPTIONS] [CONTAINER...]
```

You can limit the statistics measure to one or more specific containers by specifying a list of container IDs or names separated by a space. By default, if no containers are specified, the command will display statistics for all running containers, as you can see on the following screenshot:

| CONTAINER | CPU % | MEM USAGE / LIMIT | MEM % | NET I/O | BLOCK I/O | PIDS |
|---|---|---|---|---|---|---|
| b73f837daa7c | 0.11% | 374.8 MiB / 1.934 GiB | 18.93% | 5.11 kB / 1.14 kB | 64.7 GB / 24.6 kB | 21 |
| 70a91c44d989 | 0.08% | 318 MiB / 1.934 GiB | 16.06% | 5.76 kB / 1.14 kB | 14.2 GB / 4.1 kB | 21 |
| 06d4771d9605 | 0.08% | 305.9 MiB / 1.934 GiB | 15.45% | 13.6 kB / 1.28 kB | 3.36 GB / 4.1 kB | 21 |
| 2ac57fc82ae1 | 0.12% | 270.9 MiB / 1.934 GiB | 13.68% | 14.1 kB / 1.28 kB | 3.51 GB / 4.1 kB | 21 |
| abddf3c0d1d6 | 0.10% | 97.28 MiB / 1.934 GiB | 4.91% | 16.6 kB / 1.28 kB | 1.4 GB / 4.1 kB | 21 |
| 699ec3c495ac | 0.11% | 89.11 MiB / 1.934 GiB | 4.50% | 18.8 kB / 1.28 kB | 1.33 GB / 4.1 kB | 21 |
| 94f69cba5773 | 0.09% | 104.1 MiB / 1.934 GiB | 5.26% | 19.3 kB / 1.28 kB | 1.29 GB / 4.1 kB | 21 |

The `docker stats` command accepts options, which can include:

- `--no-stream`: This will disable streaming stats and only pull the first result
- `-a` (`--all`): This will show statistics for all (not only running) containers

The statistics can be used to see if our containers behave well when running. The information can be useful to check if we need some constraints on the resources to be applied to containers, we are going to cover the runtime constraints in a while in this chapter.

Viewing logs, container metadata and runtime statistics, give you almost infinite possibilities when monitoring your running containers. Apart from this, we can see what's happening on your docker host globally. When the docker engine on the host receives a command, it will emit an event we can observe. Let's look at this mechanism now.

# Container events

To observe the events coming to the docker engine in real time, we use the `docker events` command. If the container has been started, stopped, paused, and so on, the event will be published. This can be very useful if you would like to know what has happened during the container runtime. It's a powerful monitoring feature. Docker containers report a huge list of events, which you can list with the `docker events` command. The list includes:

```
attach, commit, copy, create, destroy, detach, die, exec_create,
exec_detach, exec_start, export, health_status, kill, oom, pause, rename,
resize, restart, start, stop, top, unpause, update
```

The `docker events` command can take the `-f` switch, which will filter the output if you are looking for something specific. If no filter is provided, all events will be reported. Currently the list of possible filters includes:

- container (`container=<name or id>`)
- event (`event=<event action>`)
- image (`image=<tag or id>`)
- plugin (experimental) (`plugin=<name or id>`)
- label (`label=<key> or label=<key>=<value>`)
- type (`type=<container or image or volume or network or daemon>`)

- volume (`volume=<name or id>`)
- network (`network=<name or id>`)
- daemon (`daemon=<name or id>`)

Take a look at the following example. The `docker events` command has been run in one console window, while the `docker run rest-example` has been issued in the separate console. As you can see in the following screenshot, `docker events` will report create, attach, connect and start events for our rest-example container:

```
C:\Users\jarek\projects\rest-example (master)
λ docker events
2017-05-06T11:11:19.252579000+02:00 container create b73f837daa7c1344f03d53c42169165a41ccca2ee5baff4c273656
72a2b16b12 (image=rest-example, name=angry_nobel)
2017-05-06T11:11:19.262586200+02:00 container attach b73f837daa7c1344f03d53c42169165a41ccca2ee5baff4c273656
72a2b16b12 (image=rest-example, name=angry_nobel)
2017-05-06T11:11:19.458280800+02:00 network connect c0760599d57588fefe9027ca1cd627263518e8afe16202e805f0303
af6bc10b1 (container=b73f837daa7c1344f03d53c42169165a41ccca2ee5baff4c27365672a2b16b12, name=bridge, type=br
idge)
2017-05-06T11:11:19.893676800+02:00 container start b73f837daa7c1344f03d53c42169165a41ccca2ee5baff4c2736567
2a2b16b12 (image=rest-example, name=angry_nobel)
```

As a result, you will get a timestamp and the name of the event, together with the ID of the container that has caused an event. The `docker events` command can take additional options, such as `--since` and `--until`, which can be used to specify a timeframe that you want to get the events from. Monitoring container events is a great tool to see what's going on the docker host. However, there's more. You can also influence, how your containers behave in case of a crash, for example. We use container restart policies for that.

# Restart policies

By using the `--restart` option with the `docker run` command you can specify a restart policy. This tells Docker how to react when a container shuts down. The container then can be restarted to minimize downtime, for example if running on a production server. However, before we explain the Docker restart policy, let's focus for a while on exit codes. The exit code is crucial information, it tells why the container failed to run or why it exited. Sometimes it's related to the contained command you will give to the `docker run` as a parameter. When the `docker run` command ends with a non-zero code, the exit codes follow the `chroot` standard, as you can see here:

- exit code `125`: The `docker run` command fails by itself
- exit code`126`: The supplied command cannot be invoked
- exit code `127`: The supplied command cannot be found
- Other, non-zero, application dependent exit code

As you may remember, in previous chapters we have been using the `docker ps` command to list running containers. To list the non-running containers as well, we can add the `-a` switch for the `docker ps` command. The exit code can be found in the output of the `docker ps -a` command in a Status column when a container completes. It's possible to automatically restart crashed containers by specifying a restart policy when starting the container. Specifying the desired restart policy is done by the -restart switch for the `docker run` command, as in the example:

```
$ docker run --restart=always rest-example
```

Currently Docker has four restart policies. Let's get to know them now one by one, starting with the simplest: `no`.

# no

The `no` policy is the default restart policy and simply will not restart a container under any case. Actually, you do not have to specify this policy, because this is the default behavior. Unless you have some configurable setup to run Docker containers, then the `no` policy can be used as an off switch.

# always

If we wanted the container to be restarted no matter what exit code the command has, we can use the `always` restart policy. Basically, it does what it says; Docker will restart the container in every case. The restart policy will always restart the container. This is true, even if the container has been stopped before the reboot. Whenever the Docker service is restarted, containers using the always policy will also be restarted, it doesn't matter whether they were executing or not.

 With the `always` restart policy, the Docker daemon will try to restart the container **indefinitely.**

# on-failure

This is a kind of special restart policy and probably the most often used. By using the `on-failure` restart policy, you instruct Docker to restart your container whenever it exits with a non-zero exit status and not restart otherwise. That's the reason we have begun explaining restart policies with the exit codes. You can optionally provide a number of times for Docker to attempt to restart the container. The syntax of this restart policy is also a little bit different, because using this policy, you can also specify a maximum number of tries that Docker will make to automatically restart the container.

Consider this example:

```
$ docker run --restart=on-failure:5 rest-example
```

The preceding command will run the container with our REST service and will try to restart it five times in the case of failure before giving up. The main benefit of the `on-failures` restart policy is that, when an application exits with a successful exit code (that means there were no errors in the application; it just finished executing), the container will not be restarted. The number of restart tries for a container can be obtained via the `docker inspect` command we already know. For example, to get the number of restarts for a container with a specific ID or name:

```
$ docker inspect -f "{{ .RestartCount }}" <ContainerID>
```

You can also discover the last time the container was started again:

```
$ docker inspect -f "{{ .State.StartedAt }}" <ContainerID>
```

You should know that Docker uses a delay between restarting the container, to prevent flood-like protection. This is an increasing delay; it starts with the value of 100 milliseconds, then Docker will double the previous delay. In effect, the daemon will wait for 100 ms, then 200 ms, 400, 800 and so on, until either the `on-failure` limit is reached, or when you stop the container using `docker stop`, or execute the force removal by executing the `docker rm -f` command.

> If a container is successfully restarted, the delay is reset to the default value of 100 milliseconds.

# unless-stopped

Again, similar to `always`, if we want the container to be restarted regardless of the exit code, we can use `unless-stopped`. The `unless-stopped` restart policy acts the same as `always` with one exception, it will restart the container regardless of the exit status, but do not start it on daemon startup if the container has been put to a stopped state before. This means that with the `unless-stopped` restart policy, if the container was running before the reboot, the container would be restarted once the system restarted. When an application within a Docker container exits, that container will be also halted. If an application that is running within a container crashes, the container stops and that container will remain stopped until someone or something restarts it.

Before you apply the restart policy to your container, it's good to think first what kind of work the container will be used to do. That also depends on the kind of software that will be running on the container. A database, for example, should probably have the `always` or `unless-stopped` policy applied. If your container has some restart policy applied, it will be shown as `Restarting` or `Up` status when you list your container using the `docker ps` command.

# Updating a restart policy on a running container

Sometimes, there's a need to update the Docker runtime parameters after the container has already started, *on the fly*. An example would be if you want to prevent containers from consuming too many resources on the Docker host. To set the policy during runtime, we can use the `docker update` command. Apart from other runtime parameters (such as memory or CPU constraints for example, which we are going to discuss later in this chapter), the `docker update` command gives you the option to update the restart policy on a running container. The syntax is quite straightforward, you just need to provide the new restart policy that you would like the container to have and the container's ID or name:

```
$ docker update --restart=always <CONTAINER_ID or NAME>
```

A new restart policy will take effect immediately after you run the `docker update` command on a container. On the other hand, if you execute the `update` command on a container that is stopped, the policy will be used when you start the container later on. The possible options are exactly the same as those you can specify when starting the container:

- `no` (which is default)
- `always`
- `on-failure`
- `unless-stopped`

> If you have more than one container running on the Docker host, and want to specify a new restart policy on all of them at once, just provide all of their IDs or names, separated by a space.

You can also see which restart policy was applied using the `docker events` command, which you already know from the previous section. The `docker events` which can be used to observe the history of runtime events that the container has reported, will also report the `docker update` event, providing you with details about what has changed. If the container has been applied the restart policy, the event will be published. If you want to check the restart policy of a running container use `docker inspect` with the container ID or name with the `--format` argument set for the path of the value:

```
$ docker inspect --format '{{ .HostConfig.RestartPolicy.Name }}'
<ContainerID>
```

The ability to set a restart policy on a container by container basis is great for those cases where your images are self-contained and you don't need to do more complex orchestration tasks. The restart policy is not the only parameter you can change on running containers.

# Runtime constraints on resources

It may be useful to restrict the Docker container usage of resources when running. Docker gives you a many possibilities to set constraints on the memory, CPU usage or disk access usage. Let's begin with setting the memory constraints.

## Memory

It's worth knowing that, by default, that is, if you use the default settings without any constraints, the running container can use all of the host memory. To change this behavior we can use the --memory (or -m for short) switch for the docker run command. It takes the usual suffixes k, m, or g for kilobytes, megabytes and gigabytes, respectively.

The syntax of the docker run command with memory constraints set will be as follows:

```
$ docker run -it -m 512m ubuntu
```

The preceding command will execute the Ubuntu image with the maximum memory that can be used by the container of half of a gigabyte.

> If you do not set the limit on memory that the container can allocate, this can lead to random issues where a single container can easily make the whole host system unstable and/or unusable. So it's a wise decision to always use the memory constraints on the container.

Apart from user memory limit, there are also memory reservation and kernel memory constraints. Let's explain what a memory reservation limit is. Under normal working conditions, a running container can, and probably will, use as much of the memory as needed, up to the limit you have set using the --memory (-m) switch for the docker run command. When memory reservation is applied, Docker will detect a low memory situation and will try to force the container to restrict its consumption up to a reservation limit. If you do not set the memory reservation limit, it will be exactly the same as the hard memory limit set with the -m switch.

Memory reservation is not a hard limit feature. There's no guarantee the limit won't be exceeded. The memory reservation feature will attempt to ensure that memory will be allocated, based on the reservation setting.

Consider the following example:

```
$ docker run -it -m 1G --memory-reservation 500M ubuntu /bin/bash
```

The preceding command sets the hard memory limit to 1g, and then sets the memory reservation to half a gig. With those constraints set, when the container consumes memory more than 500M and less than 1G, Docker will attempt to shrink container memory less than 500M.

In the next example we are going to set the memory reservation without setting the hard memory limit:

```
$ docker run -it --memory-reservation 1G ubuntu /bin/bash
```

In the preceding example, when the container starts, it can use as much memory as its processes need. The --memory-reservation switch setting will prevent the container from consuming too much memory for a long time, because every memory reclaim will shrink the container's memory usage to the size specified in the reservation.

The kernel memory is something entirely different from the user memory, the main difference is that kernel memory can't be swapped out to disk. It includes stack pages, slab pages, sockets memory pressure and TCP memory pressure. You use the --kernel-memory switch to set up the kernel memory limit to constrain these kinds of memory. As with setting the user memory limit, just provide a number with a suffix such as k, b, and g, for kilobyte, megabyte or gigabyte respectively, although setting it in kilobytes may be a really rare case.

For example, every process eats some stack pages. By restricting kernel memory, you can prevent new processes from being started when the kernel memory usage is too high. In addition, because the host cannot swap the kernel memory to disk, the container can block the whole host service by consuming too much kernel memory.

Setting the kernel memory limit is straightforward. We can set the --kernel-memory alone, without limiting the total memory with -m, as in the following example:

```
$ docker run -it --kernel-memory 100M ubuntu  /bin/bash
```

In the preceding example, the process in the container can take memory as it needs, but it can only consume `100M` of kernel memory. We can also setup the hard memory limit, as in the following command:

```
$ docker run -it -m 1G --kernel-memory 100M ubuntu /bin/bash
```

In the preceding command, we set memory and kernel memory altogether, so the processes in the container can use `1G` memory in total, and this `1G` will include `100M` of the kernel memory.

One more constraint related to the memory which can be useful when running containers, is the swappines constraint. We apply the constraint by using the `--memory-swappiness` switch to the `docker run` command. It can be helpful when you want to avoid performance drops related to memory swapping. The parameter for the `--memory-swappiness` switch is the percentage of anonymous memory pages that can be swapped out, so it takes values from `0` to `100`. Setting the value to zero, will, depending on your kernel version, disable swapping or use the minimal swap. In contrast, a value of `100` sets all anonymous pages as candidates for swapping out. For example:

```
$ docker run -it --memory-swappiness=0 ubuntu /bin/bash
```

In the preceding command, we turn the swapping completely for our `ubuntu` container.

Apart from setting the memory usage constraint, you can also instruct Docker how the processor power should be assigned to containers it's going to run.

# Processors

By using the `-c` (or `--cpu-shares` as an equivalent) for the `docker run` command switch, it's possible to specify a value of shares of the CPU that a container can allocate. By default, every new container has 1024 shares of CPU and all containers get the same part of CPU cycles. This percentage can be altered by shifting the container's CPU share weighting relative to the weighting of all other running containers. But take note, that you cannot set the precise processor speed that a container can use. This is a **relative weight** and has nothing to do with the real processor speed. In fact, there is no way to say precisely that a container should have the right to use only 2 GHz of the host's processor.

 CPU share is just a number, it's not related at all to the CPU speed.

If we start two containers and both will use 100% CPU, the processor time will be divided equally between the two containers. The reason for that is two containers will have the same number of processor shares. But if you constrain one container's processor shares to 512, it will receive just a half of the CPU time. This does not mean that it can use only half of the CPU; the proportion will only apply when CPU-intensive processes are running. If the other container (with 1024 shares) is idle, our container will be allowed to use 100% of the processor time. The real amount of CPU time will differ depending on the number of containers running on the system. It's easier to understand on a tangible example.

Consider three containers, one (let's call it Container1) has --cpu-shares set for 1024 and two others (Container2 and Container3) have a --cpu-shares setting of 512. When processes in all three containers attempt to use all of the CPU power, Container1 will receive 50% of the total CPU time, because it has half of the CPU usage allowed in comparison to the sum of other running containers (Container2 and Container3). If we add a fourth container (Container4) with a --cpu-share of 1024, our first Container1 will only get 33% of the CPU, because it now has one third of the total CPU power assigned, relatively. Container2 will receive 16.5%, Container3 also 16.5% and the last one, Container4, again, will be allowed to use 33% of the CPU.

While the -c or --cpu_shares flag for the docker run command modifies the container's CPU share weighting relative to the weighting of all other running containers, it does not restrict the container's use of CPU from the host machine. But there's another flag to limit the CPU usage for the container: --cpu-quota. Its default value is 100000 which means an allowance of 100% of the CPU usage. We can use the --cpu-quota to limit CPU usage, for example:

```
$ docker run -it  --cpu-quota=50000 ubuntu /bin/bash
```

In the preceding command, the limit for the container will be 50% of a CPU resource. The --cpu-quota is usually used in conjunction with the --cpu-period flag for the docker run. This is the setting for the CPU CFS (Completely Fair Scheduler) period. The default period value is 100000 which is 100 milliseconds. Take a look at the example:

```
$ docker run -it --cpu-quota=25000 --cpu-period=50000  ubuntu /bin/bash
```

It means that the container can get 50% of the CPU usage every 50 ms.

Limiting CPU shares and usage is not the only processor-related constraint we can set on the container. We can also assign the container's processes to a particular processor or processor core. The --cpuset switch of the docker run command comes in handy when we want to do this. Consider the following example:

```
$ docker run -it --cpuset 4 ubuntu
```

The preceding command will run the `ubuntu` image and allow the container to use all four processor cores. To start the container and only allow usage of one processor core, you can change the `--cpuset` value to `1`:

```
$ docker run -it --cpuset 1 ubuntu
```

> You can of course mix the option `--cpuset` with `--cpu_shares` to tweak you container's CPU constraints.

# Updating constraints on a running container

As with the restart policies, the constraints can also be updated when the container is already running. This may be helpful, if you see your containers eating too much of the Docker host system resources and would like to limit this usage. Again, we use the `docker update` command to do this.

As with restart policies, the syntax for the `docker update` command will be the same as when starting the container, you specify the desired constraints as an argument for the docker update command and then give the container ID (taken from the `docker ps` command output for example) or its name. Again, if you would like to change the constraints on more than one container at once, just provide their IDs or names separated by a space. Let's look at some examples of how to update constraints at runtime:

```
$ docker update --cpu-shares 512 abbdef1231677
```

The preceding command will limit the CPU shares to the value of 512. Of course, you can apply CPU and memory constraints at the same time, to more than one container:

```
docker update --cpu-shares 512 -m 500M abbdef1231677 dabdff1231678
```

The preceding command will update CPU shares and memory limits to two containers, identified by `abbdef1231677` and `dabdff1231678`.

Of course, when updating the runtime constraints, you can also apply the desired restart policy in one single command, as in the following example:

```
$ docker update --restart=always -m 300M aabef1234716
```

As you can see, the ability to set constraints gives you a lot of flexibility when running Docker containers. But it's worth noting, that applying constraints is not always possible. The reason for that is the constraint setting features depend heavily of the internals of the Docker host, especially its kernel. For example, it's not always possible to set up the kernel memory limit or `memory swappiness` for example, sometimes all you will get is `Your kernel does not support kernel memory limit or kernel does not support memory swappiness capabilities` messages. Sometimes those limitations can be configurable, sometimes not. For example if you get `WARNING: Your kernel does not support cgroup swap limit on Ubuntu`, you can tweak your Grub bootloader with the `cgroup_enable=memory swapaccount=1` setting in the Grub configuration file, this will be `/etc/default/grub` in Ubuntu, for example. It's important to read logs printed out by Docker, to make sure your constraints are in place.

> Always take note of the warnings Docker outputs during the container startup or after updating your constraints on the fly, it may happen that your constraints will not take action!

We already know how to run and observe containers using the commands available from the command line. It's not very convenient, however, if you need to spin-up your containers during the development flow, for example for integration testing. The Fabric8 Docker Maven plugin we've been using in Chapter 5, *Creating Images with Java Applications*, to build images, comes in handy if we need to run containers, as well. Let's do it now.

# Running with Maven

The plugin provides two Maven goals related to starting and stopping containers. This will be `docker:start` and `docker:stop`. Containers are created and started with the `docker:start` and stopped and destroyed with the `docker:stop`. If you need to run the container during the integration tests, the typical use case will be to include those goals in Maven build phases: the `docker:start` will be bound to the `pre-integration-test` and `docker:stop` to the `post-integration-test` phase.

# Plugin configuration

The plugin uses the configuration from the `<run>` sub-element of the `<configuration>` in the `pom.xml` file. The list of the most important configuration elements is as follows:

| | |
|---|---|
| `cmd` | Command which should be executed at the end of the container's startup. If not given, the image's default command is used. |
| `entrypoint` | Entry point for the container. |
| `log` | Log configuration for whether and how log messages from the running containers should be printed. This can also configure the log driver to use. |
| `memory` | Memory limit in bytes |
| `namingStrategy` | Naming strategy for how the container name is created:<br>• `none`: Uses randomly assigned names from Docker (default)<br>• `alias` : Uses the alias specified in the image configuration. An error is thrown, if a container already exists with this name. |
| `network` | The `<network>` element can be used to configure the network mode of the container. It knows the following sub elements:<br>• `<mode>`: The network mode, which can be one of the following values:<br>  ○ `bridge`: Bridged mode with the default Docker bridge (default)<br>  ○ `host`: Share the Docker host network interfaces<br>  ○ `container`: Connect to the network of the specified container<br>The name of the container is taken from the `<name>` element :<br>• `custom`: Use a custom network, which must be created before using Docker network create<br>• `none` : No network will be setup |
| `ports` | The`<ports>`configuration contains a list of port mappings. Each mapping has multiple parts, each separate by a colon. This is equivalent to the port mapping when using the `docker run` command with option `-p`.<br>An example entry can look same as this:<br>`<ports>`<br>`<port>8080:8080</port>`<br>`</ports>` |
| `restartPolicy` | Provides a restart policy we've been discussing earlier in this chapter. An example entry can look same as following:<br>`<restartPolicy>`<br>`<name> on-failure</name>`<br>`<retry>5</retry>`<br>`</restartPolicy>` |
| `volumes` | Volume configuration for binding to host directories and from other containers. The example configuration could look same as following:<br>`<volumes>`<br>`<bind>`<br>`<volume>/logs</volume><volume>/opt/host_export:/opt/container_import</volume>`<br>`</bind>`<br>`</volumes>` |

The complete <configuration> element of our Java REST service can look same as following. This is a very basic example, we are only configuring the runtime port mapping here:

```
<configuration>
<images>
<image>
<name>rest-example:${project.version}</name>
<alias>rest-example</alias>
<build>
<from>openjdk:latest</from>
<assembly>
<descriptorRef>artifact</descriptorRef>
</assembly>
<cmd>java -jar maven/${project.name}-${project.version}.jar</cmd>
</build>
<run>
<ports>
<port>8080:8080</port>
</ports>
</run>
</image>
</images>
</configuration>
```

Having configured our container, let's try to run it, using Maven.

# Starting and stopping containers

To start-up the container, execute the following:

```
$ mvn clean package docker:start
```

Maven will build our REST service from source, build the image and start up the container in the background. As the output, we will be given the ID of the container, as you can see on the following screenshot:

```
[INFO]
[INFO] --- maven-jar-plugin:2.6:jar (default-jar) @ rest-example ---
[INFO] Building jar: C:\Users\jarek\projects\rest-example\target\rest-example-0.1.0.jar
[INFO]
[INFO] --- spring-boot-maven-plugin:1.5.2.RELEASE:repackage (default) @ rest-example ---
[INFO]
[INFO] --- docker-maven-plugin:0.20.1:start (default-cli) @ rest-example ---
[INFO] DOCKER> [rest-example:0.1.0] "rest-example": Start container 51660084f0d8
[INFO] ------------------------------------------------------------------------
[INFO] BUILD SUCCESS
[INFO] ------------------------------------------------------------------------
[INFO] Total time: 4.420 s
[INFO] Finished at: 2017-05-06T13:33:30+02:00
[INFO] Final Memory: 41M/631M
[INFO] ------------------------------------------------------------------------

C:\Users\jarek\projects\rest-example (master)
λ
```

The container is now running in the background. To test if it's running, we could issue a
`docker ps` to list all the running containers, or just call the service by executing some HTTP
methods such as GET or POST on the mapped 8080 port. The port has been exposed in
the<build> configuration element and exposed in the <run> configuration element. This is
convenient, isn't it? But what if we would like to see the container's output instead of
running it in the background? That's also easy; let's stop it first by issuing the following
command:

```
$ mvn docker:stop
```

After 10 seconds (as you'll remember, it's a default timeout before stopping the container),
Maven will output a statement that the container has been stopped:

```
[INFO] DOCKER> [rest-example:0.1.0] "rest-example": Stop and removed
container 51660084f0d8 after 0 ms
```

Let's run the container again, this time using the Maven docker:run goal instead of
docker:start. Execute the following:

```
$ mvn clean package docker:run
```

This time, Maven Docker plugin will run the container and we will see the Spring Boot banner on the console, as you can see on the following screenshot:

```
[INFO] --- spring-boot-maven-plugin:1.5.2.RELEASE:repackage (default) @ rest-example ---
[INFO]
[INFO] --- docker-maven-plugin:0.20.1:run (default-cli) @ rest-example ---
[INFO] DOCKER> [rest-example:0.1.0] "rest-example": Start container d1d158c540d7
rest-example>
rest-example>
rest-example> /\\ /___'_ __ _ _(_)_ __ __ _ \ \ \ \
rest-example> ( ( )\___ | '_ | '_| | '_ \/ _` | \ \ \ \
rest-example> \\/ ___)| |_)| | | | | || (_| |  ) ) ) )
rest-example>  '  |____| .__|_| |_|_| |_\__, | / / / /
rest-example> =========|_|==============|___/=/_/_/_/
rest-example> :: Spring Boot ::       (v1.5.2.RELEASE)
rest-example>
rest-example> 2017-05-06 11:43:55 INFO  p.f.e.BookstoreApplication:48 - Starting BookstoreApplication v0.1.0 on d1d158c540d7 with PID 5 (/maven/
rest-example-0.1.0.jar started by root in /)
rest-example> 2017-05-06 11:43:55 DEBUG p.f.e.BookstoreApplication:51 - Running with Spring Boot v1.5.2.RELEASE, Spring v4.3.7.RELEASE
rest-example> 2017-05-06 11:43:55 INFO  p.f.e.BookstoreApplication:641 - The following profiles are active: dev
rest-example> 2017-05-06 11:43:59 INFO  p.f.e.BookstoreApplication:57 - Started BookstoreApplication in 4.357 seconds (JVM running for 4.72)
```

I guess you can identify the difference between `docker:start` and `docker:run` now. Correct, `docker:run` is the equivalent of option `-i` for the `docker run` command. The `docker:run` will also automatically switch on the `showLogs` option, so that you can see what is happening within the container. As an alternative, you can provide `docker.follow` as system property so that the `docker:start` will never return but block until *CTRL + C* is pressed, exactly the same as when you execute the `docker:run` Maven goal.

As you can see, the Fabric8 Docker Maven plugin gives you the same control as you would have when running and stopping containers from the shell or the command line. But here comes the advantage of the Maven build process itself: you can automate things. The Docker containers can be now used during the build, the integration testing, and the continuous delivery flow you may have; you name it.

# Summary

In this chapter we have learned how to manage the container's life, start it using different run modes (foreground and detached), stop or remove it. We also know how to create constraints to make our containers run exactly how we want them to, by limiting the CPU and RAM usage using runtime constraints. Having our containers running, we are now able to inspect the container's behavior in numerous ways, it will be reading log output, looking at events or browsing the statistics. If you are using Maven, and as the Java developer you probably are, you can now configure the Docker Maven plugin to start or stop containers for you automatically.

We know a lot about Docker already, we can build and run images. It's time to go further. We are going automate deployment, scaling, and management of containerized applications using Kubernetes. And this is the moment where the real fun begins.

# 7
# Introduction to Kubernetes

After reading Chapter 6, *Running Containers with Java Applications*, you now have a lot of knowledge about using Docker to package your Java applications. It's now time to move even further and focus on what we are missing--the container management and orchestration. There are some suitable tools on the market, such as Nomad, Docker Swarm, Apache Mesos, or AZK, for example. In this chapter, we will focus on probably the most popular one, Kubernetes. Kubernetes (sometimes referred to as k8s) is an open source orchestration system for Docker containers, created by Google in 2015. The first unified container management system developed at Google was the system, internally called, Borg; Kubernetes is its descendant. The list of topics covered in this chapter will be:

- Why and when we need container management
- An introduction to Kubernetes
- Basic Kubernetes concepts

Let's begin with answering the question, why do we even need Kubernetes? We will look at the reasoning behind container management and orchestration.

# Why do we need Kubernetes?

As you already know, Docker containers provide great flexibility for running Java services packaged into small, independent pieces of software. Docker containers make components of your application portable--you can move individual services across different environments without needing to worry about the dependencies or the underlying operating system. As long as the operating system is able to run the Docker engine, your Java containers can run on this system.

Also, as you remember from Chapter 1, *Introduction to Docker*, the Docker concept of isolating containers is far from the traditional virtualization. The difference is that Docker containers utilize the resources of the host operating system--they are light, fast, and easy to spin up. It's all very nice, but there are some risks. Your application consists of multiple, independent microservices. The number of services can, and probably will, grow in time. Also, if your application starts to experience a higher load, it would be nice to increase the number of containers with the same service, just to distribute the load. It doesn't mean you only need to use your own server infrastructure--your containers can go to the cloud. Today we have a lot of cloud providers, such as Google or Amazon. By having the possibility to run your containers in the cloud, it gives you a lot of advantages. First, you don't need to manage your own servers. Second, in most clouds, you pay only for the real usage. If there's a peak in the load, the cost of the cloud service will increase, of course, as you will be using more computing power. But if there is no load, you will pay nothing. This is easy to say, but monitoring your server usage, especially with an application or applications running with a huge number of components, can be tricky. You will need to look at the bill from the cloud company carefully and make sure that you don't have a container sitting in the cloud spinning and doing nothing. If the specific service is not that important for your application and does not need to respond fast, you can move it to the cheapest machine. On the other hand, if another service experiences higher loads and it's critical, you will want to move it to a more powerful machine or spin up more instances of it. Best of all, by using Kubernetes, it can be automated. By having the right tool for managing Docker containers, this can be done on the fly. Your application can adapt itself in a very agile way--the end users will probably not even be aware of where an application they're using resides. Container management and monitoring software can greatly reduce the hardware costs by better utilizing the hardware you are paying for. Kubernetes handles scheduling onto nodes in a compute cluster and actively manages workloads to ensure that their state matches the user's declared intentions. Using the concepts of labels and Pods (which we are going to cover later in this chapter), Kubernetes groups the containers which make up an application into logical units for easy management and discovery.

Having your application in the form of a set of containers running in a managed environment also changes the perspective on software development. You can work on a new version of the service and when it's ready, you can do a rolling update on the fly. This also means focusing on the application over the machines it runs on and this, as a result, allows developer teams to operate in a much more flexible, smaller, and modular manner. It allows the software development to be truly agile, which is what we always wanted. Microservices are small and independent, and the build and deployment times are dramatically lower. Also, the risk of doing releases is smaller so you can release smaller changes more often, minimizing the possibility of a huge failure which may happen if you release everything in one go.

Before we begin with basic Kubernetes concepts, let's summarize what Kubernetes gives us in a list:

- Deploying applications quickly and predictably
- Scaling on the fly
- Releasing new features seamlessly
- Fail-proofing
- Limiting hardware usage only to required resources
- Agile application development
- Portability between operating systems, hosts, and cloud providers

This is a list of features that cannot be easily beaten. To understand how this is being achieved, we need to understand the core Kubernetes concepts. So far, we know only one single concept coming from Docker--the container--which is a portable, independent unit of software. The container can contain anything we want, be it a database or a Java REST microservice. Let's get to know the remaining pieces.

# Basic Kubernetes concepts

A cluster is a group of nodes; they can be physical servers or virtual machines that have the Kubernetes platform installed. The basic Kubernetes architecture is presented in the following diagram:

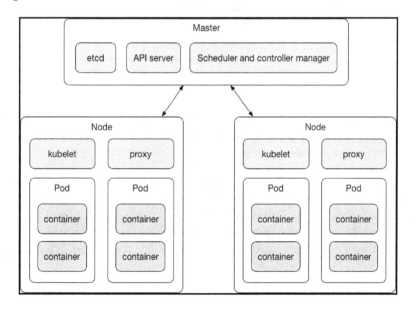

As you can see, the Kubernetes cluster consists of a Master node and a number of worker nodes with some components inside. While it may look scary and complicated at first glance, it will be easier to understand if we describe the concepts one by one, starting with the Pod.

# Pods

The Pod consists of one or more Docker containers. This is the basic unit of the Kubernetes platform and an elementary piece of execution that Kubernetes works with. A diagram of the Pod is presented as following:

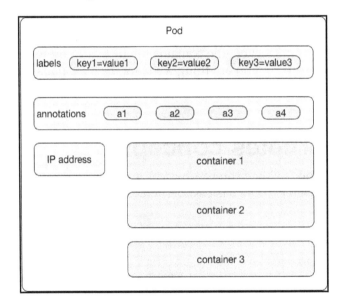

Containers running in the same Pod share the same common network namespace, disk, and security context. In fact, the communication over localhost is recommended between containers running on the same Pod. Each container can also communicate with any other Pod or service within the cluster.

As you remember from `Chapter 2`, *Networking and Persistent Storage*, you can mount volumes within Docker containers. Kubernetes also supports the concept of a volume. Volumes that are attached to the Pod may be mounted inside of one or more containers running on this Pod. Kubernetes supports a lot of different volume types as a native support for mounting GitHub repositories, network disks, local hard drives, and so on.

If your application needs a distributed storage and needs to handle large amounts of data, you are not limited only to local hard drives. Kubernetes also supports Volume Providers. Currently, the list of available Persistent Volume Providers includes:

- **GCE**: Which is a Google Cloud platform
- **AWS**: Amazon Web Services
- **GlusterFS**: A scalable network filesystem. Using GlusterFS, which is free and an open source software, you can use your existing storage hardware to create large, distributed storage solutions
- **OpenStack Cinder**: A block storage service for users of the OpenStack Nova compute platform
- **CephRBD**: A **Reliable Autonomic Distributed Object Store (RADOS)**, which provides your applications with object, block, and file system storage in a single unified storage cluster
- QuoByte
- Kube-Aliyun

Network namespace and volumes are not the only properties of the Pod. As you can see on the Pod's diagram, a Pod can have labels and annotations attached. Labels are very important in Kubernetes. They are key/value pairs that are attached to objects, in this case to Pods. The idea behind labels is that they can be used to identify objects--labels are meaningful and relevant to users. An example of the label may be:

```
app=my-rest-service
layer=backend
```

Later on, we will be using label selectors to select objects (such as Pods) having the specified label. Via a label selector, which is the core grouping primitive in Kubernetes, the client or user can identify an object or a set of objects. A selector, similar to a label, is also a key-value expression to identify resources using matching labels. For example, the selector expression `app = my-rest-service` would select all Pods with the label `app = my-rest-service`. Annotations, on the other hand, are a kind of metadata you can attach to Pods. They are not intended to be identifying attributes; they are such properties that can be read by tools of libraries. There are no rules as to what an annotation should contain--it's up to you. The annotation can contain information such as the build or release version, a timestamp, Git branch name, Git `pull` request number, or just anything, as a mobile number.

Labels are intended for identifying information about Kubernetes objects such as Pods. Annotations are just metadata attached to an object.

We've said before that a Pod is a basic unit of execution in Kubernetes. It can contain multiple containers. A real-life example of having a Pod with more than one Docker container could be our Java REST microservice Pod. For example purposes in previous chapters, our microservice has been storing its database data in memory. In real life, the data should probably go to the real database. Our Pod would probably have a container with Java JRE and the Spring Boot application itself, together with the second container with a PostgreSQL database, which the microservice uses to store its data. Two of those containers makes a Pod--a single, decoupled unit of execution that contains everything our REST service needs to operate.

The Pod's definition is a JSON or YAML file called a `Pod` manifest. Take a look at a simple example with one container:

```
apiVersion: v1
kind: Pod
metadata:
   name: rest_service
spec:
   containers:
      name: rest_service
      image: rest_service
         ports:
   - containerPort: 8080
```

The same `pod` manifest in a JSON file will look the same as the following:

```
{
   "apiVersion": "v1",
   "kind": "Pod",
   "metadata":{
      "name": "rest_service",
      "labels": {
         "name": "rest_service"
      }
   },
   "spec": {
      "containers": [{
         "name": "rest_service",
         "image": "rest_service",
         "ports": [{"containerPort": 8080}],
      }]
   }
}
```

The container's `image` is a Docker image name. The `containerPort` exposes that port from the REST service container so we can connect to the service at the Pod's IP. By default, as you remember from `Chapter 1`, *Introduction to Docker*, the entry point defined in the `image` is what will run.

It's very important to be aware that a Pod's life is fragile. Because the Pods are treated as stateless, independent units, if one of them is unhealthy or is just being replaced with a newer version, the Kubernetes Master doesn't have mercy on it--it just kills it and disposes of it.

In fact, Pods have a strictly defined lifecycle. The following list describes the phases of a Pod's life:

- `pending`: This phase means that the Pod has been accepted by the Kubernetes system, but one or more of the Docker container images has not been created. Pods can be in this phase for a while--if the image needs to be downloaded from the internet, for example.
- `running`: The Pod has been put onto a node and all of the Pod's Docker containers have been created.
- `succeeded`: All Docker containers in the Pod have been terminated with a success status.
- `failed`: All Docker containers in the Pod have been terminated, but at least one container has terminated with a failure status or was terminated by the system.
- `unknown`: This typically indicates a problem with communication to the host of the Pod; for some reason, the state of the Pod could not be retrieved.

When a Pod is being brought down, it's not only because it has failed. More often, if our application needs to handle an increased load, we need to have more Pods running. On the other hand, if the load decreases or there is no load at all, there's no point in having a lot of Pods running--we can dispose of them. Of course, we could start and stop Pods manually, but it's always better to automate. This brings us to the concept of ReplicaSets.

# ReplicaSets

ReplicaSets is the concept used in scaling your application by using replication. What is Kubernetes replication useful for? Typically, you would want to replicate your containers (which are, in fact, your application) for several reasons, including:

- **Scaling**: When load increases and becomes too heavy for the number of existing instances, Kubernetes enables you to easily scale up your application, creating additional instances as needed.
- **Load balancing**: We can easily distribute traffic to different instances to prevent overloading of a single instance or node. Load balancing comes out of the box because of Kubernetes' architecture and it's very convenient.
- **Reliability and fault tolerance**: By having multiple versions of an application, you prevent problems if one or more fail. This is particularly true if the system replaces any containers that fail.

Replication is appropriate for numerous use cases, including microservice-based applications where multiple, independent small services provide very specific functionality, or cloud native applications that are based on the theory that any component can fail at any time. Replication is a perfect solution for implementing them, as multiple instances naturally fit into the architecture.

A ReplicaSet ensures that a specified number of Pod clones, known as replicas, are running at any given time. It there are too many, they will be shut down. If there is a need for more, for example some of them died because of an error or crash, or maybe there's a higher load, some more Pods will be brought to life. ReplicaSets are used by Deployments. Let's see what Deployments are.

# Deployment

The Deployment is responsible for creating and updating instances of your application. Once the Deployment has been created, the Kubernetes Master schedules the application instances onto individual nodes in the cluster. A Deployment is a higher level of abstraction; it manages ReplicaSets when doing Pod orchestration, creation, deletion, and updates. A Deployment provides declarative updates for Pods and ReplicaSets. The Deployment allows for easy updating of a Replica Set as well as the ability to roll back to a previous deployment.

You just specify the number of replicas you need and the container to run within each Pod and the Deployment controller will spin them up. The example Deployment manifest definition in the YAML file looks the same as the following:

```
apiVersion: 1.0
kind: Deployment
metadata:
  name: rest_service-deployment
spec:
  replicas: 3
```

```
template:
  metadata:
    labels:
        app: rest_service
  spec:
    containers:
    - name: rest_service
      image: rest_service
      ports:
      - containerPort: 8080
```

In the previous example, the Deployment Controller will create a ReplicaSet containing three Pods running our Java REST service.

The Deployment is a kind of control structure that takes care of the spinning up or down of Pods. A Deployment takes care of the state of a Pod or group of pods by creating or shutting down replicas. Deployments also manage updates to Pods. Deployments are a higher abstraction, which create ReplicaSets resources. ReplicaSets watch over the Pods and make sure the correct number of replicas are always running. When you want to update a Pod, you will need to modify the Deployment manifest. This modification will create a new ReplicaSet, which will be scaled up while the previous ReplicaSet will be scaled down, providing no down-time deployment of your application.

The main purpose of Deployments is to do rolling updates and rollbacks. A rolling update is the process of updating an application to a newer version, in a serial, one-by-one fashion. By updating one instance at a time, you are able to keep the application up and running. If you were to just update all instances at the same time, your application would likely experience downtime. In addition, performing a rolling update allows you to catch errors during the process so that you can roll back before it affects all of your users.

Deployment also allows us to do an easy rollback. To do the rollback, we simply set the revision that we want to roll back to. Kubernetes will scale up the corresponding ReplicaSet and scale down the current one, and this will result in a rollback to a specified revision of our service. In fact, we will be using Deployments heavily in `Chapter 8`, *Using Kubernetes with Java*, to roll out an update of our service to the cluster.

Replication is a large part of Kubernetes' features. As you can see, the life of a Pod is delicate and ephemeral. Because Pods and their clones come and go all the time, we need something permanent and tangible, something that will stay forever so our application's users (or other Pods as well) can discover and call. This brings us to the concept of Kubernetes services. Let's focus on them now.

# Services

Kubernetes services group one or more Pods into an internal or external process that needs to be long-running and externally accessible, as our Java REST API endpoint or a database host, for example. This is where the labels we gave to our Pods become very important; a service finds Pods to group by looking for a specific label. We use label selectors to select Pods with particular labels and apply services or ReplicaSets to them. Other applications can find our service through Kubernetes service discovery.

A service is Kubernetes' abstraction to provide a network connection to one or more Pods. While (as you remember from the chapter about Docker networking), by default, Docker uses host-private networking, containers can communicate with other containers only if they are on the same host machine. In Kubernetes, cluster Pods can communicate with other Pods, regardless of which host they land on. This is possible because of the services. Each service is given its own IP address and port which remains constant for the lifetime of the service. Services have an integrated load-balancer that will distribute network traffic to all Pods. While a Pod's life can be fragile as they are being spun up or down depending on your application needs, the service is a more constant concept. Each Pod gets its own IP address, but when it dies and another one is being brought to life, the IP address can be different. This could potentially become a problem--if a set of Pods provides functionality to other Pods inside the Kubernetes cluster, one can lose track of the other one's IP address. Services, by having a lifetime-assigned IP address, solves this issue. The Service abstraction enables decoupling. Let's say we have our Java REST service running on top of the Spring Boot application. We need a way to route HTTP requests, such as `GET` or `POST`, from the internet to our Docker containers. We will do it by setting up a Kubernetes service that uses a load balancer to route requests coming from a public IP address to one of the containers. We will group the containers with the REST service into a Pod and name it, let's say, Our little REST service. Then we will define a Kubernetes service that will serve port `8080` to any of the containers in the Our little REST service Pod. Kubernetes will then use a load balancer to divide the traffic between the specified containers. Let's summarize the Kubernetes service features:

- Services are persistent and permanent
- They provide discovery
- They offer load balancing
- They expose a stable network IP address
- They find Pods to group by usage of labels

We have said that there is a service discovery mechanism built-in. Kubernetes supports two primary modes of finding a service: environment variables and DNS. Service discovery is the process of figuring out how to connect to a service. Kubernetes contains a built-in DNS server for that purpose: the kube-dns.

# kube-dns

Kubernetes offers a DNS cluster add-on, started automatically each time the cluster is started up. The DNS service runs as a cluster service itself--its SkyDNS--a distributed service for announcement and discovery of services built on top of `etcd` (you will get to know what etcd is later in this chapter). It utilizes DNS queries to discover available services. It supports forward lookups (A records), service lookups (SRV records), and reverse IP address lookups (PTR records). Actually, the service is the only type of object to which Kubernetes assigns DNS names; Kubernetes generates an internal DNS entry that resolves to a service's IP address. Services are assigned a DNS A record for a name in the form `service-name.namespace-name.svc.cluster.local`. This resolves to the cluster IP of the service. For example, for a service named `my-rest-service`, the DNS add-on will make sure that the service will be available for other Pods (and other services) in the cluster via the `my-rest-service.default.svc.cluster.local` hostname. The DNS-based service discovery provides a flexible and generic way to connect to services across the cluster.

> Note that when using the `hostNetwork=true` option, Kubernetes will use the host's DNS servers and will not use the cluster's DNS server.

There's one more concept that will appear from time to time during our Kubernetes journey--a namespace. Let's find out what it's for.

# Namespace

A namespace functions as a grouping mechanism inside of Kubernetes. Pods, volumes, ReplicaSets, and services can easily cooperate within a namespace, but the namespace provides an isolation from the other parts of the cluster. What would be the possible use case for such isolation? Well, namespaces let you manage different environments within the same cluster. For example, you can have different test and staging environments in the same cluster of machines.

This could potentially save some resources in your infrastructure, but it can be dangerous; without namespaces, it would be risky to roll out a new version of your software to test the environment, having the pre-release version running on the same cluster. By having namespaces available, you can act on different environments in the same cluster without worrying about affecting other environments.

Because Kubernetes uses the `default` namespace, using namespaces is optional, but recommended.

We have all the Kubernetes abstractions explained--we know that there are Pods, ReplicaSets, Deployments, and services. Now it's time to move to the physical, execution layer of Kubernetes' architecture. All those little, fragile Pods need to live somewhere. They live in nodes, which we are going to learn about now.

# Nodes

A node is a work horse in Kubernetes' architecture. It may be a virtual or physical machine, depending on your infrastructure. A worker node runs the tasks as instructed by the Master node, which we will explain very soon. Nodes (in the earlier Kubernetes life, they were called Minions) can run one or more Pods. They provide an application-specific virtual host in a containerized environment.

 When a worker node dies, the Pods running on the node die as well.

The following diagram shows the contents of a node:

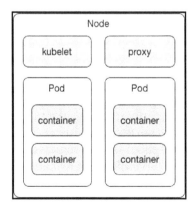

As you can see in the previous diagram, a node in Kubernetes has some processes running inside, and each is very important. Let's explain their purposes, one by one.

# Kubelet

Kubelet is probably the most important controller in Kubernetes. It's a process that responds to the commands coming from the Master node (we are going to explain what the Master node is in a second). Each node has this process listening. The Master calls it to manage Pods and their containers. The Kubelet runs Pods (which, as you already know, are collections of containers that share an IP and volumes). The Kubelet (`https://kubernetes.io/v1.0/docs/admin/kubelet/`) is responsible for what's running on an individual machine and it has one job: given a set of containers to run, to make sure they are all running. To rephrase, a Kubelet is the name of the agent and a node is what we call the machine the agent runs on. It's worth knowing that each Kubelet also has an internal `HTTP` server which listens for HTTP requests and responds to a simple API call to submit a new manifest.

# Proxy

A proxy is a network proxy that creates a virtual IP address which clients can access. The network calls will be transparently proxied to the Pods in a Kubernetes service. A service, as you already know, provides a way to group Pods into kind of a single business process, which can be reached under a common access policy. By having a proxy run on a node, we can call the service IP address. Technically, a node's proxy is a `kube-proxy` (`https://kubernetes.io/docs/admin/kube-proxy/`) process which programs `iptables` rules to trap access to the service IP address. The Kubernetes network proxy runs on each node. Without it, we would not be able to access the service.

> `kube-proxy` knows only UDP and TCP, does not understand HTTP, provides load balancing, and is just used to reach services.

# Docker

Finally, each node needs something to run. It will be a Docker container runtime, which is responsible for pulling the images and running containers.

All those nodes, as any other group of workers in the real world, need a manager. In Kubernetes, the role of the node manager is being performed by one special node: the Master node.

# The Master node

The Master node does not run any containers--it just handles and manages the cluster. The Master is the central control point that provides a unified view of the cluster. There is a single Master node that controls multiple worker nodes, which actually run our containers. The Master automatically handles the scheduling of the Pods across the worker nodes in the cluster -by taking into account the available resources on each node. The structure of the Master node is presented in the following diagram:

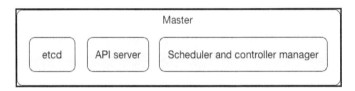

Let's dissect the Master node piece by piece, starting with etcd.

# etcd

Kubernetes stores all of its cluster state in etcd, a distributed data store with a strong consistency model. etcd is a distributed, reliable key-value store for the most critical data of a distributed system, with a focus on being:

- **Simple**: Well-defined, user-facing API
- **Secure**: Automatic TLS with optional client cert authentication
- **Fast**: Benchmarked for 10,000 writes/sec
- **Reliable**: Properly distributed using Raft

This state includes what nodes exist in the cluster, what Pods should be running, which nodes they are running on, and a whole lot more. The whole cluster state is stored in an instance of etcd. This provides a way to store configuration data reliably. Another crucial component running on the Master node is the API server.

# The API server

One of the main components residing on the Master node is the API server. It's so important that sometimes, you may find out that the Master node is being referred to as the API server in general. Technically, it's a process named `kube-apiserver` which accepts and responds to `HTTP REST` requests using JSON. It's main purpose is to validate and configure data for the API objects which are Pods, services, ReplicaSets, and others. The API server provides the frontend to the cluster's shared state through which all other components interact. The API server is the central management entity and is the only Kubernetes component that connects to etcd. All the other components must go through the API server to work with the cluster state. We will cover the Kubernetes API in detail in `Chapter 9`, *Working With Kubernetes API*.

> The Master node does not run any containers--it just handles and manages the whole cluster. The nodes that actually run the containers are the worker nodes.

# The scheduler

As we have said before, if you create a Deployment, the Master will schedule the distribution of application instances onto individual nodes in the cluster. Once the application instances are up and running, the Deployment Controller will be continuously monitoring those instances. This is kind of a self-healing mechanism--if a node goes down or is deleted, the Deployment Controller replaces it.

Now that we know what the Kubernetes specific components are that form it's architecture, let's look what tools are available for us.

# Available tools

There are a couple of tools we will be using throughout the rest of the book. Let's start with the most important one: `kubectl`.

# kubectl

`kubectl` is a command-line interface for running commands against Kubernetes clusters. In fact, this is the command used most often when working with Kubernetes. In `Chapter 8`, *Using Kubernetes with Java*, we will go through the command's syntax and possible usages. Using `kubectl`, you will be interacting with your cluster. Of course, having the API exposed by the Master node and the API server, we could do it using an `HTTP` client of our choice, but using `kubectl` is a lot faster and more convenient. `kubectl` provides a lot of functionalities, such as listing resources, showing detailed information about the resources, prints log, managing cluster, and executing commands on a container in a Pod.

# Dashboard

Kubernetes Dashboard is a nice, clean web-based UI for Kubernetes clusters. Using the Dashboard, you can manage and troubleshoot the cluster itself as well as the applications running in it. You could say it's the Kubernetes user interface. For those who prefer to use the graphical UI, the Dashboard can be a handy tool for deploying containerized applications and getting an overview of applications running on your cluster, as well as for creating or modifying individual resources such as Deployments, Pods, and services. For example, you can scale a Deployment, initiate a rolling update, restart a Pod, or deploy new applications using a deploy wizard. We will also use the Dashboard in `Chapter 8`, *Using Kubernetes with Java*.

# Minikube

Running a cluster seems to be a complicated process that needs a lot of setup. This is not necessarily the truth. Actually, it's quite easy to have the Kubernetes cluster up and running on the local machine, for learning, testing, and development purposes. The `minikube` tool, available at GitHub at `https://github.com/kubernetes/minikube`, allows you to set up the local cluster on your own machine. It's available for all major platforms, which includes Linux, macOS, and Windows. The cluster started will of course be a single node cluster, but it's more than enough to start doing real-life Kubernetes examples. In fact, in `Chapter 8`, *Using Kubernetes with Java*, before we start deploying our `REST` service into the cluster, we are going to run Kubernetes locally.

Apart from those mentioned previously, you may find a lot of other tools and utilities that work very well with Kubernetes on the internet.

# Summary

This chapter introduced a lot of new concepts. Let's briefly summarize what we have learned about the Kubernetes architecture.

Kubernetes (k8s) is an open source platform for automating container operations such as deployment, scheduling, and scalability across a cluster of nodes. Using Kubernetes, you can:

- Automate the deployment and replication of containers
- Scale up and down containers on the fly
- Organize containers in groups and provide load balancing between them
- Easily roll out new versions of application containers
- Provide fault tolerance mechanisms to your application--if a container dies it gets replaced
- Kubernetes consists of:
  - **A Cluster**: A group of nodes.
  - **Nodes**: Physical or virtual machines that act as workers. Each node runs the kubelet, proxy, and a Docker engine process.
  - **The Master node**: Provides a unified view into the cluster. It delivers the Kubernetes API server. The API server provides a REST endpoint that can be used to interact with the cluster. The Master also includes the controllers used to create and replicate Pods.
  - **Pods**: Scheduled to nodes. Each Pod runs a single container or a group of containers and volumes. Containers in the same Pod share the same network namespace and volumes and can communicate with each other using localhost. Their life is fragile; they will be born and die all the time.
  - **Labels**: Pods have labels, with key/value pairs attached. Labels are used to precisely select Pods.
  - **Services**: An abstraction that defines a set of Pods and a policy to access them. Services find their group of Pods by using label selectors. Because the IP of the single Pod can change, the service provides a permanent IP address for its client to use.

That was a piece of theory that may be a bit overwhelming. Don't worry, in `Chapter 8`, *Using Kubernetes with Java*, we are going to run the local Kubernetes cluster. Our plan will consist of creating a local Kubernetes cluster using `minikube`. We will then deploy and manage Docker containers with our Java REST microservice. By doing some practical, hands-on actions, the Kubernetes architecture will be a lot more clear. Running a local Kubernetes is not the only thing we are going to do. Later on, in `Chapter 10`, *Deploying Java on Kubernetes in the Cloud*, we will put our application in the real cloud--a place where Kubernetes really shines.

# 8
# Using Kubernetes with Java

In Chapter 7, *Introduction to Kubernetes*, we learned about the Kubernetes architecture and concepts. We know about nodes, Pods, and services. In this chapter, we will do some practical hands-on and deploy our Java REST service to a local Kubernetes cluster. For learning purposes, we will use the Minikube tool to create a cluster on the local machine. It's easier to learn Kubernetes on a local machine instead of going to the cloud in the first place. Because Minikube runs locally, instead of through a cloud provider, certain provider-specific features such as load balancers and persistent volumes, will not work out of the box. However, you can use `NodePort`, `HostPath`, persistent volumes and several addons such as DNS, or dashboard to test your apps locally before pushing to a real, production-grade cluster. In Chapter 10, *Deploying Java on Kubernetes in the Cloud*, we will run Kubernetes using **Amazon Web Services** (**AWS**) and hosted Kubernetes in Google container engine.

To follow along, we will need the following tools ready:

- `Docker` : To build the Docker images we want to deploy
- `minikube`: A local Kubernetes environment
- `kubectl`: The Kubernetes command line interface

This chapter will cover the following topics:

- Installing Minikube on macOS, Windows, and Linux
- Starting up the local Kubernetes cluster using Minikube
- Deploying a Java application on a local cluster
- Interacting with containers: scaling, autoscaling, and viewing cluster events
- Using the Kubernetes dashboard

I assume you have Docker up and running so far, so let's focus on the `minikube` utility. We have already mentioned `minikube` in the `Chapter 7`, *Introduction to Kubernetes*; now, we will go into some more details, starting with the installation process.

# Installing Minikube

The Minikube tool source code with all the documentation is available at GitHub at `https://github.com/kubernetes/minikube`.

# Installing on Mac

The following sequences of commands will download the `minikube` binary, set the executable flag and copy it to the `/usr/local/bin` folder, which will make it available in the macOS shell:

```
$ curl -Lo minikube
https://storage.googleapis.com/minikube/releases/v0.12.2/minikube-darwin-am
d64
$ chmod +x minikube
$ sudo mv minikube /usr/local/bin/
```

Alternatively, if you use Homebrew package manager (available freely at `https://brew.sh`), which is, by the way, very handy and recommended, you can just install `minikube` by typing:

```
$ brew cask install minikube
```

# Installing on Windows

Minikube for Windows is also simply a single executable file. You can always find the newest version on the Minikube's site, at `https://github.com/kubernetes/minikube`. You just need to download the latest executable, rename it `minikube.exe`, and place it in your system path to have it available from the command line.

# Installing on Linux

The installation process on Linux is identical to the macOS one. The only difference is the executable name. The following command will download the latest Minikube release, set the executable bit, and move it to the `/usr/local/bin` directory:

```
$ curl -Lo minikube
https://storage.googleapis.com/minikube/releases/latest/minikube-linux-amd64 && chmod +x minikube && sudo mv minikube /usr/local/bin/
```

That's all, a single Minikube and Docker is all we need to start the local cluster. It's time to bring it to life:

# Starting up the local Kubernetes cluster

We're using the local Kubernetes cluster provided by `minikube`. Start your cluster with:

```
$ minikube start
```

Minikube works on its own virtual machine. Depending on your host OS, you can choose between several virtualization drivers. Currently supported are `virtualbox`, `vmwarefusion`, `xhyve`, `hyperv`, and `kvm` (**Kernel-based virtual machine**). The default VM driver is virtual box. You can override this option. This is the example macOS startup command line which uses `xhyve`:

```
$ minikube start --vm-driver=xhyve
```

When starting Minikube for the first time, you will see it downloading the Minikube ISO, so the process will take a little longer. This is, however, a one-time action. The Minikube configuration will be saved in the `.minikube` folder in your `home` directory, for example `~/.minikube` on Linux or macOS. On the first run, Minikube will also configure the `kubectl` command line tool (we will get back to it in a short while) to use the local `minikube` cluster. This setting is called a `kubectl` context. It determines which cluster `kubectl` is interacting with. All available contexts are present in the `~/.kube/config` file.

As the cluster is running now and we have the `dashboard` addon enabled by default, you can take a look at the (still empty) Kubernetes dashboard with the following command:

```
$ minikube dashboard
```

It will open your default browser with the URL of the cluster's dashboard:

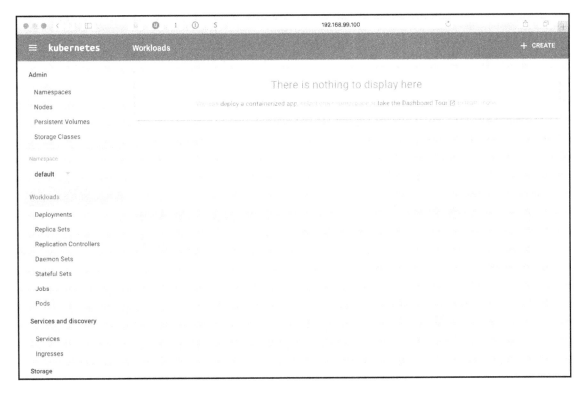

As you can see, the dashboard is empty now. If you browse to the **Namespaces** menu, you will notice that Minikube creates some namespaces, with the one available for our purposes named simply the default. The parts of the Minikube installation, such as DNS or the Dashboard, which are also running on the cluster itself, with separate namespaces such as kube-public and kube-system.

Feel free to browse the menus and sections; so far, no harm can be done, it's a local development cluster running nothing at the moment. We will get back to the dashboard in the last section of this chapter, to see how can we use it to deploy our services from the nice UI, if you prefer to do so, instead to using the shell of command line.

Of course, having the cluster running empty is quite useless, so we need a tool to manage it. While we can almost all everything using the dashboard, it's a lot more convenient to have a command line tool for that. kubectl controls the Kubernetes cluster. We will use the kubectl command line tool heavily to deploy, schedule, and scale our applications and microservices. The tool comes as a self-contained binary for Mac, Linux, and Windows. In the next section you will find installation instructions for different platforms.

# Installing kubectl

`kubectl` is available for all major platforms. Let's start with macOS installation.

## Installing on Mac

The following sequences of command will download the `kubectl` binary, set the executable flag and copy it to `/usr/local/bin` folder which will make it available in the macOS shell:

```
$ curl -O https://storage.googleapis.com/kubernetes-release/release/v1.5.2
/bin/darwin/amd64/kubectl
$ chmod +x kubectl
$ sudo cp kubectl /usr/local/bin
```

Homebrew provides the most convenient way to install `kubectl` and keep it up to date. To install, use this command:

```
$ brew install kubectl
```

To update, use the following command:

```
$ brew upgrade kubectl
```

## Installing on Windows

You can find the list of Windows `kubectl` releases on GitHub at `https://github.com/eirslett/kubectl-windows/releases`. Similar to Minikube, kubectl is just a single `.exe` file. At the time of writing this book it's `https://github.com/eirslett/kubectl-windows/releases/download/v1.6.3/kubectl.exe`. You will need to download the `exe` file and place in on your system path, to have it available in the command line.

## Installing on Linux

The installation process is, again, very similar to the macOS. The following commands will fetch the `kubectl` binary, give it an executable flag, and then move it to the `/usr/local/bin` to make it available in the shell:

```
$ curl -O https://storage.googleapis.com/kubernetes-release/release/v1.5.2
/bin/linux/amd64/kubectl
```

```
$ chmod +x kubectl
$ sudo cp kubectl /usr/local/bin/kubectl
```

To verify if your local cluster is up and running and `kubectl` is properly configured, execute the following command:

```
$ kubectl cluster-info
```

In the output, you will be given basic information about the cluster, which includes its IP address, and running Minikube addons (we will get back to addons later in this chapter):

```
 ~ — -zsh ▸ -zsh — zsh — 130×10
〉kubectl cluster-info
Kubernetes master is running at https://192.168.99.100:8443
heapster is running at https://192.168.99.100:8443/api/v1/proxy/namespaces/kube-system/services/heapster
monitoring-grafana is running at https://192.168.99.100:8443/api/v1/proxy/namespaces/kube-system/services/monitoring-grafana
monitoring-influxdb is running at https://192.168.99.100:8443/api/v1/proxy/namespaces/kube-system/services/monitoring-influxdb

To further debug and diagnose cluster problems, use 'kubectl cluster-info dump'.

〉
```

To list the nodes we have running in our cluster, execute the `get nodes` command:

```
$ kubectl get nodes
```

Of course, this is just a single node cluster, so there is no surprise in the output of the previous command:

```
 ~ — -zsh ▸ -zsh — zsh — 130×8

〉kubectl get nodes
NAME        STATUS    AGE     VERSION
minikube    Ready     2d      v1.6.0

〉
```

Our cluster is up and running; it's time to deploy our service on it.

# Deploying on the Kubernetes cluster

We begin the process of deploying our software on the Kubernetes cluster by defining a service. As you remember from Chapter 7, *Introduction to Kubernetes*, services abstract a set of Pods as a single IP and port, allow simple TCP/UDP load, and allow the list of Pods to change dynamically. Let's start with service creation.

# Creating a service

By default, each Pod is only accessible by its internal IP address within the Kubernetes cluster. To make the container accessible from outside the Kubernetes virtual network, we need to expose the Pod as a Kubernetes Service. To create a service, we are going to use the simple .yaml file, with a service manifest. YAML is a human-readable data serialization language, which is commonly used for configuration files. A sample service manifest for our Java rest-example could look the same as the following:

```yaml
apiVersion: v1
kind: Service
metadata:
  name: rest-example
  labels:
    app: rest-example
    tier: backend
spec:
  type: NodePort
  ports:
  - port: 8080
  selector:
    app: rest-example
    tier: backend
```

Note that the manifest of a service doesn't refer to a Docker image. This is because, as you remember from Chapter 7, *Introduction to Kubernetes*, a service in Kubernetes is just an abstraction which provides a network connection to one or more Pods. Each service is given its own IP address and port, which remains constant for the lifetime of the service. Each Pod needs to have a specific label, to be discovered by the service, services find Pods to group using and labels selectors. In our previous example, the selector will pick up all Pods having a label app with the value of rest-example and a label named tier with a value of backend:

```yaml
selector:
    app: rest-example
    tier: backend
```

As you remember from Chapter 7, *Introduction to Kubernetes*, every node in a Kubernetes cluster runs a kube-proxy process. The kube-proxy plays a crucial role in Kubernetes services. Its purpose is to expose a virtual IP for them. Since Kubernetes 1.2, the iptables proxy is the default. You have two options that you can use for setting up the proxy: userspace and iptables. Those settings refer to what actually handles the connection forwarding. In both cases, local iptables rules are installed to intercept outbound TCP connections that have a destination IP address associated with a service. There's an important difference between those two modes:

- Proxy-mode: userspace: In the userspace mode, the iptables rule forwards to a local port where kube-proxy is listening for connections. The kube-proxy, running in userspace, terminates the connection, establishes a new connection to a backend for the service, and then forwards requests to the backend and responses back to the local process. An advantage of the userspace mode is that because the connections are created from an application, if the connection is refused, the application can retry to a different backend.
- Proxy-mode: iptables: in this mode, the iptables rules are installed to directly forward packets that are destined for a service to a backend for the service. This is more efficient than moving the packets from the kernel to kube-proxy and then back to the kernel so it results in higher throughput and better tail latency. However, unlike the userspace mode, using iptables mode makes it impossible to automatically retry another Pod if the one it initially selects does not respond, so it depends on having working readiness probes.

As you can see, in both cases there will be a kube-proxy binary running on the node. In userspace mode, it inserts itself as the proxy; in iptables mode, it will configure iptables rather than to proxy connections itself.

The service type can have the following values:

- **NodePort**: By specifying a service type of NodePort, we declare to expose the service outside the cluster. The Kubernetes master will allocate a port from a flag-configured range (default: 30000-32767), and each node of the cluster will proxy that port (the same port number on every node) into your service
- **Load balancer**: This would create a load balancer on cloud providers which support external load balancers (for example, on Amazon AWS cloud). This feature is not available when using Minikube
- **Cluster IP**: This would expose the service only within the cluster. This is the default value which will be used if you don't provide another

Having our `service.yml` file ready, we can create our first Kubernetes service, by executing the following `kubectl` command:

```
$ kubectl create -f service.yml
```

To see if our service is created properly, we can execute the `kubectl get services` command:

```
~/projects/rest-example master*
) kubectl get services
NAME          CLUSTER-IP    EXTERNAL-IP    PORT(S)          AGE
kubernetes    10.0.0.1      <none>         443/TCP          6h
rest-example  10.0.0.214    <nodes>        8080:31141/TCP   3m

~/projects/rest-example master*
>
```

We can also list other services (including the services provided by the `minikube` cluster itself, if you are curious) by adding the `--all-namespaces` switch:

```
$ kubectl get services --all-namespaces
```

To see the details of a specific service, we use the `describe` command. Execute the following to see the details of our `rest-example` Java service:

```
$ kubectl describe service rest-example
```

In the output, we are presented with the most useful service properties, especially the endpoints (our internal container IP and port, just one in this case, because we have one Pod running in the service), service internal port, and proxied NodePort:

```
~/projects/rest-example master*
) kubectl describe service rest-example
Name:              rest-example
Namespace:         default
Labels:            app=rest-example
                   tier=backend
Annotations:       <none>
Selector:          app=rest-example,tier=backend
Type:              NodePort
IP:                10.0.0.214
Port:              <unset> 8080/TCP
NodePort:          <unset> 31141/TCP
Endpoints:         172.17.0.4:8080
Session Affinity:  None
Events:            <none>

~/projects/rest-example master*
>
```

Having all of the settings in a .yaml file is very convenient. Sometimes, though, there is a need to create a service in a more dynamic way; for example in some automation flows. In this case, instead of creating a .yaml file first, we can create a service manually, by providing all the parameters and options to the kubectl command itself. Before doing this, however, you will need have the deployment created first, because creating a service manually is just exposing a deployment using the kubectl command. After all, a service is an exposed deployment which, in fact, is just a set of Pods. The example of such exposure, which will result with service creation, looks the same as this:

```
$ kubectl expose deployment rest-example--type="NodePort"
```

# Creating a deployment

Before creating a deployment, we need to have our Docker image ready and published to a registry, the same as the Docker Hub for example. Of course, it can also be a private repository hosted in your organization. As you remember from the Chapter 7, *Introduction to Kubernetes*, each Docker container in a Pod has its own image. By default, the kubectl process in a Pod will try to pull each image from the specified registry. You can change this behavior by specifying a value for the imagePullPolicy property in a deployment descriptor. It can have the following values:

- IfNotPresent: With this setting, the image will be pulled from the registry only if not present on the local host
- Never: With this one, kubelet will use only local images

Setting imagePullPolicy with a value IfNotPresent when creating a deployment is useful; otherwise, Minikube will try to download the image before looking for an image on the local host.

Kubernetes uses the same syntax for images as Docker itself, including private registries and tags.

It is important that you provide a tag in the image name. Otherwise, Kubernetes will use the latest tag when looking for your image in a repository, the same as Docker does.

Using locally built images gets a little bit tricky when working with a local Kubernetes cluster. Minikube runs in a separate VM, hence it will not see the images you've built locally using Docker on your machine. There's a workaround for that. You can execute the following command:

```
$ eval $(minikube docker-env)
```

The previous command will actually utilize the Docker daemon running on `minikube`, and build your image on the Minikube's Docker. This way, the locally built image will be available to the Minikube without pulling from the external registry. This is not very convenient, it is certainly easier to push the Docker image to a `remote` registry. Let's push our rest-example image into the `DockerHub` registry.

1. First, we need to log in:

   ```
   $ docker login
   ```

2. Then, we are going to tag our image using the `docker tag` command (not that you will need to provide your own DockerHub username instead of `$DOCKER_HUB_USER`):

   ```
   $ docker tag 54529c0ebed7 $DOCKER_HUB_USER/rest-example
   ```

3. The final step will be to push our image to Docker Hub using the `docker push` command:

   ```
   $ docker push $DOCKER_HUB_USER/rest-example
   ```

4. Now that we have an image available in the registry, we need a deployment manifest. It's again a `.yaml` file, which can look the same as this:

```
apiVersion: extensions/v1beta1
kind: Deployment
metadata:
  name: rest-example
spec:
  replicas: 1
  template:
    metadata:
      labels:
        app: rest-example
        tier: backend
    spec:
      containers:
      - name: rest-example
        image: jotka/rest-example
        imagePullPolicy: IfNotPresent
        resources:
          requests:
            cpu: 100m
            memory: 100Mi
        env:
        - name: GET_HOSTS_FROM
          value: dns
        ports:
        - containerPort: 8080
```

To create this deployment on the cluster using `kubectl`, you will need to execute the following command, which is exactly the same as when creating a service, with a difference in the filename:

```
$ kubectl create -f deployment.yml
```

You can look at the deployment properties with:

```
$ kubectl describe deployment rest-service
```

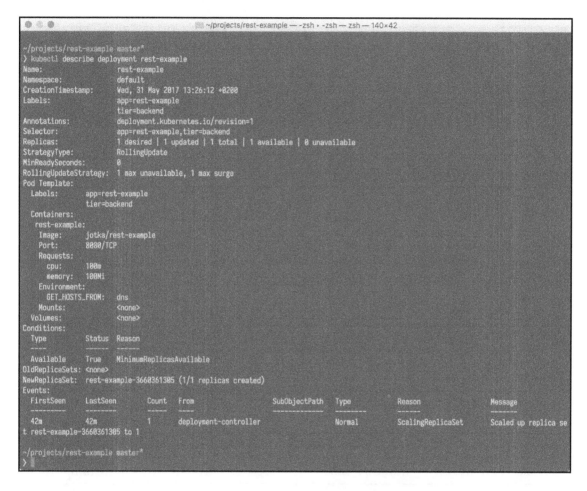

As you can see, one Pod has been created along with a ReplicaSet and the default rolling update strategy. You can also look at the Pods with:

```
$ kubectl get pods
```

The output of `get pods` command will give you the names of Pods running in the deployment. This is will be important later, because if you want to interact with a specific Pod, you will need to know its name:

```
● ● ●                    ~/projects/rest-example — -zsh ‣ -zsh — zsh — 140×8
~/projects/rest-example master*
⟩ kubectl get pods
NAME                                READY   STATUS    RESTARTS   AGE
rest-example-3660361305-gkzb8       1/1     Running   0          3m

~/projects/rest-example master*
⟩
```

As an alternative to the deployment descriptor in `.yaml` file, you can create deployments from the command line using `kubectl run` command with options, as you can see in the following example:

```
$ kubectl run rest-example --image=jotka/rest-example --replicas=1 --
port=8080 --labels="app:rest-example;tier:backend" --expose
```

Let's summarize the `kubectl` commands related to creating resources and getting information about them, with some examples, in a table:

| Example command | Meaning |
| --- | --- |
| `kubectl create -f ./service.yaml` | Create resource(s) |
| `kubectl create -f ./service.yaml -f ./deployment.yaml` | Create from multiple files |
| `kubectl create -f ./dir` | Create resource(s) in all manifest files in the specified directory |
| `kubectl create -f https://sampleUrl` | Create resource(s) from URL |
| `kubectl run nginx --image=nginx` | Start a single instance of nginx |
| `Kubectl get pods` | Get the documentation for `pod` |
| `kubectl get pods --selector=app=rest-example` | List all the Pods that match the specified label `selector` |
| `kubectl explain pods` | Show details of all Pods |
| `kubectl get services` | List all created services |
| `kubectl explain service` | Show details of specified service |

| `kubectl explain services` | Show details of all created services |
|---|---|
| `kubectl get deployments` | List all created deployments |
| `kubectl get deployment` | Show details of specified service |
| `kubectl explain deployment` | Show details of specified deployment |
| `kubectl explain deployments` | Show details of all created deployments |
| `kubectl get nodes` | List all cluster nodes |
| `kubectl explain node` | Show details of specified node |

## Calling the service

As we have seen on the `kubectl` describe service `rest-example` command output, our `rest-example service` can be accessed within the cluster via port `8080` and the domain name `rest-example`. In our case, the complete URL of the endpoint would be `http://rest-example:8080`. However, to be able to execute the service from the outside world, we have used the `NodePort` mapping, and we know that it was given the port `31141`. All we need to call the service is the IP of the cluster. We can get it using the following command:

```
$ minikube ip
```

There's a shortcut for getting to know the externally accessible service URL and a port number. We can use a `minikube service` command to tell us the exact service address:

```
$ minikube service rest-example --url
```

The output of the previous command will be the service URL with a mapped port number. If you skip the `--url` switch, `minikube` will just open the service's URL using your default web browser. This is sometimes handy.

Having the complete URL of the endpoint, we can access the service, using any of the HTTP clients, such as curl, for example:

```
● ● ●                          ~/projects/rest-example — -zsh • -zsh — zsh — 140×8
~/projects/rest-example master*
> curl "http://192.168.99.100:31141/books" -H "Content-Type: application/json"

[{"id":1,"author":"John Doe","title":"The Great Book"}]
~/projects/rest-example master*
>
```

When the service is running, application logs can often help you understand what is happening inside your cluster. The logs are particularly useful for debugging problems and monitoring cluster activity. Let's see how we can access our container logs.

# Interacting with containers and viewing logs

Most modern applications have some kind of logging mechanism. Our Java REST service, for example, uses slf4j to output logs from the REST controller. The easiest and most simple logging method for containerized applications is just to write to the standard output and standard error streams. Kubernetes supports this out of the box.

Assuming we've sent requests to our new web service using the browser or curl, we should now be able to see some logs. Prior to that, we need to have a Pods name, created automatically during deployment. To get the Pod's name, use the kubectl get pods command. After that, you can show logs of the specified Pod:

```
$ kubectl logs rest-example-3660361385-gkzb8
```

As you can see in the following screenshot, we will get access to a well-known Spring Boot banner coming from a service running in a Pod:

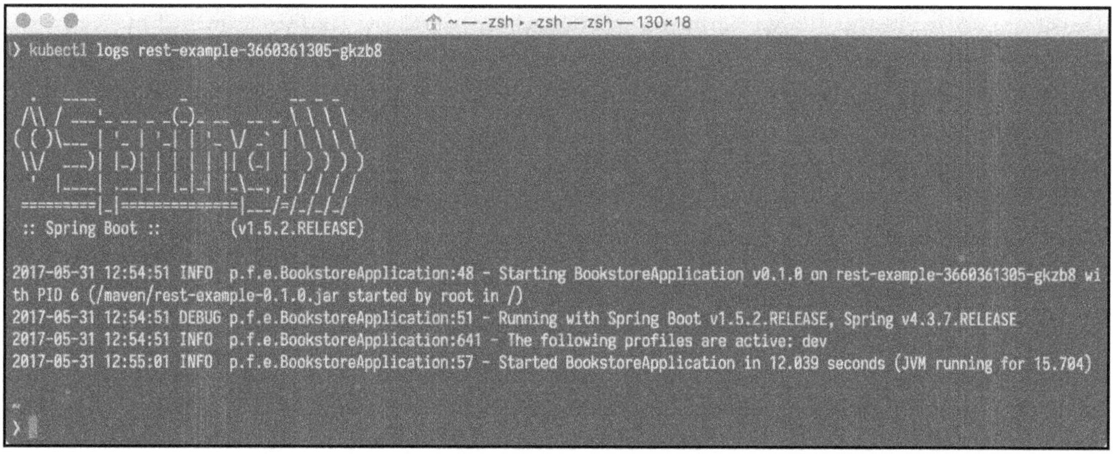

Viewing the log is not the only thing we can do with a specific Pod. Similar to Docker (a Pod is running Docker, actually), we can interact with a container by using the `kubectl exec` command. For example, to get a shell to the running container:

```
$ kubectl exec -it rest-example-3660361385-gkzb8 -- /bin/bash
```

The previous command will attach your shell console into the shell in the running container, where you can interact with it, such as listing the processes, for example, as you can see in the following screenshot:

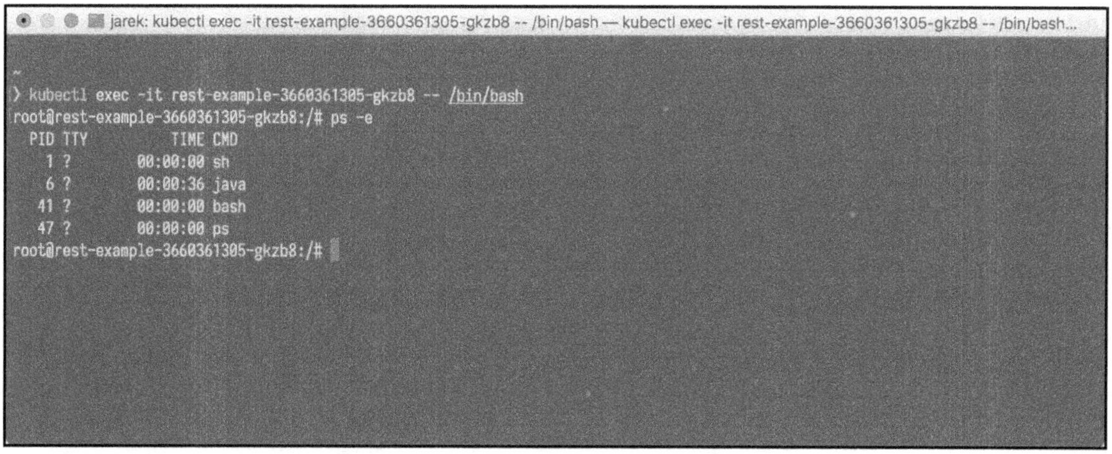

The syntax of a `kubectl exec` command is very similar to the `exec` command in Docker, with one little difference, as you remember from the Chapter 7, *Introduction to Kubernetes*, a Pod can run more than one container. In such case, we can use `--container` or `-c` command switch to specify a container in the `kubectl exec` command. For example, let's suppose we have a Pod named `rest-example-3660361385-gkzb8`. This Pod has two containers named service and database. The following command would open a shell to the service container:

```
$ kubectl exec -it rest-example-3660361385-gkzb8 --container service --
/bin/bash
```

Having the possibility to view logs and interact with the containers gives you a lot of flexibility to pinpoint potential problems you may have with running Pods. Let's summarize the `kubectl` commands related to viewing logs and interacting with the Pods in a table:

| Example command | Meaning |
| --- | --- |
| `kubectl logs myPod` | Dump `pod` logs (`stdout`) |
| `kubectl logs myPod -c myContainer` | Dump `pod` container logs (`stdout`, multi-container case) |
| `kubectl logs -f myPod` | Stream `pod` logs (`stdout`) |
| `kubectl logs -f myPod -c myContainer` | Stream `pod` container logs (`stdout`, multi-container case) |
| `kubectl run -i --tty busybox --image=busybox -- sh` | `run` `pod` as interactive shell |
| `kubectl attach myPod -i` | Attach to running container |
| `kubectl port-forward myPod 8080:8090` | Forward port 8080 of Pod to your to 8090 on your local machine |
| `kubectl exec myPod -- ls /` | `run` command in existing `pod` (one container case) |
| `kubectl exec myPod -c myContainer -- ls /` | `run` command in existing `pod` (multi-container case) |
| `kubectl top pod POD_NAME --containers` | Show metrics for a given `pod` and its containers |

As you already know, Pods and containers are fragile. They can crash or be killed. You can use kubectl logs to retrieve logs from a previous instantiation of a container with the -- previous flag, in case the container has crashed. Let's say our service is running fine, but for the reasons described in the Chapter 7, *Introduction to Kubernetes*, such as higher load, for example, you decide to increase the number of containers running. Kubernetes gives you the possibility to increase the number of Pod instances running in each service. This can be done manually or automatically. Let's focus on the manual scaling first.

# Scaling manually

When the deployment has been created, the new ReplicaSet has also been created, automatically. As you will remember from Chapter 7, *Introduction to Kubernetes*, a ReplicaSet ensures that a specified number of Pod clones, known as replicas, are running at any given time. It there are too many, some of them will be shut down. If there is a need for more, for example if some of them died because of an error or crash, new Pods will be created. Note that if you try to scale the ReplicaSet directly, then it will (for a very short time) have a new count of your desired number of Pods, for example three. But if the deployment controller sees that you have modified the replica set to three, since it knows that it is supposed to be one (defined in the deployment manifest), it will reset it back to one. By manually modifying the replica set that was created for you, you are, kind of, dealing against the system controller.

 You need to scale your deployment instead of the replica set directly.

Of course, our Java rest-example service keeps its data in memory so it's not stateless, so it may be not the best example for scaling; if another instance is brought to life, it will have its own data. However, it is a Kubernetes service, so we can use it to demonstrate scaling anyway. To scale up our rest-example deployment from one up to three Pods, execute the following kubectl scale command:

```
$ kubectl scale deployment rest-example --replicas=3
```

After a short while, in order to check, execute the following commands, you will see that now three Pods are running in the deployment:

```
$ kubectl get deployments
$ kubectl get pods
```

In the following table, you can see some more examples of `kubectl` commands related to manual scaling:

| Example command | Meaning |
| --- | --- |
| `kubectl scale deployment rest-example --replicas=3` | Scale a deployment named `rest-example` to 3 Pods |
| `kubectl scale --replicas=3 -f deployment.yaml` | Scale a resource specified in `deployment.yaml` file to 3 |
| `kubectl scale deployment rest-example --current-replicas=2 --replicas=3` | If the deployment named `rest-example` current size is 2, scale it to 3 Pods |
| `kubectl scale --replicas=5 deployment/foo deployment/bar` | Scale multiple deployments at one time |

Scaling can be done automatically by Kubernetes, if, for example, the service load increases.

# Autoscaling

With horizontal Pod auto scaling, Kubernetes automatically scales the number of Pods in a deployment or ReplicaSet based on observed CPU utilization. The Kubernetes controller periodically adjusts the number of Pod `replicas` in a deployment to match the observed average CPU utilization to the target you specified.

The Horizontal Auto Scaler is just another type of resource in Kubernetes, so we can create it as any other resource, using the `kubectl` commands:

- `kubectl get hpa`: List autoscalers
- `kubectl describe hpa`: Get detailed description
- `kubectl delete hpa`: Delete an autoscaler

Additionally, there is a special `kubectl autoscale` command for easy creation of a Horizontal Pod Autoscaler. An example could be:

```
$ kubectl autoscale deployment rest-example --cpu-percent=50 --min=1 --max=10
```

The previous command will create an autoscaler for our `rest-example` deployment, with the target CPU utilization set to 50% and the number of `replicas` between 1 and 10.

All cluster events are being registered, including those which come from scaling, either manually or automatically. Viewing cluster events can be helpful when monitoring what exactly is being performed on our cluster.

# Viewing cluster events

To view cluster events, type the following command:

```
$ kubectl get events
```

It will present a huge table, with all the events registered on the cluster:

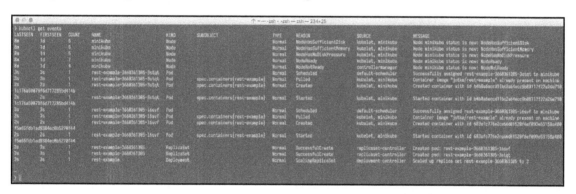

The table will include the changes in the status of nodes, pulling Docker images, events of starting and stopping containers, and so on. It can be very handy to see the picture of the whole cluster.

# Using the Kubernetes dashboard

Kubernetes dashboard is a general purpose, web-based UI for Kubernetes clusters. It allows users to manage applications running in the cluster and troubleshoot them, as well as manage the cluster itself. We can also edit the manifest files of deployment, services, or Pods. The changes will be picked up immediately by Kubernetes, so it gives us the capability to scale down or up the deployment, for example.

If you open the dashboard with the `minikube dashboard` command, it will open your default browser with a dashboard URL. From here, you can list all the resources on the cluster, such as deployments, services, Pods, and so on. Our dashboard is no longer empty, as you can see in the following screenshot; we have one deployment called `rest-example`:

If you click on its name, you will be taken to the deployment details page, which will show the same information you could get with the `kubectl describe deployment` command, with a nice UI:

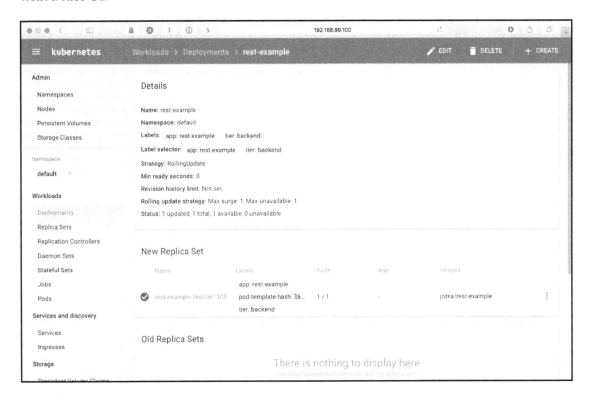

The dashboard is not only read-only utility. Each resource has a handy menu which you can use to delete it or to edit its manifest:

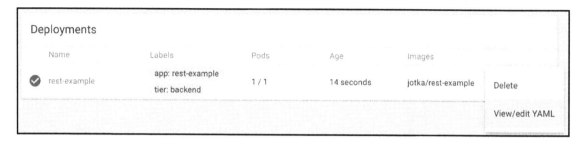

If you pick the **view/edit YAML** menu option, you will be able to edit the manifest with a handy editor:

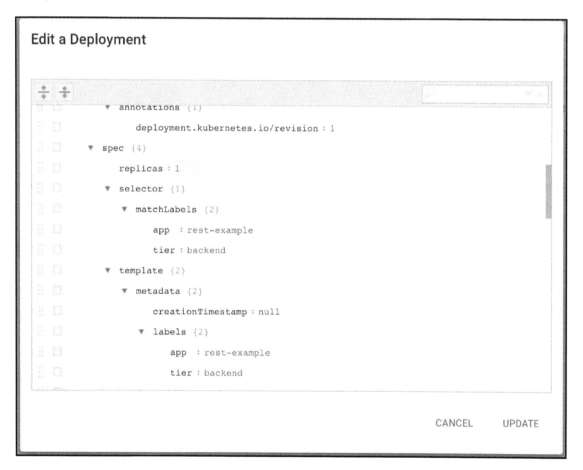

Note that if you change a value, for example the number of `replicas`, and click **Update**, the change will be sent to the Kubernetes and executed. This way you can also, for example, scale your deployment.

As deployment has created a ReplicaSet automatically, the ReplicaSet will also be visible in the dashboard:

The same applies to services. If you browse to the **Services** menu, it will present a list of all services created on a cluster:

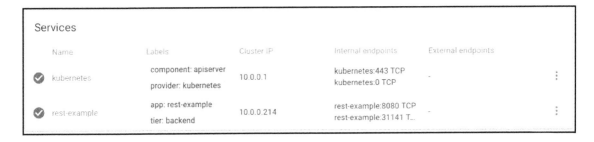

Clicking on the name of service will take you to the details page:

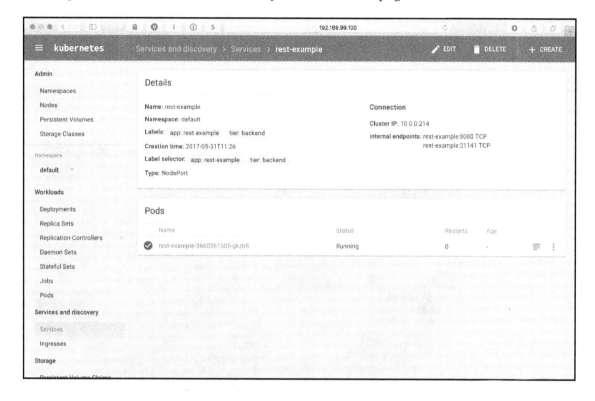

On the details screen, all important information is listed. This includes label selector, that will be used to find Pods, port type, cluster IP, internal endpoints, and of course the list of Pods running inside the service. By clicking Pod's name, you can see details of a running Pod, including its log output, as you can see in the following screenshot:

The dashboard is a very handy tool to interact with your existing deployments, services, and Pods. But there's more. If you click on the **Create** button in the top right corner of the dashboard's toolbar, you will be presented with a **Deploy a Containerized App** screen. From here, you can actually create a new deployment:

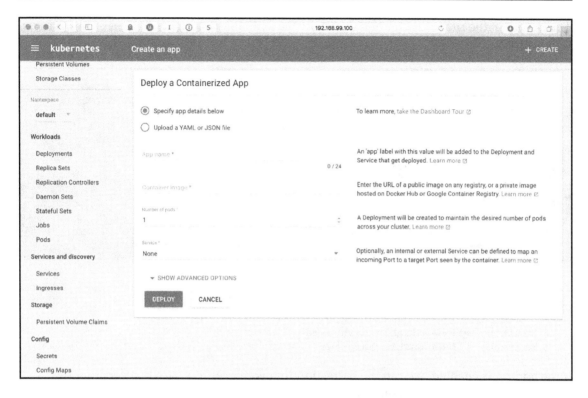

You have an opportunity to use the .yaml file, as we did before using the command line, but also you can specify details of the deployment manually, providing an application name, and container image to use and optionally create a service for the deployment. Quite handy, isn't it? The dashboard is just one of the Minikube add-ons available. Let's look at what else we have at our disposal.

# Minikube addons

Minikube comes with several add-ons, such as Kubernetes dashboard, Kubernetes DNS, and so on. We can list the available addons by executing the following command:

```
$ minikube addons list
```

The output of the previous command will list the available addons with their current status, for example:

```
  ● ● ●                    ⬆ ~ — -zsh ‣ -zsh — zsh — 104×12
~
❭ minikube addons list
- kube-dns: enabled
- heapster: enabled
- ingress: disabled
- registry-creds: disabled
- addon-manager: enabled
- dashboard: enabled
- default-storageclass: enabled

~
❭ ▌
```

To enable or disable the addon, we use `minikube addons disable` or `minikube addons enable`, respectively, for example:

```
$ minikube addons disable dashboard
$ minikube addons enable heapster
```

If the add-on is enabled, we can the corresponding web user interface by executing the `addon open` command, for example:

```
$ minikube addons open heapster
```

# Cleaning up

If you finish playing with your deployment and services or would like to start from the beginning, you can do some cluster cleaning by removing the deployment or services:

```
$ kubectl delete deployment rest-example
$ kubectl delete service rest-example
```

This code can also be combined in one command, for example:

```
$ kubectl delete service,deployment rest-example
```

The `kubectl delete` supports label `selectors` and namespaces. Let's see some other examples of the command in a table:

| Example command | Meaning |
|---|---|
| `kubectl delete pod,service baz foo` | Delete pods and services with same names `baz` and `foo` |
| `kubectl delete pods,services -l name=myLabel` | Delete pods and services with label `name=myLabel` |
| `kubectl -n my-ns delete po,svc --all` | Delete all pods and services in namespace `my-ns` |

To stop the `minikube` cluster, issue simply:

```
$ minikube stop
```

If you would like to delete the current `minikube` cluster, you can issue the following command to do it:

```
$ minikube delete
```

# Summary

As you can see, the Minikube is an easy way to try out Kubernetes and use it for local development. Running the local cluster is not as scary as it may have seemed at the beginning. Best of all, the local `minikube` cluster is a valid Kubernetes cluster. If you get to know Kubernetes by playing with it locally, you will be able to deploy your applications in the real cloud without any issues. Let's summarize the steps that we need to perform to make our Java application run on the Kubernetes cluster.

First, we need to write some code for our microservice. This can be based on whatever you want, it can be a microservice running on Tomcat, JBoss, or Spring Bootstrap. It doesn't matter, you just choose the technology you want your software to run with:

- Next, put the code into Docker image. You can do it by hand by creating a Dockerfile or you can use Docker Maven plugin to automate this
- Create Kubernetes metadata, such as deployment manifest and service manifest
- Apply the metadata by rolling out the deployment and creating the service
- Scale your applications to your needs
- Manage your cluster either from the command line or from the dashboard

In `Chapter 9`, *Working with Kubernetes API*, we will take a look at the Kubernetes API. This is a great way of interacting with Kubernetes cluster. Because of API, the possibilities are almost endless, you can create your own development flows, such as continuous delivery using Jenkins, for example. Having the API, you are not limited only to existing tools to deploy your software to Kubernetes. Things can get more interesting.

# 9
# Working with the Kubernetes API

In Chapter 7, *Introduction to Kubernetes*, and Chapter 8, *Using Kubernetes with Java*, we learned about the Kubernetes concepts and used them in practice by installing local Kubernetes clusters with minikube. We know all the pieces of Kubernetes architecture, such as pods, nodes, deployment, and services, for example. We have also mentioned one of the main components residing on the Master node, which is the API server. As you remember from Chapter 7, *Introduction to Kubernetes*, the API server is technically a process named kube-apiserver that accepts and responds to HTTP REST requests using JSON. The API server's main purpose is to validate and process data of cluster resources, such as Pods, services, or deployments. The API Server is the central management entity. It's also the only Kubernetes component that directly connects to etcd, a distributed key-value data store where Kubernetes stores all its cluster state.

In previous chapters, we've been using a kubectl command-line tool to manage our cluster. Kubectl is a useful utility, whenever we want to execute commands against our cluster, either for creating, editing, or removing resources. In fact kubectl also communicates with the API server; you may have noticed that almost every action in Kubernetes that changes something is basically editing a resource. If you want to scale up or down your application, this will be done by modifying the deployment resource. Kubernetes will pick up the change on the fly and apply it to the resource. Also, read-only operations such as listing Pods or deployments, will execute the corresponding GET request.

In fact, you can see what REST calls are being made by the kubectl command if you run it with a higher level of verbosity, with the --v=6 or --v=9 option, we will get back to it later in this chapter. We can access the API using kubectl, client libraries, or by making REST requests. When can the REST API be useful? Well, you can create a REST call in every programming or scripting language. This creates a whole new level of flexibility, you can manage Kubernetes from your own Java application, from your continuous delivery flow in Jenkins, or from the build tool you are using, let it be Maven for example. Possibilities are almost endless. In this chapter, we will get to know the API overview, its structure, and example requests. We will be doing this using the REST calls with the command-line curl utility. This chapter will cover the following topics:

- Explanation about the API versioning
- Authentication (determining who is who)
- Authorization (determining who can do what)
- Using the API by making some example calls
- OpenAPI Swagger documentation

Let's gets started with an API overview.

# API versioning

Kubernetes grows continuously. Its features change and this results in the API changing as well. To deal with those changes and to not break compatibility with existing clients over an extended period of time, Kubernetes supports multiple API versions, each with a different API path, such as /api/v1 or /apis/extensions/v1beta1. There are three API levels in the Kubernetes API specification: alpha, beta, and stable. Let's get to know the difference.

# Alpha

The alpha version level is disabled by default, as with the other software, an alpha version should be considered as buggy and not production ready. Also, you should note that any featured introduced in the alpha version might not always be available later, in the stable version. Also, the changes in the API may be incompatible in the next release. You should not use the alpha version, unless you are very eager to test new features or do some experiments.

# Beta

The beta level totally different from the `alpha` level of the API, code is tested (it still may have some bugs, as it is still not the `stable` release). Also, in contrast to the `alpha` level, features in `beta` will not be dropped in the future releases. If there is a breaking, not backward compatible change in the API, Kubernetes team will provide a guide on how to migrate. Using `beta` on a production environment is not the best idea, but you can safely use `beta` on a non-business critical cluster. You are also encouraged to provide feedback from using `beta`, this will make Kubernetes better for everyone of us using it. A version name in the `beta` level will contain the word `beta`, such as `v1beta1` for example.

# Stable

The stable level of the API is a tested, production-ready software. The version name in the stable API will be `vX` where `X` is an integer number, such as `v1` for example.

Kubernetes API utilizes a concept of API groups. API groups have been introduced to make it easier to extend the Kubernetes API in the future. The API group is specified in a `REST` path and in the `apiVersion` field of a call's JSON payload. Currently, there are several API groups in use: core, batch, and extensions. The group name is a part of the `REST` path of an API call: `/apis/$GROUP_NAME/$VERSION`. The core group is an exception, it does not show up in the `REST` path, for example: `/api/v1`. You can find the full list of supported API groups in the Kubernetes API reference.

By using the API, you can do almost anything with your cluster, as you would normally do using the `kubectl` command. This can be dangerous; that's why Kubernetes supports authentication (determining who you are) and authorization (what you can do). The basic flow of calling the API service is presented in the following diagram:

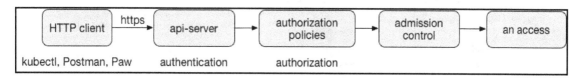

Let's begin with the authentication.

# Authentication

By default, the Kubernetes API server serves HTTP requests on two ports:

- **Localhost, unsecured port**: By default, the IP address is localhost and a port number is 8080. There is no TLS communication, all requests on this port bypasses authentication and authorization plugins. This is intended for testing and bootstrap, and for other components of the master node. This is also used to other Kubernetes components such as scheduler or controller-manager to execute API calls. You can change the port number with the --insecure-port switch, and the default IP by using the --insecure-bind-address command-line switch.

- **Secure port**: The default port number is 6443 (it can be changed with the ` --secure-port switch), usually it's 443 on Cloud providers. It uses TLS communication. A certificate can be set with a --tls-cert-file switch. A private SSL key can be provided with a --tls-private-key-file switch. All requests coming through this port will be handled by authentication and authorization modules and admission control modules. You should use the secure port whenever possible. By having your API clients verify the TLS certificate presented by the api-server, they can verify that the connection is both encrypted and not susceptible to man-in-the-middle attacks. You should also be running the api-server where the insecure port is only accessible to localhost, so that connections that come across the network use HTTP's.

- With minikube, to access the API server directly, you'll need to use the custom SSL certs that have been generated by minikube. The client certificate and key are typically stored in ~/.minikube/apiserver.crt and ~/.minikube/apiserver.key. You'll have to load them into your HTTP'S client when you make HTTP requests. If you're using curl use the --cert and the --key options to use the cert and key file.

> The access to the API server can be simplified through the proxy, which we will start later in this chapter.

If you want to send requests to the Kubernetes API from a different domain, you will need to enable cors on api-server. You do that by adding a --cors-allowed-origins=["http://*"] argument to kube-apiserver configuration, typically in the /etc/default/kube-apiserver file and restart kube-apiserver.

Note that Kubernetes cluster does not manage users by itself. Instead, users are assumed to be managed by an outside, independent service. There is no resource in Kubernetes cluster that represents normal user accounts. That's why users cannot be added to a cluster through an API call.

 Kubernetes does not manage user accounts by itself.

The Kubernetes API supports multiple forms of authentication: HTTP basic auth, bearer token, and client certificates. They are called authentication strategies. When launching the api-server, you can enable or disable each of these authentication strategies with command-line flags. Let's look what's possible, starting with the simplest, basic auth strategy.

# HTTP basic auth

To use this authentication strategy, you will need to start the api-server with the --basic-auth-file=<path_to_auth_file> switch. It should be a csv file with the following entry for each user:

```
password, user name, userid
```

You can also specify an optional fourth column containing group names, separated by a comma. If there is more than one group for the user, the whole column contents must be enclosed in double quotes, for example:

```
password, user, userid, "group1,group2,group3"
```

If the api-server utilizes the basic auth strategy, it will expect all REST calls to be made with the Authorization header containing username and password encoded in BASE64 (similar to ordinary basic auth protected web calls), for example:

```
BASE64ENCODED (USER:PASSWORD)
```

To generate the authorization header value, you can use the following command in the shell, it will generate the value for user having password secret:

```
echo -n "user:secret" | base64
```

Note that any changes to the basic `auth` file will require a restart of the `api-server` to pick up the changes.

`HTTP` basic auth is typically used as default when running Kubernetes in the cloud. For example, once you launch your container cluster on Google Container Engine, you will have a master running the `api-server` on a VM in your GCP project. If you run a `gcloud preview container clusters` list, you will see the endpoint at which the `api-server` listens for requests as well as the credentials needed to access it. You will find more on running Kubernetes in the cloud in `Chapter 10`, *Deploying Java on Kubernetes in the Cloud*.

# Static token file

To make `api-server` use this scheme, it needs to be started with the `--token-auth-file=<PATH_TO_TOKEN_FILE>` switch. Similar to the `HTTP` basic auth strategy, the provided file is a `csv` file with a record for every user. The record needs to be in the following format:

```
token, user, userid, group
```

Again, the group name is optional and if there is more than one group for the user, you will need to separate them with a comma and enclose them in double quotes. The token is just a `base64` encoded string. An example command to generate a token on Linux can be as follows:

```
$ echo `dd if=/dev/urandom bs=128 count=1 2>/dev/null | base64 | tr -d
"=+/" | dd bs=32 count=1 2>/dev/null`
```

The output will be a token, which you then enter into the `token` file, for example:

```
3XQ8W6IAourkXOLH2yfpbGFXftbH0vn,default,default
```

When using this strategy, `api-server` will be expecting an `Authorization` header with a value of `Bearer <TOKEN>`. In our example, this will looks the same as the following:

```
Authorization: Bearer 3XQ8W6IAourkXOLH2yfpbGFXftbH0vn
```

Tokens last indefinitely, and the token list cannot be changed without restarting API server.

# Client certificates

In order to use this scheme, the `api-server` needs to be started with the following switch:

```
--client-ca-file=<PATH_TO_CA_CERTIFICATE_FILE>
```

The `CA_CERTIFICATE_FILE` must contain one or more certificates authorities that can be used to validate client certificates presented to the `api-server`. The /CN (common name) of the client certificate is used as the username. Client certificates can also indicate a user's group memberships using the organization fields. To include multiple group memberships for a user you will need to include multiple organization fields in the certificate. For example, using the `openssl` command-line tool to generate a certificate signing request:

```
$ openssl req -new -key user.pem -out user-csr.pem \
-subj "/CN=user/O=group1/O=group2"
```

This would create a certificate signing request for the username `user`, belonging to two groups, `group1` and `group2`.

# OpenID

OpenID connect 1.0 is a simple identity layer on top of the OAuth 2.0 protocol. You can read more about OpenID connect on the internet at `https://openid.net/connect`. It allows clients to verify the identity of the end-user based on the authentication performed by an authorization server, as well as to obtain basic profile information about the end-user in an interoperable and REST-like manner. All cloud providers, including Azure, Amazon, and Google support OpenID. The main difference with `OAuth2` is the additional field returned with the access token called an `id_token`. This token is a **JSON Web Token (JWT)** with well-known fields (user's email for example), signed by the server. To identify the user, the authenticator uses the `id_token` from the `OAuth2token` response as a bearer token. To use the OpenID authentication, you will need to log in to your identity provider, which will provide you with an `id_token` (and also standard OAuth 2.0 `access_token` and a `refresh_token`).

Since all of the data needed to do the authentication is contained within the `id_token`, Kubernetes does not need to make an additional call to the identity provider. This is very important from the scalability purposes, every request is stateless.

To provide a token value to the `kubectl` command, you will need to use the `--token` flag. Alternatively, you can add it directly to your `kubeconfig` file.

This is the simplified flow of things that will happen if you execute a `HTTP` call to your `api-server`:

- `kubectl` will send your `id_token` in an `authorization` header to the API server
- The API server will validate the JWT signature by checking against the certificate named in the configuration
- The API server will check to make sure the `id_token` hasn't expired
- The API server will make sure the user is authorized, and returns a response to `kubectl` if so

By default, anyone who has access credentials to the `api-server` has full access to the cluster. You can also configure more fine grained authorization policies, let's look at authorization now.

# Authorization

The next step after the successful authentication is to check what operations are allowed for the authenticated user. Kubernetes supports four types of authorization policy schemes as of today. To utilize the specific authorization schema, use the `--authorization-mode` switch when starting `api-server`. The syntax is:

```
$ kube-apiserver --authorization-mode <mode>
```

The `<mode>` parameter contains an ordered list of authorization plugins that Kubernetes is supposed to authenticate users with. When multiple authentication plugins are enabled, the first one that will successfully authenticate the request will make Kubernetes skip executing all remaining plugins.

The default authorization mode is `AlwaysAllow`, which allows all requests.

The following authorization schemes are supported:

- Attribute-based control
- Role-based control
- Webhook
- `AlwaysDeny`
- `AlwaysAllow`

Let's describe them, one by one, briefly.

# Attribute-based access control

**Attribute-Based Access Control (ABAC)** policy will be used if you start the `api-server` with the `--authorization-mode=ABAC` option. This policy uses local files in which you can, in a flexible way, define permission every user should have. There is an additional option to provide a policy file: `--authorization-policy-file`, so the complete syntax to use this policy will be:

```
$ kube-apiserver --authorization-mode=ABAC \
--authorization-policy-file=<PATH_TO_ POLICY_FILE>
```

Note that any changes to policy file will require a restart of the `api-server`.

As you remember from `Chapter 7`, *Introduction to Kubernetes*, Kubernetes clusters use the concept of namespaces to group related resources, such as Pods, deployments, or services. The authorization schemas in the `api-server`'s make use of these namespaces. The `ABAC` policy file syntax is rather clear and readable. Each entry is a JSON object describing the authorization rule. Consider the following entry in the policy file, which gives user `john` complete access to the namespace `myApp`:

```
{
    "apiVersion": "abac.authorization.kubernetes.io/v1beta1",
    "kind": "Policy",
    "spec": {
        "user":"john",
        "namespace": "myApp",
        "resource": "*",
        "apiGroup": "*",
        "nonResourcePath": "*"
    }
}
```

The next example will give user `admin` complete access to all the namespaces:

```
{
    "apiVersion": "abac.authorization.kubernetes.io/v1beta1",
    "kind": "Policy",
    "spec":{
        "user":"admin",
        "namespace": "*",
    "resource": "*",
    "apiGroup": "*",
    "nonResourcePath": "*"
    }
}
```

And finally, an example that gives all users read-only access to the entire cluster:

```
{
    "apiVersion": "abac.authorization.kubernetes.io/v1beta1",
    "kind": "Policy",
    "spec": {
        "user":"*",
        "namespace": "*",
        "resource": "*",
        "apiGroup": "*",
        "nonResourcePath": "*",
        "readonly":true
    }
}
```

# Role-based access control (RBAC)

The **Role-Based Access Control** (**RBAC**), policy implementation is deeply integrated into Kubernetes. In fact, Kubernetes uses it internally for the system components, to grant the permissions necessary for them to function. RBAC is 100% API driven, roles and bindings are API resources that an administrator can write and create on the cluster such as other resources such as Pods, deployments, or services. Enabling RBAC mode is as easy as passing a flag to `kube-apiserver`:

```
--authorization-mode=RBAC
```

This mode allows you to create and store policies using the Kubernetes API. In the RBAC API, a set of permission is represented by the concept of role. There is a distinction between namespace roles, represented by a `Role` resource, and a whole cluster role, represented by a `ClusterRole` resource. A `ClusterRole` can define the same all permissions a `Role` can define, but also some cluster-related permission, such as managing cluster nodes or modifying resources across all available namespaces. Note that once RBAC is enabled, every aspect of the API is disallowed access.

Permissions are additive; there are no deny rules.

This is an example of role that gives the whole set of available permissions to all operations on all resources:

```
apiVersion: rbac.authorization.k8s.io/v1beta1
metadata:
  name: cluster-writer
rules:
  - apiGroups: ["*"]
    resources: ["*"]
    verbs: ["*"]
    nonResourceURLs: ["*"]
```

The Role is a resource, as you remember from Chapter 8, *Using Kubernetes with Java*, to create resource using the file, you execute the `kubectl create` command, for example:

```
$ kubectl create -f cluster-writer.yml
```

A `Role` and `ClusterRole` defines the set of permissions, but does not assign them to users or groups directly. There is another resource for that in Kubernetes API, which is `RoleBinding` or `ClusterRoleBinding`. They bind `Role` or `ClusterRole` to the specific subject, which can be user, group, or service user. To bind the `Role` or `ClusterRole`, you will need to execute the `kubectl create rolebinding` command. Take a look at the following examples. To grant the `adminClusterRole` to a user named `john` in the namespace `myApp`:

```
$ kubectl create rolebinding john-admin-binding \
--clusterrole=admin --user=john --namespace=myApp
```

The next one will grant the `cluster-admin ClusterRole` to a user named `admin` across the entire cluster:

```
$ kubectl create clusterrolebinding admin-cluster-admin-binding \
--clusterrole=cluster-admin --user=admin
```

The equivalent YAML file to use with `kubectl create -f` will be as follows:

```
apiVersion: rbac.authorization.k8s.io/v1beta1
kind: ClusterRoleBinding
metadata:
  name: admin-cluster-admin-binding
roleRef:
  apiGroup: rbac.authorization.k8s.io
  kind: ClusterRole
  name cluster-admin
subjects:
- kind: User
  name: admin
```

# WebHook

When the `api-server` is started with the `--authorization-mode=Webhook` option, it will make calls to external HTTP server to authorize the user. This gives you the capability to create your own authorization servers. In other words, a WebHook is an HTTP callback mode that allows you to manage authorization using a remote REST server, either developed on your own, or a third-party authorization server.

When doing the authorization check, the `api-server` will execute a HTTP POST request, with a JSON payload containing a serialized `api.authorization.v1beta1.SubjectAccessReview` object. This object describes the user making request to the `api-server`, the action which this user would like to execute, and the details about the resource being the subject of this action. An example request payload could look like the following example:

```
{
    "apiVersion": "authorization.k8s.io/v1beta1",
    "kind": "SubjectAccessReview",
    "spec": {
      "resourceAttributes": {
        "namespace": "rest-example",
        "verb": "get",
        "resource": "pods"
      },
      "user": "john",
      "group": [
        "group1",
        "group2"
      ]
    }
}
```

The remote authorization server should provide a response, saying if this user is authorized to execute the specified action on a specified resource. The response should contain the `SubjectAccessReviewStatus` field, specifying if the `api-server` should either allow or disallow access. A permissive JSON response would looks the same as the this:

```
{
    "apiVersion": "authorization.k8s.io/v1beta1",
    "kind": "SubjectAccessReview",
    "status": {
      "allowed": true
    }
}
```

The negative response will appear as in the following example:

```
{
  "apiVersion": "authorization.k8s.io/v1beta1",
  "kind": "SubjectAccessReview",
  "status": {
    "allowed": false,
    "reason": "user does not have read access to the namespace"
  }
}
```

Having the possibility to delegate the authorization to another service makes the authorization process very flexible, imagine your own software that authorizes a user to do certain things in your cluster depending on the roles they have in the corporate LDAP directory for example.

# AlwaysDeny

This policy denies all requests. If will be used if you start the api-server with a --authorization-mode=AlwaysDeny switch. This can be useful if you are doing some testing or would like to block incoming requests without actually stopping the api-server.

# AlwaysAllow

If you start the api-server with --authorization-mode=AlwaysAllow, all requests will be accepted, without using any authorization schema. Use this flag only if you do not require authorization for your API requests.

As you can see, the authentication and authorization possibilities in Kubernetes are very flexible. On the diagram at the beginning of this chapter we have seen the third phase of the API call flow: the admission control. What role does the admission control play? Let's find out.

# Admission control

An admission control plug-in intercepts requests to the Kubernetes API server after the request is authenticated and authorized, but prior to making any changes to the API resource. These plug-ins run in sequence, before a request is accepted into the cluster. The Kubernetes API server supports a flag, `admission-control` that takes a comma-delimited, ordered list of admission control plugins.

Now that we have an overview of how the API call looks the same, let's actually make some use of it.

# Using the API

The API reference is a detailed document, available on the internet `https://kubernetes.io/docs/api-reference/v1.6/;` of course the API version will change in the future, v1.6 was the current one at the time of writing.

Before we make some actual calls to the `api-server`, it's worth knowing that `kubectl` also communicates with Kubernetes cluster using the API. As we mentioned earlier, you can see what `REST` calls are being made by the `kubectl` command. Looking at what's being sent to the server during the usage of `kubectl` is a great way to become familiar with Kubernetes API.

> To see `REST` requests being executed by `kubectl`, run it with a higher level of verbosity, for example with a `--v=6` or `--v=9` option.

Before we start making actual `REST` calls, let's briefly see what API operations are possible.

# API operations

Kubernetes API defines the CRUD (create, update, read, and delete) set of operations:

- `Create`: Create operations will create the resource in the cluster. The JSON payload that you will need to provide with your `REST` call is the resource manifest. It's the equivalent of the YAML file we've been constructing in the `Chapter 8`, *Using Kubernetes with Java*. This time, it will be in the JSON format.

- `Update`: The update operation can be either `Replace` or `Patch`. A `Replace` will simply replace the whole resource object (a Pod, for example) with the provided spec. A `Patch`, on the other hand, will apply a change only to a specific field.
- `Read`: A read operation can be either `Get`, `List`, or `Watch`. By executing `Get`, you will be given a specific resource object by its name. Executing `List` will retrieve all resource objects of a specific type within a namespace. You can use the selector query. A special form of the `List` operation is `List All Namespaces`, as the name says this will retrieve resources across all namespaces. A `Watch` operation will stream results for an object or a of list objects as they are updated.
- `Delete`: Will simply delete a resource.

Kubernetes `api-server` also exposes some additional, resource-specific operations. This includes `Rollback`, which rollbacks a Pod template to a previous version or read /write scale, which reads or updates the number of replicas for the given resource.

# Example calls

In the following examples, we will be using a command-line `HTTP` client, `curl`. You are not limited to `curl`, you can freely use the `HTTP` client you find convenient. Using the `HTTP` client with the user interface is often very handy, they usually present the `HTTP` response in a structured form and sometimes also do some request validation, if it's well formed. My recommended GUI clients will be Postman (for Windows, Linux, or Mac), or PAW for Mac.

Before making any calls, let's first start a proxy to the Kubernetes API server. The `kubectl` needs to be configured first, to be able to communicate with your cluster. In our local Kubernetes installation with `minikube`, the `kubectl` command will be automatically configured. To start a proxy to the `api-server`, execute the following command:

```
$ kubectl proxy --port=8080
```

While the proxy session is running, any request sent to `localhost:8000` will be forwarded to the Kubernetes API server. To check if our `api-server` is running, let's ask for the API version it supports:

```
$ curl http://localhost:8080/api/
```

If the `api-server` is running and waiting for incoming requests, it should give you an output similar to this one:

```
> curl http://localhost:8080/api/
{
  "kind": "APIVersions",
  "versions": [
    "v1"
  ],
  "serverAddressByClientCIDRs": [
    {
      "clientCIDR": "0.0.0.0/0",
      "serverAddress": "10.0.2.15:8443"
    }
  ]
}
>
```

It seems to be running fine; let's continue and make some use of the exposed API, starting, the same as previously, by creating a service.

# Creating a service using the API

First, let's create a service manifest file. Note that if you have your services, deployments, and Pods created in Chapter 8, *Using Kubernetes with Java*, by using the kubectl, you will need to delete them using kubectl or the Kubernetes dashboard. We are going to use the same names for the service and a deployment. When using curl with larger payloads, it's more convenient to have the payload in the external file and not type it in the command-line. The JSON file that we will use as the payload is very similar to the one we have been using when creating a Pod with kubectl, but in JSON format this time. Let's create a file named service.json:

```
{
  "apiVersion": "v1",
  "kind": "Service",
  "metadata": {
    "name": "rest-example",
    "labels": {
      "app": "rest-example",
      "tier": "backend"
    }
  },
```

```
  "spec": {
    "type": "NodePort",
    "ports": [
      {
        "port": 8080
      }
    ],
    "selector": {
      "app": "rest-example",
      "tier": "backend"
    }
  }
}
```

Note that the contents of the JSON file are basically identical to the one we've been using when we were creating resources using YAML files. Yes, you can clearly see how the `kubectl` command is implemented, it just creates a JSON payload from the file input, there is no magic behind the scenes, at all.

> You can convert between YAML to JSON and vice-versa using one of the YAML/JSON converters available online. The Kubernetes `api-server` will accept such JSON as `kubectl` accepts the YAML file.

Having our JSON file ready, the next step is to create the service resource in our cluster by invoking the following command:

```
$ curl -s http://localhost:8080/api/v1/namespaces/default/services \
-XPOST -H 'Content-Type: application/json' -d@service.json
```

Having our service defined, let's create a deployment.

# Creating a deployment using the API

Creating a deployment is very similar to creating a service, it's creating another type of Kubernetes resource, after all. All we need is a proper JSON payload file that we will be sending to the `api-server` using the `POST HTTP` method. Our `rest-example` deployment manifest in JSON can look as follows:

```
{
  "apiVersion": "extensions/v1beta1",
  "kind": "Deployment",
  "metadata": {
    "name": "rest-example"
  },
```

```
"spec": {
  "replicas": 1,
  "template": {
    "metadata": {
      "labels": {
        "app": "rest-example",
        "tier": "backend"
      }
    },
    "spec": {
      "containers": [
        {
          "name": "rest-example",
          "image": "jotka/rest-example",
          "imagePullPolicy": "IfNotPresent",
          "resources": {
            "requests": {
              "cpu": "100m",
              "memory": "100Mi"
            }
          },
          "env": [
            {
              "name": "GET_HOSTS_FROM",
              "value": "dns"
            }
          ],
          "ports": [
            {
              "containerPort": 8080
            }
          ]
        }
      ]
    }
  }
}
```

Let's save the file using the `deployment.json` filename. Again, all we need to do now is to post this file to the `api-server`. This process is very similar to the creation of the service, it will be just a `POST` to the different endpoint with a different payload. To create a deployment from the shell using `curl`, execute the following command:

```
$ curl -s \
http://localhost:8080/apis/extensions/v1beta1/namespaces/default/deployment
s -XPOST -H 'Content-Type: application/json' \
-d@deployment.json
```

In the preceding example, you should note that deployment related API commands are in another API group: `extensions`. That's why the endpoint will have a different `REST` path.

After executing those two `REST HTTP` requests, we should have our service and deployment created in the cluster. Of course, because of the deployment manifest contains the number of replicas with the value `1`, one Pod will be created as well. Let's check if it's true, by executing the following commands:

```
$ kubectl get services
$ kubectl get deployments
$ kubectl get pods
```

As you can see in the following screenshot, all of the resources exist on our cluster. This time, however, they were created by two simple `HTTP POST` requests to the Kubernetes `api-servers`, without using `kubectl`:

We have said before that we can observe what HTTP requests are being executed by the kubectl tool. Let's verify that. We will execute the last command to get the list of Pods, but with additional verbosity level, the same as this:

```
$ kubectl get pods -v6
```

The output should be similar to the following:

There's a bunch of log lines about getting information from the cluster cache, but the last line is especially interesting, it contains the actual HTTP request being made by kubectl:

```
GET https://192.168.99.100:8443/api/v1/namespaces/default/pods
```

If you now run the curl GET command using this URL, all the authentication and authorization mechanisms would come into play. But having the api-server proxy running, we can skip authorization and authentication by executing the call on the proxied port (note that curl executes the GET method by default):

```
$ curl http://localhost:8080/api/v1/namespaces/default/pods
```

As the output, you will be given the JSON response containing detailed information about Pods in your cluster. The API is working, as you can see in the following screenshot:

# Deleting a service and deployment

If you decide it's time to do some clean up, you may delete the service and the deployment by executing the HTTP DELETE request, for example:

```
$ curl http://localhost:8000/ \
apis/extensions/v1beta1/namespaces/default/deployments/rest-example \
-XDELETE
$ curl http://localhost:8080/ \ api/v1/namespaces/default/services/rest-
example -XDELETE
```

Finding out the proper API operation REST paths (endpoints) can be very inconvenient just by looking at the web documentation or by spying what URLs are being called by kubectl. There's a better way of doing this; OpenAPI specification of the Kubernetes api-server. Let's look at how we can get this specification.

# Swagger docs

The Kubernetes `api-server` provides the list of available API commands by utilizing the OpenAPI specification. The OpenAPI Specification defines a standard, language-agnostic interface to `REST` APIs that allows both humans and computers to discover and understand the capabilities of the service without access to source code, documentation, or through network traffic inspection. It's very convenient to browse the API commands catalogue using the SwaggerUI tool that comes with Kubernetes `api-server`. You can also execute the `HTTP` commands using SwaggerUI.

Note that the SwaggerUI is not enabled by default if you are running the local cluster using Minikube. You will need to enable it during the cluster startup, using the following command:

```
$ minikube start --extra-config=apiserver.Features.EnableSwaggerUI=true
```

Having the `api-server` proxy still running using port `8080`, visit the following host in your web browser to see the SwaggerUI screen:

```
http://localhost:8080/swagger-ui/
```

You will be presented with a list of available API commands, grouped into API groups:

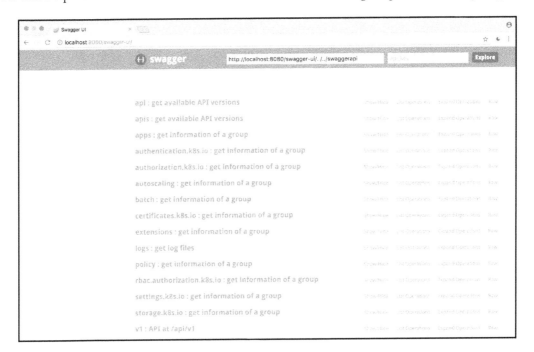

Expanding each API section will give you all the available endpoints with the description of each operation. The SwaggerUI is a great tool to explore an API in a clear and readable form.

# Summary

As you can see, the API exposed by Kubernetes is a very powerful tool in your arsenal. Any task that can be performed through the dashboard or kubectl client is exposed as an API. You can do almost anything with your cluster simply by utilizing HTTP calls. Kubernetes takes an API-first approach that makes it programmable and extensible. As we have seen it is easy to get started with the API. Our service and deployment creating examples, may be simple but should give you an idea how to experiment with the api-server. Using the API you can create and retrieve cluster resources not only from the command-line using kubectl, but also from your own application, build scripts, or continuous delivery pipelines. Only your imagination and the sky is the limit, and speaking of the sky, it's time to move there and see how Kubernetes can be used in the cloud.

# 10
# Deploying Java on Kubernetes in the Cloud

In previous chapters, we have managed to run the Kubernetes cluster locally. Using `minikube` is a great way to learn Kubernetes and experiment on your own machine. The `minikube` powered cluster behaves exactly the same as the normal cluster that runs on the server. However, if you decide to run your clustered software in a production, the cloud is one of the best solutions. In this chapter, we will briefly cover the advantages of using cloud environments in the context of microservices running on Docker. Next, we are going to deploy our Kubernetes cluster on the Amazon AWS. Configuring AWS and running Kubernetes on it is not the easiest and most straightforward process from the start but, following this chapter will give you an overview of the process, you will be able to run your own cloud cluster quickly and deploy your own or third-party Docker images on it.

The list of topics covered includes:

- The benefits of using cloud, Docker, and Kubernetes
- Installing the needed tools
- Configuring AWS
- Deploying the cluster

Let's begin with the advantages of using a cloud-deployed Kubernetes cluster.

# Benefits of using the cloud, Docker, and Kubernetes

Having an application deployed on a Kubernetes cluster has its advantages. It's fail resilient, scalable, and has efficient architecture. What's the difference between having your own infrastructure and using the cloud? Well, it comes down to couple of factors. First, it can be a significant cost reduction. For small services or applications, which could be shut down when not in use, the price of deploying applications in the cloud can be lower, due to lower hardware costs, there will be more effective usage of physical resources. You will not have to pay for the nodes that do not use the computing power or network bandwidth.

Having your own servers requires you to pay for the hardware, energy, and operating system software. Docker and Kubernetes are free of charge, even for commercial purposes; so, if you run it in the cloud, the cloud provider fee will be the only cost. Cloud providers update their software stack often; you can benefit from this by having the latest and greatest versions of the operating system software.

When it comes to the computing power or network bandwidth, large cloud providers such as, Amazon or Google cannot be easily beaten. Their cloud infrastructure is huge. Since they provide services to many different clients, they buy large, high-performance systems that offer performance levels much higher than a small company can afford to run internally. Also, as you will see in the next sections of this chapter, cloud providers can spin up new servers or services in minutes or even seconds. As a result, if there's a need, new instances will be brought to life in a way that is almost transparent for the users of your software. If your application needs to handle a lot of requests, sometimes having it deployed in the cloud can be the only option.

As for fault-tolerance, because cloud providers have their infrastructure spread out over the whole world (such as AWS zones, as you will see later in this chapter), your software can be fail-proof. No single accident such as power outage, fire, or an earthquake, can stop your application from running. Adding Kubernetes to the equation can scale the deployment up or down and will increase the fault tolerance of your application, even reducing the chance of complete failure to zero.

Let's move our software to the cloud. To do this, we need to create a toolset first, by installing the required software.

# Installing the tools

To be able to manage Kubernetes cluster on Amazon EC2, we will need to install some command-line tools first. Of course, using the Amazon EC2 web interface is also possible. Spinning up a cluster is quite a complicated process; you will need to have a user with proper access and permissions, storage for a cluster state, EC2 instances to run your Kubernetes master and worker nodes, and so on. Doing everything manually is possible, but can be time consuming and error prone. Luckily, we have tools that can automate most of the things for us, this will be the AWS command-line client (`awscli`) and `kops`, Kubernetes operations, production Grade K8s installation, upgrades, and management. There are some requirements though. `Kops` runs on Linux and macOS, it's written in Go, like Docker. The `awscli` is written in Python, so let's focus on Python installation first.

# Python and PIP

To run the AWS command-line tools (`awscli`), we will need `python3` present on our machine.

It may be present already, you can verify that using the command:

```
$ python3 --version
```

If the output is `command not found`, the fastest way of installing it will be using the package manager you have on your system, such as `apt` on Debian/Ubuntu, `yum` on Fedora, or Homebrew on macOS. If you work on macOS and do not have Homebrew installed, I highly recommend doing so; it's a wonderful tool that gives you the possibility to easily install thousands of packages together with all the needed dependencies. Homebrew is available freely at `https://brew.sh/`. To install it, execute the following:

```
$ ruby -e "$(curl -fsSL
https://raw.githubusercontent.com/Homebrew/install/master/install)"
```

From now on, you should have the `brew` command available in your macOS terminal.

To install Python on Linux using the `apt` package manager (on Debian or Ubuntu), execute the following commands:

```
$ sudo apt-get update
$ sudo apt-get install python3.6
```

On macOS, this will be the following command:

```
$ brew install python3
```

The process of installing Python depends on the speed of your machine and internet connection, but it should not take long. Once Python is installed, we will need another tool, which is `pip`. `pip` is the recommended tool for installing Python packages. It's written in Python itself. You can install it using the package manager of your choice, executing the following, for example, on Ubuntu or Debian:

```
$ sudo apt-get install python3-pip
```

An alternative way of installing `pip` is using the installation script. In this case, the process is exactly the same for Linux and macOS. First, we need to download the installation script using the following command:

```
$ curl -O https://bootstrap.pypa.io/get-pip.py
```

After a while, we need to run the installation script by executing the following:

```
$ python3 get-pip.py -user
```

After a while, `pip` should be available for you in the terminal shell. To verify if it's working, execute the following command:

```
$ pip -V
or
$ pip --version
```

Now that we have Python and pip installed and working properly, it's time to move on to more interesting things, installing Amazon AWS command-line utilities.

# AWS command-line tools

The Amazon **AWS command-line tool** (**awscli**) interface is a unified tool for managing your AWS services. The `awscli` is built on top of the AWS SDK for Python, which provides commands for interacting with AWS services. With minimal configuration (actually, providing login id and a secret is enough, we will do it in a while), you can start using all of the functionality provided by the AWS Management Console web interface. Moreover, the `awscli` is not only about EC2, which we will be using to deploy our cluster on, but also other services such as S3 (a storage service) for example.

To install `awscli`, execute the following `pip` command:

```
$ pip3 install --user --upgrade awscli
```

After a while, `pip` will download and install the necessary files in the `python3` folder structure on your drive. It will be `~/Library/Python/3.6/bin` in case of macOS and Python 3.6. It's very convenient to add this folder to your `PATH` environment variable, to make it available from anywhere in the shell. This is straightforward; you will need to edit the `PATH` variable in one of those files, depending on the shell you use:

- **Bash**: `.bash_profile`, `.profile`, or `.bash_login`
- **Zsh**: `.zshrc`
- **Tcsh**: `.tcshrc`, `.cshrc` or `.login`

An example `PATH` entry could look the same as this, on macOS:

```
export PATH=~/Library/Python/3.6/bin/:$PATH
```

After logging back in or launching a new terminal, you can verify if the `aws` command is available, by executing the following command:

```
$ aws -version
```

As you can see in the output, this will give you a detailed `aws` command-line tools version also with the Python version it's running on:

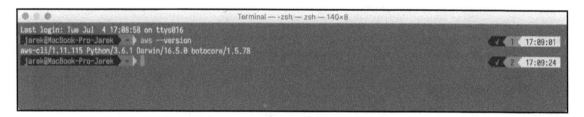

The `awscli` is ready to use, but we have one more tool to add to our tool setup. It will be Kubernetes `kops`.

# Kops

Kubernetes operations or `kops`, for short, is the production grade Kubernetes installation, upgrades, and management tool. It's a command-line utility that helps you create, destroy, upgrade, and maintain highly available Kubernetes clusters on AWS. AWS is officially supported by the tool. You can find the `kops` releases on GitHub: `https://github.com/kubernetes/kops/releases`

To install on either macOS or Linux, you will just need to download the binary, change the permission to executable and you are done. To download, execute, for example:

```
$ wget \
https://github.com/kubernetes/kops/releases/download/1.6.1/kops-darwin-amd6
4
$ chmod +x kops-darwin-amd64
$ mv kops-darwin-amd64 /usr/local/bin/kops
```

Alternatively, if you are using Linux, execute the following command:

```
$ wget \
https://github.com/kubernetes/kops/releases/download/1.6.2/kops-linux-amd64
$ chmod +x kops-linux-amd64
$ mv kops-linux-amd64 /usr/local/bin/kops
```

Alternatively, again, using the package manager will be the easiest way to get the latest `kops` binary, for example using `brew` on macOS:

```
$ brew update && brew install kops
```

Note that you must have `kubectl` (`https://kubernetes.io/docs/tasks/tools/install-kubectl/`) installed in order for `kops` to work. If you use the package manager, the dependency to `kubectl` will be probably defined in the `kops` package, so the `kubernetes-cli` will be installed first.

The last tool is the `jq`. Although not mandatory, it's very useful when dealing with JSON data. All the AWS, Kubernetes, and `kops` commands will post and receive JSON objects, so having a tool for parsing JSON comes in handy, I highly recommend installing `jq`.

# jq

`jq` is a command-line JSON processor. It works like `sed` for JSON data; you can use it to filter, parse, and transform structured data with the same ease that `sed`, `awk`, or `grep` let you do with raw text. `Jq` is available on GitHub at `https://stedolan.github.io/jq/`. The installation is very simple; it's just a single binary, available for Windows, macOS, and Linux. Just download it and copy it into the folder available on your system `PATH` to be able to run it from the shell or command-line.

Assuming we have all the tools installed before we start using kops, we will need to configure our AWS account first. This will be creating an administrative user and then, using the `aws` command-line tool, creating the user for running `kops`.

# Configuring Amazon AWS

The configuration of AWS before setting up a Kubernetes cluster goes down to creating a user, basically. All the rest will be done more or less automatically by the `kops` command. Before we can use `kops` from the command-line, it's good to have a user dedicated to `kops`. But first, we will need to create an administrator user. We will do it from the Web Management Console.

# Creating an administrative user

Depending on the AWS region you have chosen, the AWS Management Console is available at a subdomain of `console.aws.amazon.com`, this will be `https://eu-central-1.console.aws.amazon.com`, for example. After logging in, go to the **IAM** page of the **Security, Identity, and Compliance** section, then switch to the **Users** page, then click on the **Add user** button.

You will be presented with the user creation screen:

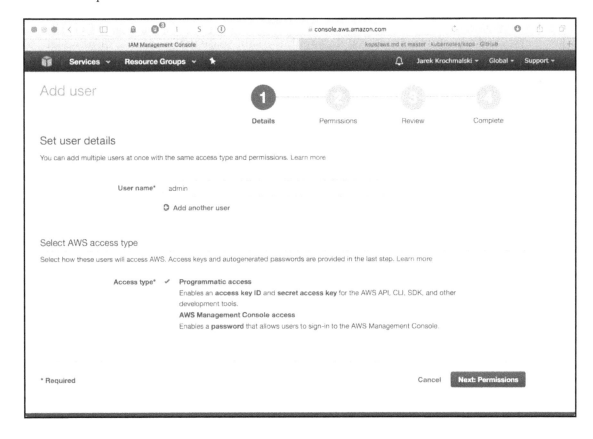

We will need this user for using `awscli`, so the only option we need to mark is the **Programmatic Access**. After clicking on **Next: Permissions**, let's give our `admin` user full administrative rights by adding him to the `admin` group:

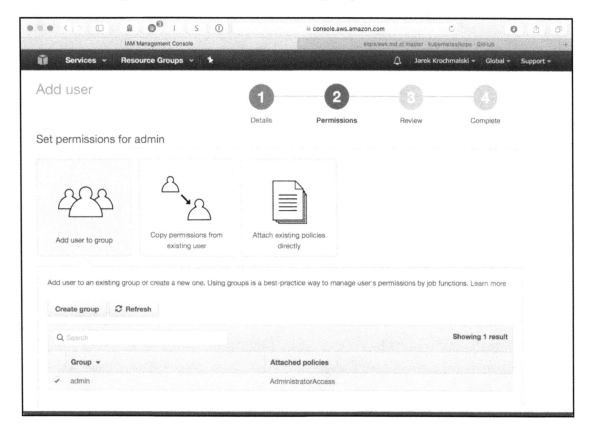

On the last page of the user creation wizard, you will be able to see the **Access key ID** and **Secret access key ID**. Do not close the page, we will need both in a short while to authenticate using `awscli`:

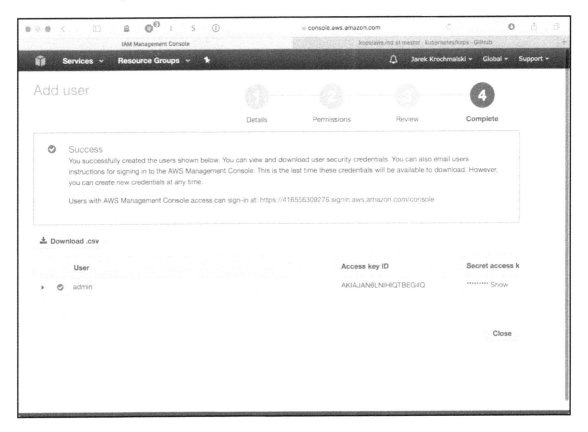

That's it. We have created an admin user with all the administrative rights and have the access keys. It's all we need to manage our AWS instances using `awscli`. Running `kops` using the `admin` user is probably not the best idea, so let's create a separate user for that. This time, however, we will do it from the command-line. It will be a lot easier in comparison to UI clicking on the **Web Console**. First, let's authenticate using the admin user's **Access key ID** and `Secret access key ID`, presented on the last page of the user creation wizard.

# Creating a user for kops

The `kops` user will need to have the following permissions in AWS to function properly:

- `AmazonEC2FullAccess`
- `AmazonS3FullAccess`
- `AmazonRoute53FullAccess`
- `IAMFullAccess`
- `AmazonVPCFullAccess`

First, we are going to create a group named `kops` and give the needed permissions to the group. Execute the following list of commands to create a group and assign permissions:

```
$ aws iam create-group --group-name kops

$ aws iam attach-group-policy --policy-arn $
arn:aws:iam::aws:policy/AmazonEC2FullAccess --group-name kops

$ aws iam attach-group-policy --policy-arn
arn:aws:iam::aws:policy/AmazonS3FullAccess --group-name kops

$ aws iam attach-group-policy --policy-arn
arn:aws:iam::aws:policy/AmazonRoute53FullAccess --group-name kops

$ aws iam attach-group-policy --policy-arn
arn:aws:iam::aws:policy/IAMFullAccess --group-name kops

$ aws iam attach-group-policy --policy-arn
arn:aws:iam::aws:policy/AmazonVPCFullAccess --group-name kops
```

The `create-group` command will give you some JSON response, but there will be no response when attaching a permission (group policy) to the group if all goes well:

Next, let's create the `kops` IAM user and add the user to the `kops` group, using the following commands:

```
$ aws iam create-user --user-name kops
$ aws iam add-user-to-group --user-name kops --group-name kops
```

If you are curious you can now login into the web AWS console. You will see that our `kops` user has all the permissions we need:

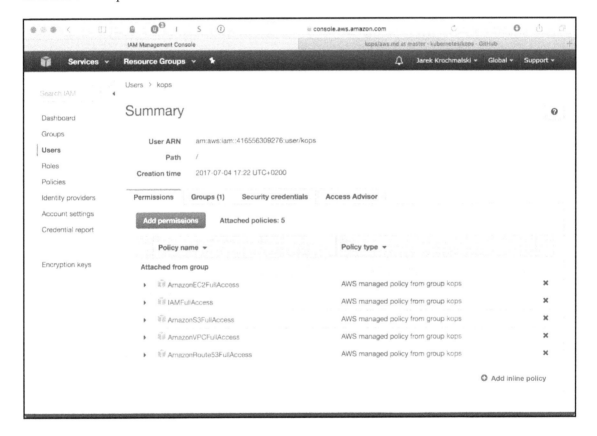

To list all the registered users, execute the following command:

```
$ aws iam list-users
```

As you can see in the following screenshot, we should now have two users: `admin` and `kops`:

```
●  ●  ●                          Terminal — -zsh — zsh — 140×20
jarek@MacBook-Pro-Jarek   ~ ▸ aws iam list-users                                          ✓  23   17:23:49
{
    "Users": [
        {
            "Path": "/",
            "UserName": "admin",
            "UserId": "AIDAIVXM6O2AGI5BGS32Q",
            "Arn": "arn:aws:iam::416556309276:user/admin",
            "CreateDate": "2017-07-04T15:19:51Z"
        },
        {
            "Path": "/",
            "UserName": "kops",
            "UserId": "AIDAJMBABKOQLTOQFOQPC",
            "Arn": "arn:aws:iam::416556309276:user/kops",
            "CreateDate": "2017-07-04T15:22:21Z"
        }
    ]
}
jarek@MacBook-Pro-Jarek   ~ ▸ █                                                           ✓  24   17:24:06
```

The last thing we need to do regarding our new `kops` user is to generate the access keys. We will need them to authenticate using the `aws configure` command. Execute the following to generate the access keys for the `kops` user:

```
$ aws iam create-access-key --user-name kops
```

As you can see in the following screenshot, AWS will answer with the JSON response containing `AccessKeyId` and `SecretAccessKey`; we will need both when authenticating using the `aws configure` command:

```
●  ●  ●                          Terminal — -zsh — zsh — 140×18
jarek@MacBook-Pro-Jarek   ▸ aws iam create-access-key --user-name kops                    ✓  20   17:22:45
{
    "AccessKey": {
        "UserName": "kops",
        "AccessKeyId": "AKIAJQ6SIGRGLGB5JCIQ",
        "Status": "Active",
        "SecretAccessKey": "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",
        "CreateDate": "2017-07-04T15:22:49.225Z"
    }
}
jarek@MacBook-Pro-Jarek   ~ ▸ aws configure                                               ✓  21   17:22:49
AWS Access Key ID [****************E640]: AKIAJQ6SIGRGLGB5JCIQ
AWS Secret Access Key [****************TJE1]: 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
Default region name [None]:
Default output format [None]:
jarek@MacBook-Pro-Jarek   ~ ▸ █                                                           ✓  22   17:23:37
```

All we need to do now is to authenticate using the `aws configure` command, providing the `AccessKeyId` and `SecretAccessKey` we got in the response. Execute the following:

```
$ aws configure
```

Because the `aws configure` command doesn't export these variables for `kops` to use, we need to export them now:

```
$ export AWS_ACCESS_KEY_ID=<access key>
$ export AWS_SECRET_ACCESS_KEY=<secret key>
```

That's it, we have authenticated with our new user named `kops`, which has all the permissions needed to spin up a Kubernetes cluster. From now on, every `kops` command we execute will use the AWS `kops` user. It's time to get back to the point and create our cluster, eventually.

# Creating the cluster

We are going to create a simple cluster with one master node and two worker nodes. To do it using `kops`, we will need:

- A user profile declared in `~/.aws/credentials` (this is done automatically if you authenticate using `aws configure`).
- An S3 bucket to store `kops` cluster state. In order to store the representation of our cluster and its state, we need to create a dedicated S3 bucket for `kops` to use. This bucket will become the source of truth for our cluster configuration.
- DNS configured. This means we will need a Route 53 hosted zone in the same AWS account. Amazon Route 53 is a highly available and scalable cloud **Domain Name System** (**DNS**) web service. Kops will use it to create records needed by the cluster. If you are using newer kops (1.6.2 or later), then DNS configuration is optional. Instead, a gossip-based cluster can be easily created. For the purposes of the example's simplicity, we will use the gossip-based cluster. To make it work, the cluster name must end with `k8s.local`. Let's look at other options we have regarding DNS setup, though.

# DNS settings

Four scenarios are possible for our cluster's domain, basically: the root domain, which is hosted on AWS, the subdomain of the domain hosted on AWS, using Amazons Route 53 for a domain hosted elsewhere, and finally, a subdomain for your cluster set up in Route 53 while having the root domain elsewhere. Let's briefly look at those setups now.

## Root domain on AWS hosted domain

If you have your domain bought and hosted on AWS, you will probably have the Route 53 configured for you automatically already. If you would like to use this root level domain for your cluster, you need do nothing to be able to use that domain name with your cluster.

## The subdomain of the domain hosted on AWS

If you have your domain bought and hosted on AWS, but would like to use the subdomain for the cluster, you will need to create a new hosted zone in Route 53 and then delegate the new route to this new zone. This is basically about copying the NS servers of your subdomain up to the parent domain in Route 53. Let's assume our domain is `mydomain.com`; we need to get some information first. Note that the `jq` command-line tool comes in handy now, when executing `aws` commands. First, we need the ID of our main parent zone:

```
$ aws route53 list-hosted-zones | jq '.HostedZones[] \
| select(.Name=="mydomain.com.") | .Id'
```

To create a new subdomain, execute the following:

```
$ aws route53 create-hosted-zone --name myservice.mydomain.com \
--caller-reference $ID | jq .DelegationSet.NameServers
```

Note that the previous command will list the name servers of the new domain. If you created the subdomain before, and would like to list the name servers (to copy the NS servers list to the parent zone, we will need to know them first), execute the following command to get the subdomain zone ID:

```
$ aws route53 list-hosted-zones | jq '.HostedZones[] | \ select(.Name="
myservice.mydomain.com.") | .Id'
```

Having the ID of the subdomain zone, we can list its name servers, by executing the following command:

```
$ aws route53 get-hosted-zone --id <your-subdomain-zoneID> \
| jq .DelegationSet.NameServers
```

So far, we have our parent's zone ID, subdomain zone's ID and a list of subdomain's name servers. We are ready to copy them into the parent. The most convenient way will be to prepare the JSON file, as it's quite a long input. The file will look the same as the following:

```
{
  "Changes": [
    {
      "Action": "CREATE",
      "ResourceRecordSet": {
        "Name": "myservice.mydomain.com",
        "Type": "NS",
        "TTL": 300,
        "ResourceRecords": [
          {
            "Value": "ns-1.awsdns-1.com"
          },
          {
            "Value": "ns-2.awsdns-2.org"
          },
          {
            "Value": "ns-3.awsdns-3.com"
          },
          {
            "Value": "ns-4.awsdns-4.net"
          }
        ]
      }
    }
  ]
}
```

You will need to save this as a file, let's say `my-service-subdomain.json`, and execute the last command. It will copy the name servers list into the parent zone:

```
$ aws route53 change-resource-record-sets
--change-batch file://my-service-subdomain.json \
--hosted-zone-id <your-parent-zone-id>
```

After a while, all network traffic to `*.myservice.mydomain.com` will be routed to the correct subdomain hosted zone in AWS Route 53.

# Route 53 for a domain purchased with another registrar

If you bought your domain elsewhere, and would like to dedicate the entire domain to your AWS hosted cluster, things can get a little complicated, as this setup requires you to make crucial changes in another domain registrar.

 If the registrar for your domain is also the DNS service provider for the domain (which is, actually, very often the case), it's recommended to transfer your DNS service to Amazon Route 53 before you continue with the process to transfer the domain registration.

The reason for that is that when you transfer the registration, the previous registrar might disable the DNS service for the domain, as soon as they receive a transfer request from Route 53. As a result, any service you have on this domain, such as a web application or an email, might become unavailable. To transfer the domain registration to Route 53 from another registrar, you will need to use the Route 53 console, available at `https://console.aws.amazon.com/route53/`. In the navigation pane, choose **Registered Domains** and then **Transfer Domain**, and enter the name of the domain which you would like to transfer and click on **Check**. If the domain is unavailable for transfer, the console will list the probable reasons and a recommended way to handle them. If everything is ok and the domain is available for transfer, you will have an option to add it to the cart. You will need to enter some details then, such as your contact information, the authorization code for transfer (you should get it from the previous registrar) and the name server settings. I highly recommend selecting the Route 63 managed DNS server, as it's quite easy to configure and reliable. The Route 63 will take care of communication with your previous registrar, but you may receive some emails requiring you to confirm some things. The transfer process can take a longer time, but when it's done, you may proceed with configuring the domain for your AWS based cluster in the same way as in the previous two cases.

# Subdomain for cluster in AWS Route 53, the domain elsewhere

If you have your domain registered at a registrar other than Amazon and would like to use the subdomain of that domain to point to your cluster, you will need to modify your name servers entries in your registrar. This would require a new hosted zone subdomain to be created in Route 53 and then migration of this subdomain's name server records to your registrar.

Similar to the subdomain on the AWS-hosted domain, let's create a subdomain first, by executing the following command:

```
$ aws route53 create-hosted-zone \
--name myservice.mydomain.com \
--caller-reference $ID | jq .DelegationSet.NameServers
```

The output of the previous command will list the name servers for the subdomain. You will need to log in to your registrar's settings page and create a new subdomain, providing the four name server records received from the previous command. You can find detailed instructions on how to edit the name servers for your domain in your specific registrar help guides.

The previous guides should make your cluster available under a specific domain or subdomain. For the rest of our chapter, however, we will be running the gossip-based cluster.

Before we create anything on AWS, we must see what zones are available for use. You should know that Amazon EC2 is hosted in multiple locations world-wide. These locations are composed of regions and availability zones. Each region is a separate geographic area. Each region has multiple, isolated locations known as availability zones. You can pick the location you want, but first, you will need to check the zones availability. Let's do that now.

# Checking the zones' availability

To list the zones available for the specific region, execute the following command:

```
$ aws ec2 describe-availability-zones --region eu-central-1
```

As you can see on the following screenshot, AWS will give you the list of zones in the response:

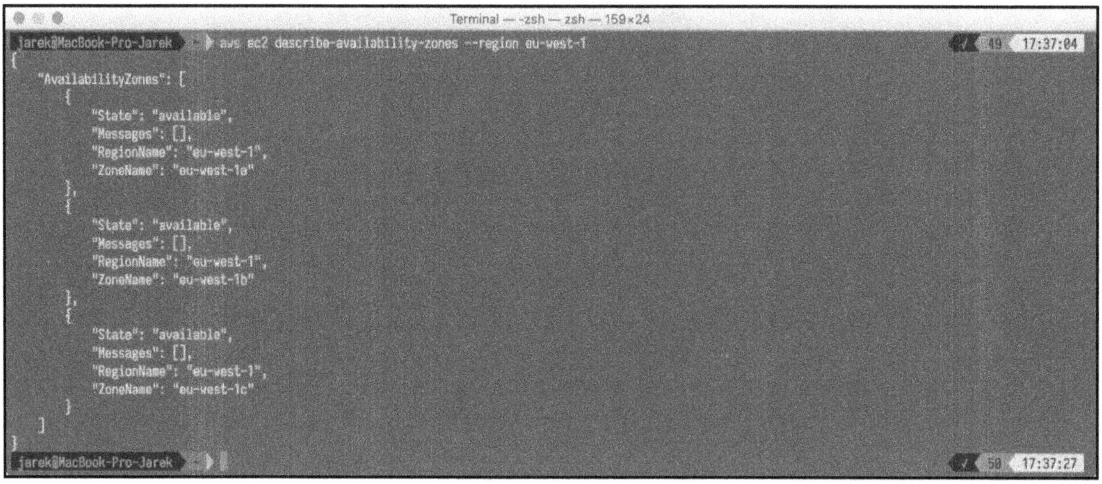

# Creating the storage

Our cluster needs to store its state somewhere. Kops uses Amazon S3 buckets for that purpose. An S3 bucket is a logical unit of storage in the **Amazon Web Services** (**AWS**) object storage service, **Simple Storage Solution** (**S3**). Buckets are used to store objects, which consist of data and metadata that describes the data. To create a bucket, execute the following `aws` command:

```
$ aws s3api create-bucket \
--bucket my-cluster-store \
--region eu-central-1 \
--create-bucket-configuration LocationConstraint=eu-central-1
```

As you will see on the following screenshot, AWS will give you back the concise information about the location of the store:

```
● ● ●                          Terminal — -zsh — zsh — 159×16

jarek@MacBook-Pro-Jarek  ➤ aws s3api create-bucket --bucket my-cluster-store --region eu-west-1 --create-bucket-configuration LocationConstraint=eu-west-1
{
    "Location": "http://my-cluster-store.s3.amazonaws.com/"
}
jarek@MacBook-Pro-Jarek  ➤ █                                                                                               ✔ 41  17:33:10
```

Having the store created, we will need to make it available for `kops` when creating a cluster. To do this, we need to export the bucket's name into the `KOPS_STATE_STORE` environment variable to:

```
$ export KOPS_STATE_STORE=s3://my-cluster-store
```

We are now ready to create a cluster.

> As you remember, we are going to use a gossip-based cluster instead of configured DNS, so the name must end with `k8s.local`.

# Creating a cluster

Let's first export our cluster name to the environment variable. This will be useful, because we are going to refer to the cluster's name often. Execute the following command to export the cluster name:

```
$ export NAME=my-rest-cluster.k8s.local
```

The `kops create cluster` is the command we are going to use to create our cluster. Note that this will not affect our Amazon EC2 instances yet. The outcome of the command will be just a local cluster template which we can review and edit before rolling out real, physical changes on the AWS.

The syntax of the command is very simple:

```
$ kops create cluster [options]
```

The command takes a lot of options; you can always find the up-to-date description on GitHub
at `https://github.com/kubernetes/kops/blob/master/docs/cli/kops_create_cluster.m`
d. Let's focus on the most important ones:

| Option | Description |
|--------|-------------|
| `--master-count [number]` | Sets the number of master nodes. The default is one master node per master-zone. |
| `--master-size [string]` | Sets instance size for masters, for example: `--master-size=t2.medium`. |
| `--master-volume-size [number]` | Sets instance volume size for master nodes in gigabytes. |
| `--master-zones [zone1,zone2]` | Specifies AWS zones in which to run masters (this must be an odd number). |
| `--zones [zone1,zone2 ]` | Zones in which to run the cluster, for example: `--zones eu-central-1a,eu-central-1b`. |
| `--node-count [number]` | Sets the number of nodes. |
| `--node-size [string]` | Sets instance size for nodes, for example: `--node-size=t2.medium`. |
| `--node-volume-size int32` | Sets instance volume size (in GB) for nodes. |

If you would like to make your cluster private (it's public by default) you will need to consider using these options additionally:

| Option | Description |
|--------|-------------|
| `--associate-public-ip [true|false]` | Specifies if you want your cluster to have a public IP assigned or not. |
| `--topology [public|private]` | Specifies the internal networking topology for the cluster, it can be `public` or `private`. |

| --bastion | The --bastion flag enables a bastion instance group. The option is valid only with the private topology. It will generate a dedicated SSH jump host for SSH access to cluster instances. A jump host provides a point of entry into a private network of your cluster. It can be started and stopped to enable or disable inbound SSH communication from the internet. |
|---|---|

Let's create our cluster now, using the following command:

```
$ kops create cluster --v=0 \
--cloud=aws --node-count 2 \
--master-size=t2.medium \
--master-zones=eu-central-1a \
--zones eu-central-1a,eu-central-1b  \
--name=${NAME} \
--node-size=t2.medium
```

In the response, kops will list all the details of the configuration that has been created and suggest some next steps you can take with your new cluster configuration:

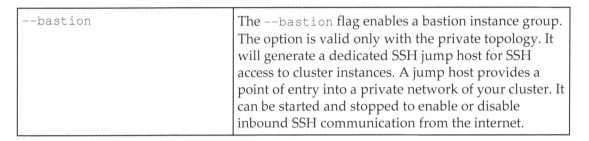

After running the command, `kops` will configure your `kubectl` Kubernetes client to point to your new cluster; this will be `my-rest-cluster.k8s.local` in our example.

As we have said before, at this stage, only the cluster's template is created, not the cluster itself. You can still change any option by editing your cluster:

```
$ kops edit cluster my-rest-cluster.k8s.local
```

This will bring up the default editor you have defined in your shell, where you can see the cluster template that has been generated. It will contain a lot more settings, not only those you have specified when running the `cluster create` command:

```
● ● ●                    Terminal — vi • kops edit cluster my-rest-cluster.k8s.local — zsh — 124×19
# Please edit the object below. Lines beginning with a '#' will be ignored,
# and an empty file will abort the edit. If an error occurs while saving this file will be
# reopened with the relevant failures.
#
apiVersion: kops/v1alpha2
kind: Cluster
metadata:
  creationTimestamp: 2017-07-04T15:53:58Z
  name: my-rest-cluster.k8s.local
spec:
  api:
    loadBalancer:
      type: Public
  authorization:
    alwaysAllow: {}
  channel: stable
  cloudProvider: aws
  configBase: s3://my-cluster-store/my-rest-cluster.k8s.local
"/var/folders/qt/jvv17hmd3bb10mv8xdns1_rw0000gn/T/kops-edit-fpllnyaml" 52L, 1281C
```

If you are satisfied with your cluster template, it's time to spin it up to create real cloud-based resources, such as networks and EC2 instances. Once the infrastructure is ready, `kops` will install Kubernetes on the EC2 instances. Let's do it.

# Starting up clusters

To start the cluster and spin up all the necessary EC2 instances, you will need to execute the update command. It's recommended in the kops manual that you should do it first in the preview mode without the --yes switch. This will not spin up any EC2 instances:

```
$ kops update cluster ${NAME}
```

If all is looking correct, execute the update command with the --yes switch:

```
$ kops update cluster ${NAME} --yes
```

```
Terminal — kops update cluster --name=my-rest-cluster.k8s.local --yes — zsh — 124×19
jarek@MacBook-Pro-Jarek  ~  kops update cluster --name=${NAME} --yes                          ✓  69  17:49:46
I0704 17:49:54.732061   21467 apply_cluster.go:396] Gossip DNS: skipping DNS validation
I0704 17:49:55.252617   21467 executor.go:91] Tasks: 0 done / 69 total; 32 can run
I0704 17:49:56.196981   21467 vfs_castore.go:422] Issuing new certificate: "kops"
I0704 17:49:56.232940   21467 vfs_castore.go:422] Issuing new certificate: "kube-proxy"
I0704 17:49:56.312472   21467 vfs_castore.go:422] Issuing new certificate: "kube-scheduler"
I0704 17:49:56.500122   21467 vfs_castore.go:422] Issuing new certificate: "kubelet"
I0704 17:49:56.755896   21467 vfs_castore.go:422] Issuing new certificate: "kube-controller-manager"
I0704 17:49:56.797244   21467 vfs_castore.go:422] Issuing new certificate: "kubecfg"
I0704 17:49:58.110841   21467 executor.go:91] Tasks: 32 done / 69 total; 14 can run
I0704 17:49:58.980137   21467 executor.go:91] Tasks: 46 done / 69 total; 19 can run
I0704 17:49:59.936095   21467 launchconfiguration.go:320] waiting for IAM instance profile "masters.my-rest-cluster.k8s.loca
l" to be ready
```

Your cluster is starting and should be ready in a few minutes. If you now log in into the WAS Management Console, you will see your EC2 instances starting up, as you can see in the following screenshot:

You can also check the whole cluster state, issuing the following command:

```
$ kops validate cluster
```

The output will contain information about the number and status of the cluster's nodes, including the master node:

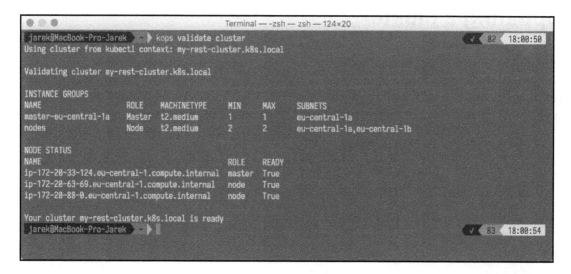

Of course, as the `kubectl` is now configured to act on our AWS cluster, we can list nodes using `kubectl get nodes` command, exactly the same as we did in the `Chapter 9,` *Working with Kubernetes API*, with `minikube` base cluster. Execute the following command:

```
$ list nodes: kubectl get nodes --show-labels
```

You will be given the information about the name and status of your cluster's nodes:

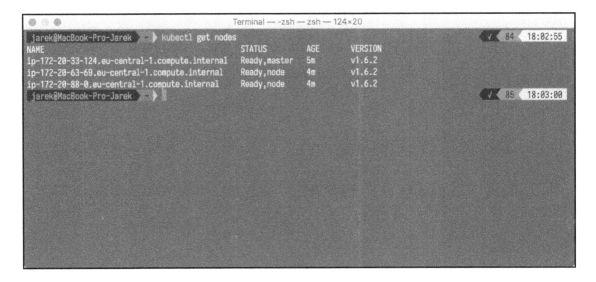

# Updating a cluster

`Kops` behaves similarly to `kubectl`; you can edit the configuration files in the editor before actually doing any changes on the cluster. The `kops update` command will apply configuration changes, but will not modify the running infrastructure. To update the running cluster, you will need to execute the `rolling-update` command. The following will start the update or recreation process of the cluster's infrastructure:

```
$ kops rolling-update cluster -yes
```

Our fresh cluster is running, but it's empty. Let's deploy something.

# Installing the dashboard

Having the cluster running, it would be nice to have a dashboard deployed, to see the status of your services, deployments, pods and so on. The dashboard is included in the `minikube` cluster by default, but on our brand new Amazon cluster we will need to install it manually. This is a straightforward process. As we have `kubectl` configured to act on the remote cluster, we can execute the following `kubectl create` command with the `kubernetes-dashboard.yaml` template as an input:

```
$ kubectl create -f \
https://rawgit.com/kubernetes/dashboard/master/src/deploy
kubernetes-dashboard.yaml
```

The next thing would be to proxy the network traffic, using the following `kubectl proxy` command we already know:

```
$ kubectl proxy
```

That's it! After a while the dashboard will be deployed and we will be able to access it using the localhost address:

`http://localhost:8001/`, as you can see in the following screenshot, is the same dashboard we have already seen in the `Chapter 9`, *Working with Kubernetes API*:

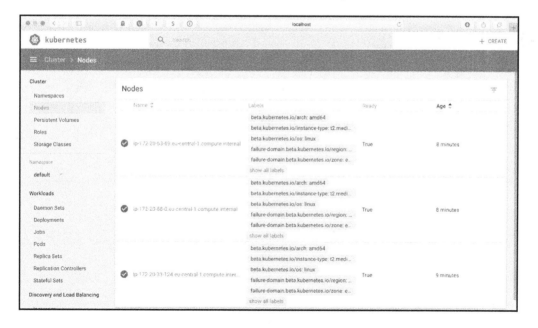

From now on, you can use the `kubectl` and the dashboard to manage your cluster as we did before in the `Chapter 9`, *Working with Kubernetes API*. All the `kubectl create` commands will work the same as with the local cluster. This time, however, your software will go to the cloud.

If you decide to remove the cluster, execute the following command:

```
$ kops delete cluster –name=${NAME} --yes
```

Note that if you just created the cluster template, without executing `kops update cluster ${NAME} --yes` first, you can also delete the cluster, as you can see in the following screenshot:

If the cluster is already created on Amazon, the process of deleting it will take longer, as all EC2 instances for master and worker nodes needs to be shutdown first.

# Summary

In this chapter, we have set up a cluster in the real cloud, Amazon AWS. `Kops` is one of the best tools that we have available right now to manage Kubernetes on AWS. Using it, you can easily create and manage clusters on AWS. It can be a test or a production-grade cluster; `kops` will make the creation and management of it a breeze.

# 11
# More Resources

We are at the end of our Docker and Kubernetes journey. After reading this book, you should already know how Kubernetes compliments Docker. You may think of them as of different layers of your software stack; Docker sits below, serving single containers, while Kubernetes orchestrates and manages them in a cluster. Docker becomes more and more popular and a lot of people use it during the development or production deployments. Just to name a few big ones, it is used by PayPal, General Electric, Groupon, Spotify, and Uber. It's mature enough to be run on production and I hope you will use it too to deploy and run your Java applications with success.

To further extend your knowledge about Docker and Kubernetes, there's plenty of information. The trick is to find the valuable information. In this chapter, I will present the most useful if you want to further extend your Docker and Kubernetes knowledge.

## Docker

The first one on our list will be the awesome Docker list.

## Awesome Docker

Awesome Docker available on GitHub at `http://veggiemonk.github.io/awesome-docker/` . The author updates the list often, so you can clone the Git repository locally and do periodical updates to see what's new. Awesome Docker contains sections such as an introduction to Docker, tools (with the groups such as developer tools, testing, or utilities). The Videos section can be especially useful when learning Docker, you can find tutorials and trainings here. Apart from this list, it's really hard to find some more that could be useful.

# Blogs

The first blog I would recommend to continue learning about Docker will be Arun Gupta's blog, available at `http://blog.arungupta.me`. Arun, who first started blogging about Docker in July 2014, is the VP of developer advocacy at Couchbase, a Java champion, a JUG leader, and a Docker captain. He writes about many things on his blog; you can filter the content to only related to Docker using the `#docker` tag, using the link: `http://blog.arungupta.me/tag/docker/`.

You will find a lot of useful stuff here, related to Java development and Docker. He also authored a great Docker tutorial, available on GitHub: `https://github.com/arun-gupta/docker-tutorial`.

Next comes the official Docker blog, available at `https://blog.docker.com`. You will not find many tutorials on how to use Docker, but there will be announcements about new releases and their features, more advanced Docker usage tips, and community news such as Docker events.

The Red Hat developer program, under the category containers, available at `https://developers.redhat.com/blog/category/containers/` also contains a lot of useful articles around Docker and container technology in general.

# Interactive tutorials

There are many Docker tutorials available on the web, but I find one of them especially interesting. It's Katakoda's interactive Docker learning course, available at `https://www.katacoda.com/courses/docker`. You will find the complete feature set of Docker here, starting with deployment of a single container and going through subjects such as adding labels, inspecting containers, and optimizing your image builds. It's interactive; all you need is a modern browser, you do not even need to install Docker on your local machine. It's very complete and fun to learn with. The other one is `http://training.play-with-docker.com`. It comes with three sections: beginner, which covers the basics such as running single containers, intermediate, covering networking for example, and advanced, covering Docker security. Some of the course tasks are interactive, you can execute them straight in your browser.

# Kubernetes

When Docker started to gain more popularity the need for containers management platform started to gain attention. Thus, more resources regarding Kubernetes started to pop up on the internet.

## Awesome Kubernetes

Similar to its Docker counterpart, the awesome Kubernetes list, available at GitHub `https://github.com/ramitsurana/awesome-kubernetes` contains a lot of useful resources regarding Kubernetes. You will find a lot here; staring from the introduction to Kubernetes, through the list of useful tools and developer platforms, up to the enterprise Kubernetes products. There's even a link to the tutorial on how to install Kubernetes cluster using Raspberry Pi devices!

## Tutorials

The official Kubernetes site contains a lot of interesting tutorials, starting from the basics and going through the whole Kubernetes feature lists. The list of tutorials is available at `https://kubernetes.io/docs/tutorials/`. If you haven't followed our Minikube install guide, I highly recommend doing so, using Kubernetes official Bootcamp, it's an interactive web based tutorial and its goal is to deploy a local development Kubernetes cluster using Minikube. It's available at `https://kubernetes.io/docs/tutorials/kubernetes-basics/cluster-interactive/`.

## Blogs

The official Kubernetes blog is available at `http://blog.kubernetes.io/`. You will find announcements about new releases, useful technical articles, and interesting case studies here.

The Red Hat enterprise Linux blog also contains a lot of interesting articles regarding Kubernetes. They are tagged with the Kubernetes tag, so you can easily filter them out by using the link `http://rhelblog.redhat.com/tag/kubernetes/`.

# Extensions

As you know, Kubernetes supports extensions. There is a nice resource tracking a number of Kubernetes, available at `https://github.com/coreos/awesome-kubernetes-extensions`. If you need, for example, to integrate some cert manager into your architecture, you will probably find a proper extension there.

# Tools

Apart from useful articles and tutorials, there are also a couple of useful tools or platforms that make using Kubernetes more enjoyable. Let's briefly present them now.

# Rancher

Rancher, available at `http://rancher.com`, is a platform that deserves a separate section in our book. It's open source software that makes it easy to deploy and manage Docker containers and Kubernetes in production on any infrastructure. You can easily deploy and run containers in production on any infrastructure with the most complete container management platform.

# Helm and charts

Kubernetes Helm (available on GitHub at `https://github.com/kubernetes/helm`) introduces the concept of charts, which are packages of pre-configured Kubernetes resources, curated application definitions for Kubernetes. Helm is a tool for managing charts; it streamlines installing and managing Kubernetes applications. Think of it as an `apt/yum/homebrew` package manager for Kubernetes. You can use it to find and use popular software packaged as Kubernetes charts, share your own applications as Kubernetes charts, and create reproducible builds of your Kubernetes applications. There's a separate repository for charts, of course, on GitHub: `https://github.com/kubernetes/charts`. Currently, the chart binary repository is available on Google Cloud at `https://console.cloud.google.com/storage/browser/kubernetes-charts/` and contains a lot of useful prepackaged tools such as Ghost (`node.js` blogging platform), Jenkins, Joomla, MongoDb, MySQL, Redis, Minecraft, and just to name a few.

# Kompose

Kompose (`https://github.com/kubernetes/kompose`) is a tool to help move Compose configuration files into Kubernetes. Kompose is a tool for defining and running multi-container Docker applications. If you are a Kompose user, you can use it to move your multi-containers configuration straight into Kubernetes setup by translating a Docker Compose file into Kubernetes objects. Note that the transformation of the Docker Compose format to Kubernetes resources manifest may not be exactly precise, but it helps tremendously when first deploying an application on Kubernetes.

# Kubetop

Kubetop, again available on GitHub `https://github.com/LeastAuthority/kubetop`, is the same as the `top` command for Kubernetes cluster. It's extremely useful; it lists all your cluster's running nodes, all pods on them and all containers in those pods. The tool gives you information about the CPU and memory utilization for each node, similar to the Unix/Linux `top` command. If you need to know quickly what's consuming the most resources on your cluster, the quick command-line tool is a very handy option.

# Kube-applier

Available on GitHub at `https://github.com/box/kube-applier`, `kube-applier` enables automated deployment and declarative configuration for your Kubernetes cluster. It runs as a Kubernetes service, takes a set of declarative configuration files hosted in a Git repository, and applies them for a Kubernetes cluster.

The `kube-applier` runs itself as a Pod in your cluster and continuously watches the Git repository to ensure that the cluster objects are up to date with their associated `spec` files (JSON or YAML) in the repository. The tool also contains a status page and provides metrics for monitoring. I find it extremely useful in the daily development, where your deployment, services, or pod definition change often.

As you can see, there are a lot of useful resources for Docker and Kubernetes around the web. After reading this book, you will probably want to skip most of the beginnings and go straight to more advanced topics. The best thing about all of those resources is that they are free of charge, so basically nothing stops you from exploring the wonderful world of managed containers. Try and learn, and if the time comes, go ahead and use Docker and Kubernetes to deploy your production ready Java software, either on your own infrastructure or on the cloud. It will be amazing to see how your Java application scales itself and becomes fail proof. Docker and Kubernetes enable it and you now have the knowledge to use it. Docker, together with Kubernetes, has radically changed the face of the technology landscape and I hope it will also change your development and release flow for the better.

# Index

www.ingramcontent.com/pod-product-compliance
Lightning Source LLC
Chambersburg PA
CBHW080625060326
40690CB00021B/4814